TWENTIETH-CENTURY DICTATORSHIPS

Also by Paul Brooker

DEFIANT DICTATORSHIPS: Communist and Middle Eastern
  Dictatorships in a Democratic Age
THE FACES OF FRATERNALISM: Nazi Germany, Fascist Italy,
  and Imperial Japan

Twentieth-Century Dictatorships

The Ideological One-Party States

Paul Brooker
Lecturer in Politics
Victoria University of Wellington

M
MACMILLAN

First published 1995 by
MACMILLAN PRESS LTD
Houndmills, Basingstoke, Hampshire RG21 2XS
and London
Companies and representatives
throughout the world

ISBN 0–333–61110–1

A catalogue record for this book is available
from the British Library.

10   9   8   7   6   5   4   3   2   1
04   03   02   01   00   99   98   97   96   95

Printed and bound in Great Britain by
Antony Rowe Ltd
Chippenham, Wiltshire

Contents

Introduction

As with many other political terms the meaning of 'dictatorship' has changed markedly over the years. The original meaning dates back to the ancient Roman office of Dictator, which conferred virtually unlimited powers on a temporary ruler installed by his fellow citizens to deal with an emergency. Nowadays any regime is likely to be called a dictatorship if it is neither a democracy nor one of the few remaining monarchies. Using this more recent and wider meaning of the term, it is easy to claim that the twentieth century has been the century of dictatorship. For certainly dictatorship has been the most common form of regime, much more common than democracy.

However, one reason for there having been so many dictatorships is that most of them have been short-lived regimes. In fact often they claim, in a manner reminiscent of the older conception of dictatorship, to be intending to rule only temporarily. The military dictatorships are especially prone to present themselves in this fashion. They usually proclaim that the military have intervened in politics solely to save the nation and will return to the barracks as soon as possible. Such apparently temporary, emergency dictatorships are not really equivalents or rivals of any form of regime that, like monarchy and democracy, seeks to be a permanent fixture. But after the First World War there emerged a modernized form of dictatorship with a longer-term perspective than the previous forms. Although it would never be as numerous as the old-style dictatorships continued to be, the modernized form of dictatorship became a real contender for the title of being the century's pre-eminent form of regime. Certainly it was the distinctively twentieth-century form of dictatorship, and its examples can be viewed as being in that sense *the* twentieth-century dictatorships.

The characteristic feature of the modernized, twentieth-century dictatorships was their possession of an official ideology and political party. In some cases this involved simply an otherwise old-fashioned military dictatorship establishing

1

an official ideology and party, as in the case of Primo de Rivera's and Franco's regimes in Spain. But many other examples were produced by an ideologically committed political party seizing power and establishing a dictatorship, as in the case of the Communist regime in Russia and the Fascist and Nazi regimes in Italy and Germany. There were also a few instances of ideologically committed armies seizing power and later establishing an official party, as in Mexico in the 1920s and in Burma forty years later. The presence of an official ideology and political party indicated much more reliably than any public pronouncement could that these modernized dictatorships intended to be more than temporary, emergency regimes. And the possession of an ideology and a party also increased their chances of achieving that degree of permanency.

The fact that these modernized, twentieth-century dictatorships appeared in several different guises probably explains why they have been categorized by political scientists under several different headings. For example, the concept of 'totalitarianism' was normally used to highlight the peculiarities and novelty of only the more extreme examples of the new form of dictatorship. The other examples were usually categorized as not totalitarian but 'authoritarian' – a term which is often given such a wide meaning that it seems to include virtually any non-democratic regime. A narrower and more appropriate category was that of 'one-party state', which at least was based upon one of the characteristic features of the twentieth-century form of dictatorship. However, for some reason the term was not applied to any examples which had been established by the military, despite the fact that these dictatorships met the criterion of having one – and only one – political party. Instead they were categorized as military regimes like all the old-style, party-less military dictatorships.

The most accurate categorical or conceptual description of the twentieth-century form of dictatorship would be to term it an 'ideological one-party state'. But the long-established prejudice against referring to any military dictatorship as a one-party state means that separate civilian and military sub-categories have to be created to make it clear that military dictatorships equipped with an official ideology and party are being categorized as ideological one-party states. Therefore, the terms 'party-state' and 'military-party' will be used from here on to describe respectively the civilian and the military type of ideological one-party state.

The ideological one-party states vary and differ so much that they are best studied through a case-study (rather than a thematic or topical) approach. In all, sixteen case studies will be presented in the following chapters. They will cover the whole era from the 1920s to the 1980s and be drawn from several different regions of the world – from Latin America, Black Africa, the Middle East, and Asia, as well as Europe. In addition to presenting examples the party-state and military-party types in Parts I and II respectively, this set of case studies will, in Part III, provide examples of a dictatorship transforming itself from one type to the other while retaining the basic form of an ideological one-party state. A number of not very systematic but familiar subheadings, such as fascist, Communist, and Third World, will be used to organize the presentation of the party-state and military-party case studies. Within each case study there will be a few standard topic or section headings to ensure that the description and analysis are focused on such key topics as the ideology and the party.

Such an extensive range of case studies should provide students and political observers with a historical and comparative context in which to view not only the few remaining examples of the twentieth-century form of dictatorship, but also the new examples which will probably emerge in the near future or next century. At the very least, providing a set of case studies which includes many of the most famous and interesting examples of this century's dictatorships should prevent students and observers of politics from having the same sort of gap in their knowledge that students of zoology would have if they knew little about the dinosaurs. Like the dinosaurs, a few of the extinct dictatorships still attract a great deal of public and academic interest. But often the public interest in these regimes, notably Hitler's and Stalin's, seems to be based on a ghoulish fascination with the genocide or other mass atrocities that they perpetrated. For the interest does not extend to examples of 'benevolent' dictatorships, such as those of

Cárdenas in Mexico and Kemal Atatürk in Turkey, or to the many examples of regimes that have fallen somewhere in between the two extremes of benevolent and mass-murdering dictatorship.

There is also little awareness in the 1990s of for how long and how closely the twentieth-century dictatorships rivalled the democracies for ideological and political pre-eminence. It is difficult now to comprehend that the new form of dictatorship had democracy on the defensive for virtually half of the twentieth century. Indeed first fascism in the 1930s and then Communism in the 1950s seemed for a time to have replaced democracy as the 'wave of the future'. As late as the 1970s the twentieth-century dictatorships were still capable of attracting converts in the Third World to their regime format of dictatorship supported by an official ideology and party.

In fact democracy's victory over the twentieth-century form of dictatorship is somewhat surprising and even incongruous when viewed from a neutral and 'scientific' standpoint. For not only is ideological and party-equipped dictatorship a newer form of regime than democracy but also it has shown much greater political variety and creativity than democracy. In this variety and creativity lies much of the fascination of the twentieth-century dictatorships for those who study them and their place in the world's political development during a tumultuous century.

1 The Twentieth-Century Dictatorships' Challenge to Democracy

The modern form of democracy emerged much earlier than the twentieth-century form of dictatorship and was also a much earlier user of ideology and political parties. Modern democracy was actually characterized by the development of a party system in which competing parties selected their candidates for public office and sought to win support for them among a mass electorate. A few democracies had also pioneered the use of ideology as a means of legitimating a regime, notably when ideologies developed in the American and French Revolutions were later used to help legitimate the American and French democracies. By the beginning of the twentieth century the modern form of democracy seemed to be about to sweep aside the old-fashioned monarchies and dictatorships and make this the democratic century. The inevitability of democracy's triumph seemed to be confirmed by the otherwise disastrous First World War of 1914–18. For the democratic Allies, led by Britain, France and the United States, had been victorious over the monarchical Central Powers of Germany, Austria-Hungary and the Turkish Ottoman Empire. In the West the war was actually depicted as being fought and won 'to make the world safe for democracy'.

But the 1920s saw the first wave of a political and ideological challenge to the democracies' position by a new, modernized form of dictatorship, equipped with an ideology and a political party. The potential strength of the new form of dictatorship was revealed by the Communist regime which had originated in the 1917 October Revolution in Russia and had successfully fought a bitter Civil War in 1918–21 against the counter-revolutionaries. By the early 1920s it was clear that the dictatorship established by the Communists was not a temporary, (civil) wartime measure but instead was

5

intended to be a permanent regime. Then the establishment of Mussolini's Fascist regime in Italy revealed that
the new, ideological and party-equipped form of dictatorship could also be adopted by a radically right-wing regime. What is more, the decision by General Primo de Rivera
in Spain to add a party, the Patriotic Union, and an ideology, Primoderriverismo, to his military dictatorship produced the first example of a military version or type of
modernized dictatorship.

The establishment of the Kuomintang (National People's
Party) dictatorship in China in 1928 showed that the new
form of dictatorship would not be confined to Europe and
surrounding areas. And a year later the military regime in
Mexico showed that the new form of dictatorship could also
disguise itself as a democracy by allowing other parties to
compete with the regime's official party in fraudulent elections. Already both the Kuomintang regime and Kemal's military regime in Turkey had shown that examples of the new
form of dictatorship might espouse the idea of eventually introducing Western-style democracy. But the Mexican regime
had gone one step further and was actually operating behind
a democratic façade. All around the world the modernized
form of dictatorship was already indicating what a problem
it would pose for the democracies in the decades ahead.

1   THE MODERNITY OF THE NEW FORM OF DICTATORSHIP

The new form of dictatorship was a more modern regime
than democracy – and not just in the sense of being newer
or more recent. For it was pioneering not only new uses for
ideologies and parties but also the new practice of having
an ideology or party perform more than one role for its
regime. Previously they had usually performed only a political role. Ideologies had helped to legitimate some of
the democratic regimes; political parties had helped all
the democracies with their electoral processes. But the
ideologies and parties of the modernized dictatorships usually
performed social and/or governing as well as political roles.
The social role of the ideology would be to help build

social solidarity, often by expressly emphasizing solidarity and always by offering a (potentially) widely shared set of beliefs that could create social solidarity in the same way as a widely accepted religion might do. The party would perform its social role by helping to indoctrinate members of society in this solidarity-building ideology. The governing role of the ideology would be to justify or legitimate the regime's policies, often even its foreign policy. The party would perform its governing role by taking charge (through its political committee) of the regime's governmental policy making and by supervising the state's implementation of the regime's policies.

The use of ideologies and parties in social and governing as well as political roles was not just a matter of putting existing political tools to new uses; the tools were being provided with a new, additional capacity that enabled them to be used in such a fashion. The modernized dictatorships created this extra, 'multi-role' capacity in their ideology and party components partly by giving them an effective monopoly, whether in law, in fact, or just in effectiveness. But in addition to enjoying an effective monopoly these official ideologies and parties were also more extensive and more disciplined than their democratic counterparts. The official ideology was extensive enough in its scope to include not only the solidarity-building content required for its social role but also the policy goals and guidelines required for its governing role. Similarly, the official party had an extensive enough membership and administrative apparatus of party officials to be able to play an indoctrinating social role and a supervisory governing role. As for discipline, the official ideology was clearly more disciplined than ideologies used by democracies, if only because its presentation and interpretation were closely controlled by the regime's approved ideologists. The official party, too, was a disciplined organization, more like a bureaucracy or even an army than like any political party in a democracy.

These disciplined, extensive, monopolistic, and multi-role parties and ideologies gave the new dictatorships appearing in the 1920s an unequalled modernity and the sort of advantage that they needed in order to mount an effective challenge to the newly victorious democracies. Another advantage enjoyed by the modernized dictatorships was their greater political creativity than the democracies.

2 THE VARIETY AND POLITICAL CREATIVITY OF THE TWENTIETH-CENTURY DICTATORSHIPS

Even as early as the 1920s the modernized dictatorships were clearly showing much more variety than the democracies. There were already at least two different types of the new form of dictatorship – those established by a party and those established by the military. And there were also indications of a similar difference or distinction in forms of leadership from that between the presidential and the parliamentary forms of government, namely individual leadership by a party or military figure as distinct from collective leadership by the political committee of a party or a military force. However, the great variety to be found among the modernized dictatorships would be most obvious at the level of their components and instruments of rule, such as the political party. As will be shown by the case studies included in the following chapters, there is a surprising degree of variation and uniqueness visible among their parties and other political or administrative structures. What is more, many of these unusual or unique features were the regimes' innovations, not legacies from the past, and thus are clear-cut examples of political creativity.

The same variety and capacity for innovation is visible in the range of ideas, and combinations of ideas, that are to be found in the ideologies developed by these regimes. The obvious illustration of this is the contrast between the radical leftism of the Communist dictatorships and the radical rightism of the fascist dictatorships. But as the case studies will show, there are many other variations, often too subtle or complex to describe in a left-wing versus right-wing context.

In comparison to the twentieth-century dictatorships' ideological variety and creativity the democracies appear quite sterile, relying upon the nineteenth century for their equivalent of ideological justifications for democratic rule and practices. It is true that the ideological justifications of a purely political regime like democracy have less scope for innovation than do ideologies that cover social and economic matters as well. Yet even the purely or narrowly political content of the dictatorships' ideologies – irrespective of their social and economic content – shows greater variation and creativity than do the democracies' attempt at an equivalent of ideological justification. Many of the dictatorships' ideologies have included a 'personality cult' glorifying a particular dictator, while the Nazi *Führerprinzip* (leader principle) and Peronist Conductor (leader) doctrine have justified dictatorial rule by any appropriate leader figure. Party dictatorship has been justified by the Leninist doctrine that the Communist Party is the vanguard of the proletariat, and there were also justifications for party rule in Touré's ideology in Guinea and in the Kuomintang's doctrine of political tutelage. Even military dictatorship has been justified by the Nasserist doctrine of the military's being the vanguard of the revolution and by the 'dual function' doctrine of the Indonesian army.

3 THE FAILURE OF THE CHALLENGE TO DEMOCRACY: THE PERSONALIST FLAW

The ideological and structural creativity of the modernized, twentieth-century dictatorships raises the obvious question of why the democracies, despite having the less modern and less creative form of regime, eventually emerged victorious. The answer to this question may well lie outside the political realm, in the relative failure of the dictatorships' economies. But the twentieth-century form of dictatorship also suffered from a major political weakness that severely reduced its ability to compete with democracy.

For the modernized, twentieth-century dictatorships were plagued by a tendency to degenerate into personal dictatorships, which in turn meant the loss of their advantages in political modernity and creativity and the acquiring of some major disadvantages. Each regime had been established by an organization, either a party or a military force, and was at this stage an 'organizational' dictatorship – a party or military dictatorship. The regime's leadership, whether an individual or a political committee, acted as the agent of the ruling organization, whether the party or the military. But usually, and sooner rather than later, the regime was transformed from a case of party or military rule into one of personal rule by an individual who originally had been only an agent of the party or the military. The original principal-agent relationship not only had come to an end but also may even have been reversed, with the formerly ruling organization now becoming the agent of the personal ruler.

The transformation from organizational to personal dictatorship did not remove the ideology and party components which are the basis for classing the regime as an example of the twentieth-century form of dictatorship. But while its outward form remained modern, in essence the regime was reverting to a very old type of rule. For a personal dictator is the modern equivalent of a monarch and often of a distinctly absolutist monarch. He might differ from a monarch in not attempting to establish a hereditary dynasty but the personal dictator nevertheless represented a retreat from modernity and a return to the outdated practice of rule by a person rather than by an organization or by the people. The modernity of the outward form of the regime was being counterbalanced by this old-fashioned personalist element, and the resulting decline in overall modernity meant the loss of one of the advantages the regime appeared to have over democracy.

What is more, personal rule usually meant a reduction in the political creativity of the regime. For the innovative capacity of the ruler would almost inevitably decline with the passing years and there was no mechanism for peacefully replacing him with a new leader or leaders. Consequently, many of the twentieth-century dictatorships saw a distinct decline in their political creativity as the regime aged along with its personal ruler. Once again one of their apparent advantages was being lost.

In addition to undermining the strengths of the modernized form of dictatorship, the establishment of personal dictatorship brought with it the weaknesses that have long been known to be associated with rule by an individual's will and whim. For example, a tendency towards wishful thinking and losing touch with reality would often be apparent in these personal dictators. If this tendency took the form of attempts to implement grandiose schemes, it could actually counteract the tendency towards a loss of political creativity. But such unrealistic schemes could also seriously weaken the regime and even lead to its destruction, as was clearly revealed by the fate of the two fascist dictatorships that were in the forefront of the challenge to democracy in the 1930s.

During the 1930s the increasingly prominent challenge to the democracies posed by the new, modernized form of dictatorship was due largely to the rise of its fascist and quasi-fascist examples. To Mussolini's Italy and Primo de Rivera's Spain were added such new examples as Hitler's Germany and neighbouring Austria – both of them former democracies. Old-fashioned forms of non-democratic regime in Portugal, Hungary, Yugoslavia and Poland also began developing varieties of dictatorship which showed some resemblances to Mussolini's or Primo de Rivera's regimes. The striking and symbolic culmination of the fascist trend of the 1930s was the 1936–9 Spanish Civil War, which saw the destruction of the young Spanish democracy by a military-led revolt that replaced it with General Franco's modern, Falangist dictatorship. None of the democracies, only the Communist regime of the Soviet Union, had been prepared to assist those fighting against Franco's rightist revolt, and this aid had been matched by the men and material Franco had received from the Fascist and Nazi regimes.

These two regimes were leading the strong fascist challenge to democracy by the new form of dictatorship. But they had already succumbed to the twentieth-century dictatorship's tendency to personal rule, and their personal dictators, Mussolini and Hitler, would soon provide two of the best examples of the dangers of personal rule. For each would bring about the destruction of his regime by pursuing grandiose schemes for territorial expansion that eventually involved Italy and Germany in a world war they could not win. The Second World War provided the opportunity for the two regimes to be destroyed through military means by a coalition of the democracies and the Communist dictatorship in the Soviet Union. They were able to eliminate the fascist challenge in a rapid and comprehensive fashion that would not have been possible in peacetime, as the survival of Franco's quasi-fascist regime into the 1970s confirms. The fatal flaw of the twentieth-century form of dictatorship was never better exposed than in the virtual self-destruction of these two fascist regimes by their personal rulers.

The same flaw seriously weakened the next great challenge to democracy by the twentieth-century form of dictatorship. Although the Second World War destroyed the Nazi and Fascist regimes, it also resulted in the Communist takeover of Eastern Europe, North Korea and China by the end of the 1940s. On the face of it the new, Communist challenge to democracy seemed more dangerous than the fascist had been, for in this post-war period the Communists had rapidly won control of a large proportion of the world's territory and population. Yet the Communist challenge soon lost momentum. In particular, the dissolving of the old colonial empires into dozens of independent states during the 1950s and 1960s failed to add significantly to the number of Communist regimes. It is true that only a few of the newly independent states became stable democracies. But the rest usually either succumbed to the old-fashioned form of military dictatorship or created new varieties of the twentieth-century form of dictatorship, rejecting its Communist as well as fascist varieties. Among the many reasons for this loss of Communist momentum was the harm that had been done to the image of Communism by the personal ruler of the Soviet Union, Josef Stalin, until his death in 1953. Stalin's refusal during the post-war period to liberalize his totalitarian Soviet Union or to introduce any other innovatory policies reduced the potential appeal of Communism. Nor did the tyrannical control he exercised over Eastern European Communist regimes encourage newly independent states to join the bloc of Communist regimes.

Therefore the challenge to democracy was divided from the 1950s onwards between Communist and non-Communist varieties of the twentieth-century form of dictatorship. The non-Communist varieties were the main rival of democracy in what became known as the Third World, the very large group of states which had recently emerged from colonialism or foreign domination and had no desire to join the Western or Communist blocs. Not until the 1970s was there a burst of Communist expansion in the Third World. In addition to the conquest of South Vietnam, Laos and Cambodia by conventional or guerrilla armies, the decade saw the establishment of several avowedly Marxist–Leninist regimes in Africa, notably in Angola and Ethiopia.

Yet it was also in the 1970s that democracy began a somewhat surprising, almost anachronistic, resurgence. During the later 1970s and the 1980s a wave of democratization swept through Portugal, Spain, much of South America, the Philippines, South Korea, Pakistan, and ultimately into the Communist bailiwick of Eastern Europe. The Communist challenge was to experience almost as rapid and comprehensive a defeat as the fascist challenge did in the Second World War. By the end of the 1980s most of the East European states had renounced their former belief in Communist Party domination of state and society and were preparing for multi-party elections. Even the Soviet Union itself was showing signs of impending democratization. The aura of historical inevitability that democracy had enjoyed seventy years earlier had returned and all forms of dictatorship seemed in danger of extinction.

2 Analyzing the Ideological One-Party States: Components, Leadership and Types

The chapters that follow will use a small set of basic concepts or terms in analyzing their case studies of the twentieth-century form of dictatorship, the ideological one-party state. Its distinctive components, the official ideology and political party, in turn have their own distinctive characteristics, such as their monopoly privileges and their multirole capacity. But the case studies will also focus upon other features of these regimes, notably the tendency to personal rule. Furthermore, the case studies will be categorized as examples of one or other of the two different types of ideological one-party state – the party-state and military-party types.

1 COMPONENTS

An *ideology* is similar to a religion in holding certain things to be sacred. As with a religion, such sacred things can include not only particular doctrines but also particular texts, symbols, events and people. There are two major differences, though, between a religion and an ideology. The first is that ideology is primarily concerned with ideas, goals and principles, while a religion may consist solely of sacred rituals and symbols. The second is that religion is focused on spiritual, 'other worldly' matters, while ideology is concerned with 'this worldly' matters, such as politics, economics, social structure, and even international relations.

As was mentioned in the previous chapter, the official ideologies of ideological one-party states tend to be monopolistic, extensive, disciplined and multi-role. But the case studies will be concerned only with the actual *content* of a regime's ideology and with its two legitimating roles – the governing role of legitimating the regime's policies and the political role of legitimating the regime itself. (Furthermore, there will be no attempt to estimate how wide a section of society accepted the legitimation as valid and morally binding.) No attention will be paid to the ideology's other, social role of strengthening social solidarity through its solidarity-building content.

The political party, the *regime party*, of an ideological one-party state is publicly or implicitly recognized by the regime as its official party. However, the regime party does not always call itself a political party, sometimes preferring instead the title of 'Union' or 'Front'. Nor is the regime party always the *only* party allowed to exist – whether in law (*de jure*) or in fact (*de facto*) – in an ideological one-party state. For in addition to the standard, *literal* one-party states, where literally only one party is allowed to exist, there are many supposedly 'multi-party' regimes which differ only in form rather than substance from a literal one-party state. In these *substantive* one-party states the regime party is given a monopoly in *effectiveness* rather than in law or in fact – one or more other parties are allowed to exist alongside the regime's official party but are not allowed to compete effectively with it.

Another important distinction is the difference between the *non*-competitive and the *semi*-competitive variants of the 'multi-party', substantive one-party state. The Communist 'people's democracies' were the most common examples of the non-competitive variant. They tried to maintain a multi-party, democratic façade by preserving one or more non-Communist parties and even giving them token parliamentary representation. However, these parties had been taken over by the regime to use for its own purposes – they were *puppet* parties – and they did not in any way compete with or oppose the official party. The semi-competitive variant of the one-party state has been less common but has produced much more convincing façades of multi-party democracy. Examples of this variant, such as in Mexico, Indonesia and Perón's Argentina, not only allow other parties to exist alongside the regime party but also allow them to retain a degree of autonomy and to compete with the official party in supposedly democratic elections. The regime makes sure that its party enjoys a monopoly in effectiveness, though, by providing special advantages for the regime party and hampering the competing parties. The special advantages have ranged from simply rigging the vote in favour of the regime party to using state patronage – public funds, works and jobs – to buy voting support for the regime party. The hampering of competing parties has ranged from simply arresting their leaders to restricting their access to the mass media.

The political role of the regime party in a 'multi-party', substantive one-party state is in some ways the same as a party's role in a democracy – selecting candidates for election to public office and mobilizing voting support for them from the mass electorate. However, even semi-competitive examples of the substantive one-party state offer only unfair and unfree electoral competition. The non-competitive examples offer no competitive element at all, presenting voters with only one candidate (or list) for each constituency, to vote for or against. The semblance of representativeness is maintained in these one-candidate elections by including members of the puppet parties among the list of parliamentary candidates. (One-candidate elections are also quite commonly held in the literal one-party states, such as the former Soviet Union, where the candidates all belong to the official and sole party or are token non-party representatives approved by the party.) The lack of a competitive element is not the only difference between a regime party's political role and that of a party in a democracy. Many of the public offices sought by the regime party's electoral candidates have no real power or even influence and are basically only ceremonial or symbolic. Parliaments in particular are almost invariably only rubber-stamping institutions. Together with the uncompetitive nature of elections, this political irrelevancy of most elected public offices greatly reduces the significance of the party's political role.

However, the political role is usually not the only role performed by a regime party, and this *multi-role* aspect of regime parties will be very evident in the case studies that follow. As with the coverage of ideology, most attention will paid to the governing role – the party's governmental policy making and supervision of the implementation of the regime's policies by the state apparatus. Less attention will be paid to its political role and to its social role of helping (not always very effectively) to indoctrinate the society in the solidarity-building ideology, to instil the ideology in the hearts and minds of the people.

The case studies will also examine the *monopolistic, extensive* and *disciplined* nature of the party component of an ideological one-party state. What sort of monopoly did the party enjoy? How extensive was the party? Did it have a very large membership, many attached organizations, and an extensive administrative apparatus? How disciplined was the party – to a quasi-military or just a quasi-bureaucratic degree? Did it have a military-style hierarchical structure, with a highly disciplined chain of command stretching from the highest to the lowest ranking member? Or did it have a less disciplined and less hierarchical structure, more like that of a bureaucracy? In looking at such questions the case studies will be able to 'flesh out' what has so far been only a skeletal description of the new type of political party developed by the ideological one-party states.

2 INDIVIDUAL/COLLECTIVE LEADERSHIP AND PERSONAL DICTATORSHIP

As was pointed out in the previous chapter, the ideological one-party states are plagued by a tendency towards personal rule. Dictatorship by an organization, whether by a party or a military force, tends to be transformed into personal dictatorship. The tendency towards personal rule has often taken the shape of a dictatorship's recognized regime leader (who usually holds the post of head of state or head of government) transforming himself from an agent of the party or military into a personal dictator. However, the tendency towards personal rule has also quite often taken the shape of a personal dictator emerging from a regime which has a *collective* leadership rather than an individual leader.

Collective leadership of an ideological one-party state usually takes the form of a party or military's *political committee* acting as the collective agent of that organization's dictatorship. In the case of party dictatorships the most common example of this political committee is a Communist Party's Political Bureau, usually known simply as the Politburo. In the case of military dictatorships the political committee of the military is an *ad hoc* group of leading military men that is commonly referred to by political observers as a 'junta', the Spanish-American word for 'council'. Juntas give themselves such titles as the Military Council, the Revolutionary Command Council, or even the State Law and Order Restoration Committee. While a junta may consist of simply the heads of the three armed services, quite often it includes a dozen or so other senior officers, and it may even consist entirely of middle-ranking officers if they, not the high command, have led the military seizure of power.

When a personal dictator emerges from a situation of collective leadership, there can be some difficulty in judging the progress of his transformation into a personal ruler. It is quite common for one member of a political committee to exercise a dominant influence within or over it. In the case of Stalin and the Soviet Union's Politburo or of Nasser and the Egyptian RCC junta this dominant member of the committee eventually became a personal ruler. But it is difficult to say exactly when it was that he achieved this status – when exactly did he become more than just an agent of the party or the military? More importantly, in many cases the dominant individual in a political committee never achieved such an obvious degree of personal power as Stalin eventually acquired. In these examples it can be difficult to decide whether the dominant individual ever became a personal ruler. For there are several degrees of personal rule and the difference between an example of weak personal rule and one of individual regime leadership is not always easy to discern.

In assessing to what extent a regime succumbed to personal rule, the case studies will be concerned not just with the question of *whether* personal rule occurred but also with estimating and describing the *degree* of personal rule. For example, how secure or absolutist was the personal ruler, and did he actually reverse rather than just escape from the principal-agent relationship with the party or military? In making their assessment the case studies will use as indicators and explanations the three main bases on which a position of personal rule is built. As indicators of personal rule they could be summed up as, first, whether the apparently dominant individual occupies a governing office, such as President, that is constitutionally endowed with extensive powers and prestige; secondly, whether he is the leader of the military and/or the official party; thirdly, whether he has much standing with the public, or at least is the subject of an official 'personality cult'. However, the question of whether or not – and to what degree – a regime succumbed to personal rule is irrelevant when it comes to deciding which of the two *types* of ideological one-party state that regime belongs to. For the two types are distinguished not by the presence or absence of personal rule but by the *party/military* distinction.

3 THE PARTY-STATE AND MILITARY-PARTY TYPES

The two types of ideological one-party state are the *party-state* and *military-party* regimes. In a party-state regime the ruler is either the regime party or a party figure. In a military-party regime the ruler is either the military or a military figure, who may have retired or resigned from the military. Thus within each of these two types of twentieth-century dictatorship there is the distinction between personal rule by a dictator, either a party or military figure, and dictatorship by an organization, either the party or the military.

Although the terms 'party-state' and 'military-party' are being used simply to make a party/military distinction between types of one-party state, they beg the question of what exactly is the relationship between party and state and between military and party in these two types of dictatorship. The simple answer is that the relationship varies from one example to the next. It is not a topic that will be explicitly included in the case studies but in each case of party-state regime it is implicitly covered by the assessment of the party's governing role – that is, the extent to which the party performs the twin roles of governmental policy making and supervision of the state's implementation of the regime's policies. In looking at governmental policy making the key question is whether the party's political committee has replaced the state's governing body – its Cabinet or Council of Ministers – as the real government of the country, with the legal government reduced only to implementing the governmental policy decisions of the party's political committee.

In looking at party supervision the key question is what the party's officials can do in the way of supervising the state's implementation of the regime's policies. If as in the Italian Fascist regime they do not exercise any control over the state, the party's supervisory role is reduced to no more than *monitoring* the state's implementation of policy. All that the party can do is pass on information about misimplementation to the regime's leadership or personal ruler. The party obviously would have a much stronger supervisory role if it could exercise at least the 'negative' control of being able to *veto* decisions by members of the state apparatus. And the party would have a powerful supervisory role if it could actually *direct* the state's implementation of policy. The distinction between vetoing and directing is very evident in the case of Communist regimes, where the party's supervisors of the military arm of the state are never allowed more than a right of veto (over military officers' orders) but where some of the party's supervisors of the civilian state apparatus are able to issue directives to state officials.

As for the relationship between military and party in a military-party regime, this is implicitly covered in the case studies of military-party regimes in a special section on the military which has been added to the usual section describing the regime party. In each case there is an assessment of the part that the military has played in this particular military-party regime. Invariably the military prefers to leave electoral and indoctrinating roles to the regime party. However, sometimes the military has adopted a governmental policy-making role (through its junta political committee) and, more often, a supervisory role – which has normally encompassed not just the civilian state apparatus but also the regime party itself.

Part I
The Party-State Type

3 The Fascist Examples

1 MUSSOLINI'S REGIME IN ITALY

The first example of a fascist one-party state was the Fascist party-state regime established in Italy in the 1920s – a regime which gave its name to the generic term of 'fascism'. After the First World War some of the more right-wing war veterans established the small *fasci di combattimento* (groups of combatants) movement and its paramilitary wing, the 'squads'. The *fasci* found their political mission in a very violent response to the social unrest that plagued the kingdom of Italy as it moved towards a truly democratic form of constitutional monarchy.[1] What became known as the *biennio rosso* (red years) of 1919–20 saw constant expressions of revolutionary rhetoric as the Marxist Socialists and other leftists mobilized the masses into trade unions and political parties. In fact the Fascist regime would later propagate the myth that the *fasci* movement's violent attack – through its squads of street fighters – on the left-wing parties and trade unions had saved Italy from 'Bolshevism', from a leftist revolution like the one which the Bolsheviks had staged in Russia in October 1917.

However, the Fascist movement became an effective counter-revolutionary force only in 1921, *after* the revolutionary impulse among the workers had been extinguished by the failure of their move to take over the factories.[2] (The Fascist movement had a membership of only some 20 000 at the end of 1920 but by the end of 1921 the newly created Fascist Party could boast a membership of almost 250 000.[3]) Nevertheless, the fear and class hatred that had been aroused during the 'red years' was a major factor in stimulating upper- and middle-class support for the Fascists and in winning over the support of much of the state apparatus, many of whose members assisted or allowed the Fascists to perpetrate their lawless violence against the left. Finally, in October 1922 the Fascists staged a weak attempt at a coup, the March on Rome. The constitutional government resigned

23

and left the King to make the crucial decision of whether to use the army against the Fascists or find a political solution. He chose to end the crisis by appointing the Fascists' leader, Mussolini, to be his new Prime Minister.

Despite the Fascist description of the March on Rome as a revolution, there was to be no social revolution and for a time there was no political revolution either. The leader of the Fascist Party had been undemocratically but quite constitutionally appointed Prime Minister and proceeded to rule according to the provisions of the existing Constitution. Mussolini seems initially to have been seeking a political arrangement in which the Fascist Party would share power with amenable allies behind a façade of competitive multi-party democracy – and under his rule as Prime Minister. But from 1925 onwards he set about establishing a one-party state and propagating an official ideology, Fascism.

Fascist Ideology

Fascism was an extensive ideology that covered everything from economics to aesthetics but it was based upon the sacred principles or values of nationalism and statism. A foreign observer of the regime came to the conclusion that 'the Nation as the supreme ethical unit dominates the Fascist scheme of values'.[4] The concern for national solidarity was used to support the regime's anti-liberalism and anti-socialism, while nationalism was used to support the imperialist strand in Fascist ideology. Italy was depicted as being a young, 'proletarian' nation exploited and constricted by the older nations, such as Britain and France, that had acquired their empires in earlier times and now wished to prevent Italy, too, from acquiring an empire. And as Fascist nationalism emphasized Italy's ancient Roman heritage, the desire for a Mediterranean colonial empire was presented as the desire for a new Roman Empire. Similarly, the ancient Roman values were used to support Fascism's fervent militarism, displayed in Mussolini's famous pronouncements that 'War alone... puts the stamp of nobility upon the peoples who have the courage to meet it', and that Fascism was 'education for combat'.[5]

The imperialism and militarism espoused in Fascist ideology legitimated the regime's imperialist and bellicose foreign policy of the mid-1930s onwards. The invasion and conquest of Ethiopia in 1935–6 was the first outward sign of the serious intent of the new foreign policy. It was followed by military intervention in the Spanish Civil War and then by the invasion and conquest of Albania. By 1938 Mussolini was publicly proclaiming that Italians were now 'permanently mobilized for war', and in private he was setting the goal of having the economy prepared for a major war.[6] (In fact his foreign policy was already having a major effect on the regime's economic policy, which was by now aimed at rearmament and an autarkic, self-sufficient economy.) However, Nazi Germany initiated a full-scale European war in 1939, several years ahead of Mussolini's schedule. His initial, prudent policy of staying out of the war was hard to justify after the bellicose ideological and propaganda emphasis of recent years. But his later disastrous decision of June 1940 to join his German ally in apparently finishing off the defeated French and British – and dismembering their empires – could easily be legitimated by Fascist ideology.

Statism was almost as important as nationalism in Fascist ideology, and in fact Mussolini in 1932 depicted the Fascist State as being the 'keystone' of Fascist doctrine.[7] The extremist nature of Fascist statism was epitomized by the Fascist notion of the 'totalitarian State', summed up in Mussolini's famous slogan, 'Everything in the State, nothing outside of the State, nothing against the State'.[8] Such statism was also evident in the development and implementation of Fascism's economic doctrine of the Corporative (or Corporate) State.

The Fascist doctrine of the Corporative State was regarded by many foreign observers as Fascism's main claim to be an ideology equal in significance to liberal democracy or to Communism.[9] Fascist corporativism envisaged an economy organized into combined employer–employee syndicates or corporations, each covering a particular branch of industry or sector of the economy. Originally it was envisaged that these syndicates or corporations would collectively manage the economy, but in the mid-1920s the corporativist ideal was given a more statist interpretation. Any idea of economic self-government by the corporations was no longer taken seriously except in the regime's propaganda. The creation by law in 1926 of thirteen syndicates was aimed not at introducing a degree of corporativist economic management but instead at providing the means and ideological justification for instituting state control over labour contracts and disputes. (Moreover, these syndicates were not the originally envisaged combined employer–employee bodies; there were separate syndicates for employers and for employees.) In 1934 the regime did establish twenty-two combined employer–employee corporations with powers to regulate prices and production as well as labour relations and wages. But these powers were ultimately controlled by the state, and the new corporations were in practice no more than state-controlled forums for discussing industry or sector problems and plans.

A new and important component was added to the ideology in 1929 when the atheist Mussolini signed a Treaty and Concordat with the Vatican and began a mutually beneficial alliance with the Catholic Church. The strong anticlerical wing and tradition of the Fascist Party were silenced and Catholicism was incorporated into the Fascist ideology as one of the things Fascism held to be sacred.[10] By the mid-1930s Fascist Italy 'was a confessional state, unique among the great powers of contemporary Europe'.[11] The new relationship between Church and Fascist state began stormily and was strained by the regime's adoption of Nazi-style racism and anti-Semitism in the late 1930s.[12] But the ideologically recognized alliance with the Church certainly succeeded in increasing the regime's legitimacy in the eyes of the Catholic section of the population.

Finally, while the Fascists clearly had a basically negative attitude to democracy, Fascist ideology did not completely renounce any claim to incorporate some kind of democracy. Mussolini strongly attacked not only the form of democracy practised by contemporary Western states but also the very principles of majority rule and of political equality – as manifested in the practice of universal suffrage. Yet he went on to argue that 'if democracy may be conceived in diverse forms', then 'Fascism may write itself down as "an organized, centralized and authoritative democracy"'.[13]

The Fascist Party

The March on Rome did not lead immediately to any sort of monopoly for the Fascist Party, the Partito Nazionale Fascista. A relatively democratic multi-party system continued operating until the 1924 elections, when it became clear that the Fascist Party was being guaranteed a monopoly in effectiveness by Mussolini's government. Then in October 1925, almost exactly three years after the March on Rome, the Socialist Party was banned, and in 1926 the new Law for the Defence of the State was (mis)used to ban all the remaining non-Fascist parties, including Catholic and liberal parties.[14]

By the time it had acquired this legally enforced but not legally recognized monopoly, the Fascist Party had almost doubled in size, from 500 000 members in October 1922 to 940 000 in November 1926.[15] Some of these new members were acquired through a merger with the small Nationalist Party but most of the new members were opportunists or careerists jumping on the Fascist bandwagon. Therefore the Party decided to limit its extensiveness in order to preserve its pretensions to being a revolutionary élite. It took the innovatory step of banning any further adult enrolment in the Party and allowing only graduates of the Fascist youth groups to acquire Party membership. In 1932, though, the ban on adults joining the Party was lifted and membership was opened to all state employees – in fact Party membership became obligatory for civil servants. The Party lost any pretension to being a committed élite of 'combatants' and became a state party, incorporating the hundreds of thousands of state bureaucrats. (The danger that the Party might be taken over by the state employees was removed by the simple but again innovatory step of prohibiting these new members from holding any leadership post within the Party.[16]) The ban on adult enrolment was then reimposed and continued until 1936, when volunteers for the war in Ethiopia were permitted to apply. At the end of the decade the Party's membership stood at more than 2.6 million – some 6 per cent of the population.[17]

A distinctive feature of the Fascist Party was that it remained an exclusively male organization. However, a separate

network of women's *fasci* units was established and by 1936
the Fasci Femminili organization had a membership of
583 000.[18] In addition to this attached women's organization, the Party acquired control in the 1930s of the massive, multi-million-member Dopolavoro leisure organization.
On the other hand, the large Fascist trade union movement
had been transformed into state-supervised employee syndicates. Similarly, the Party's youth organization, the Balilla,
had been transformed into a state organ under the authority
of the Ministry of Education. The only Fascist youth groups
retained by the Party were those aimed at young adults. Not
until near the end of the 1930s did the Party take control of
a new youth organization, the GIL, which covered all age
groups and quickly became compulsory.

To administer what became a multi-million-member party
– supplemented by some sizeable attached organizations –
the Fascists had to develop an extensive administrative apparatus.[19] It was headed by a national Secretary, whose national headquarters' staff included administrative and
political secretariats and other specialist organs. At the
regional level each provincial administrative apparatus was
headed by one of the ninety-four provincial Party secretaries. Beneath them were the some 7300 local Party secretaries who each headed a *fascio di combattimento*. These
administrative secretaries – national, provincial, and local
– were also political leaders. They constituted the leadership corps that directed the life of the Party on behalf of
the ultimate leader, the Duce (leader), who headed the
Party as a whole.

The Fascist Party was hierarchical and disciplined in both
theory and practice. Fascist ideology included a 'principle
of hierarchy', and the Party's leadership corps were called
gerarchi (hierarchs).[20] Its first Party statute had declared
its keystones to be 'order, discipline and hierarchy'.[21] Hierarchy and discipline were also to be expected in a party
with such a military flavour – composed of 'groups of
combatants', having its members wear a black-shirted uniform, and officially entitled a 'voluntary militia placed at
the service of the nation'.[22] In 1926 the elective element in
the Party's organization, the election from below of the
local *fascio* secretary and the provincial secretary, was re-

placed in theory and practice by appointment from above.[23]

At the top of the Party hierarchy was Mussolini, the Duce of the Party, who chose the national Secretary of the Party – in fact Mussolini chose and replaced four different national Secretaries from 1925 to 1939.[24] The national Secretary in turn not only nominated the provincial secretaries but also could transfer them from one province to another. He was able to enforce a bureaucratic, though not quasi-military, discipline upon the provincial secretaries, who in turn were enforcing it upon the secretaries of the local *fasci*. It is true that some veteran provincial leaders of Fascism, who had risen to power in their provinces by their own efforts, enjoyed so much independent power after the March on Rome that they were referred to informally as *ras*, the Ethiopian word for a feudal chief. But most of these *ras* were removed in the later 1920s or surrendered to the discipline imposed by the national Secretary. By the 1930s the national Secretary had won complete control over nearly all of the provincial secretaries, as was shown when almost half of them were 'kicked upstairs' into the Chamber of Deputies by the national Secretary.

The Fascist Party did not provide a very good example of the multi-role capacity of a regime party. The initial political role of the Party was perhaps the most significant and effective role that it played. In the 1924 elections it had to produce victory for the 'government list' of candidates (including a number of non-Fascist conservatives) in a hard-fought and in many cities truly competitive multi-party election.[25] But the Party's political role steadily declined in importance. By the time of the 1929 elections a literal one-party state had been established and the Party was engaged in a referendum-like 'single list' election to a parliament that had lost much of its power and political significance. Ten years later the parliament's elected Chamber of Deputies was actually replaced by a Chamber of Fasci and Corporations, thereby removing any requirement for the Party to engage in electoral activities of any kind.

There was no similar decline in the Party's social role of strengthening social solidarity by instilling Fascist ideology in the hearts and minds of the people. If anything, the regime's emphasis on indoctrination increased during the

1930s. But the Party was hampered by the weakness of its organizational presence in the south of Italy and by the fact that several of the organizations propagating Fascism, such as the youth organizations and the syndicates, were not under the direction of the Party. Therefore, it is not surprising that the Party appears to have been quite ineffective in converting Italians into Fascists.[26]

The Party's lack of a significant governing role, though, was its most striking failing as a multi-role party. The weakness of its governing role was only to be expected considering the statism of Fascist ideology and the statist bias of the official pronouncements on the place of the Party within the regime's political structure. For example, in 1927 a well-publicized circular by Mussolini to the state's Prefects (provincial Governors) stated that the Party was 'only an instrument conscious of the will of the State' and consequently that all Fascists were to 'subordinately collaborate' with the Prefect of their province.[27] Similarly, a law of 1932 stated that the Fascist Party was a 'Civilian Militia at the orders of the Duce, in the service of the Fascist State'.[28] By then the Party's own constitution had explicitly acknowledged the 'conscious and definitive subordination of the Party to the State, both at the centre and at the periphery'.[29]

Any possibility of the Party's performing a policy-making governing role was ended when the nearest thing the Party had to a political committee, the Grand Council of Fascism, was transformed into a state-dominated institution. The Grand Council had been established at the end of 1922 and was declared in the new Party Statute of 1926 to be the supreme policy-making organ of Fascism.[30] In an innovatory move the Fascist regime in 1928 conferred constitutional status upon this Party organ – indeed it acquired a legal authority second only to the King's and superior to the Council of Ministers'. However, Mussolini stated that the new, constitutionally recognized Grand Council was to be 'the collective synthesis of the various organizations of the State'.[31] This not only suggested that the Party was a state organization but also meant that the Grand Council had to include representatives of the various other state organizations. To the Party's national Secretary, Vice-Secretary and four senior Fascist leaders were added, *ex officio*, no fewer than sixteen holders of high state offices. Mussolini himself was now in law the powerful chairman of the Grand Council (with the right to set its agenda and convene it at his discretion) only because he was head of government, not because he was Duce of the Party.

In the light of the regime's statist bias it is hardly surprising that the Party did not acquire any supervisory powers over the state apparatus. Although in 1932 the civil servants were drafted into the Party, the national Secretary and his staff were never given any authority by Mussolini to supervise the civil service.[32] The most they could do was unofficially monitor its activities and put in a good word for active Fascists seeking promotion. At the regional level the Party's position was even weaker. The 1927 circular to the Prefects clarified the relationship between them and the provincial Party secretaries by making it quite clear that the Prefect was superior to the provincial Party secretary in not only state matters but even in Party matters. The circular specified that the Prefect was the 'highest political representative of the Fascist regime' at the provincial level and was 'to stimulate and coordinate the activities of the Party in its various manifestations' within his province.[33] This was the first and only time that a party-state regime gave state officials control over the regime party.

Nor did the Party perform a significant supervisory role in its dealings with the military arm of the state apparatus. The opening of the Party to civilian state employees in the early 1930s was accompanied by a less coercive opening of the Party to the military that authorized rather than forced the officer corps to join the Party.[34] Most army officers did join the Party and it successfully interfered in the promotions process on behalf of Party members it held in high regard.[35] There was also a 'Fascistization' of the military through the introduction of Fascist indoctrination and celebrations and in such relatively trivial matters as the adoption of the Fascist salute and goose-step.[36] Yet such Fascistization and the widespread Party membership do not seem to have involved the Party in performing much more of a supervisory role than it performed in relation to the civil service – at most an unofficial monitoring of how the regime's policies were being implemented.

The lack of Party supervision of the military might have appeared more politically significant if the Party had not also possessed some form of counterbalance – the Militia – to the army's military power. One of the regime's major innovations was the creation of a Fascist state Militia.[37] Not long before the March on Rome the Fascists had formed a militia out of the paramilitary squads attached to the local *fasci*. In January 1923, this militia was replaced by the legally recognized and empowered but still highly political Voluntary Militia for National Security (MVSN). The law which established the MVSN defined its function as helping the police and the army to maintain public order and depicted it as being a voluntary force drawn from the Fascist Party's militia and from suitable volunteers approved by the Party and MVSN leaders. By 1928 it was taking part in the annual military manoeuvres as an independent force operating alongside the army. The Militia had become a separate (albeit part-time) army, tens of thousands of whose members would later fight overseas, in Ethiopia and Spain, in their own Militia divisions and battalions. Moreover, the Militia's membership had grown to 461 000 by 1934 and no less than 764 000 by 1938.[38] But the Militia was not as powerful a Party counterbalance to the army's military power as may at first appear. The dual nature of the Militia as both a state and a political organization meant that it swore allegiance to the King as well as to Mussolini. More importantly, by the 1930s the Militia had also lost its independence from the army and become subject to a degree of control by the military.[39]

Mussolini's Personal Rule

Mussolini provided the earliest example of personal rule over a party-state regime, albeit a limited and insecure form of personal rule. From the time he became Prime Minister he sought to be more than just an agent of the Fascist Party, and within a few years he was making a serious effort at establishing a position of personal rule. A distinctive feature of this effort was that it involved subordinating the Party to the state, despite the fact that he was the Party's leader. Mussolini was the founder of the Fascist movement, the acknowledged Duce of the Party since its inception, and had seen his formal leadership position over the Party officially recognized in the new Party Statute of 1926.[40] Yet instead of transforming the Party into a powerful agent or instrument of his personal rule he converted his Party into an instrument of the *state* by such moves as in 1927 subordinating the Party in the provinces to the state Prefects and in 1928 transforming the Party's Grand Council of Fascism into a state-dominated institution. In doing so, Mussolini was reducing the political significance of his position as leader of the Party and was increasing his reliance upon his state post as head of the government.

However, this state office of Chief of the Government, which was created for him by a law of December 1925, was a very powerful post.[41] Unlike his previous state office of Prime Minister, it placed Mussolini in complete charge of the Council of Ministers and gave him autonomy from and some dominance over the parliament's Chamber of Deputies. (So he was no longer dependent in any way upon the Party's performing its political role and stacking the Chamber with his supporters.) As Chief of the Government he also took control of the new legislative powers conferred upon the government in 1926 by a law which allowed it to issue 'juridical rules' or decree-laws that would have the force of law for two years from their date of promulgation.[42] Furthermore, as was mentioned earlier, the Chief of the Government was the chairman and virtual controller of the constitutionally empowered Grand Council of Fascism.

In addition to being Chief of the Government, Mussolini personally held the key ministerial posts in the government, such as Minister of the Interior, and in fact at one time he held no fewer than eight of the thirteen ministerial posts.[43] Among the key Ministries that he headed were the three military, armed-service Ministries. But being a civilian who had never held a higher rank than corporal, Mussolini could not expect to enjoy much personal authority over the military. His lack of real authority over the military was an obvious weakness in not only his control of the state apparatus but also his position as a personal ruler.

From the later 1920s onwards his personal position was

strengthened by the effort of the Party and other propagandists to boost Mussolini's public standing – to have the public view him as Duce of Italy as well as of the Party. By the 1930s the national Secretary of the Party had become, in a modern historian's description, the 'high priest' of a 'cult of the *Duce*'.[44] And some foreign observers gained the impression that *mussolinismo*, as it was called, had actually replaced Fascism.[45] All the regime's successes, real or exaggerated, were credited to the Duce by the Fascist propagandists, producing the colloquial maxim that 'everything bad is the fault of the Fascists and all that is good is due to Mussolini'.[46] Newsreels of Mussolini declaiming and posturing to a crowd from the balcony of his office made the oratorical or demagogic aspect of *mussolinismo* internationally famous. By the 1930s he was also clearly the leading, if not the sole, official ideologist of the Fascist regime. His role as intellectual ideologist was included in the mass media campaign to depict Mussolini as truly a man of many parts and talents, including hard-working head of government, international statesman, military leader, intellectual, and family man. Nevertheless, a few real 'achievements' probably did as much as the propaganda cult of the Duce to increase Mussolini's prestige. His public standing reached its high points after the signing of the Treaty and Concordat with the Vatican in 1929 (even the Pope referred to him as 'the man sent by Providence') and after Italy's conquest of Ethiopia and defiance of the League of Nations in 1935–6.[47]

Yet although Mussolini had established some degree of personal rule, his personal position had a very serious underlying weakness – the constitutionally supreme position of the King as head of state. For example, the King was the titular Commander-in-Chief of the armed forces, and not until June 1940 did he delegate this titular supreme command to Mussolini.[48] Not only the military but also the civil service and police swore their oath of loyalty to the King.[49] Although Mussolini was Chief of the Government, in theory and law it was not 'his' government but the King's government that he headed and directed. The government decrees issued by Mussolini took the form of Royal Decrees, and the special decree-laws issued by the government after 1926 were promulgated in the name of the King's government. Most important of all, the law of 1925 that established the new office of Chief of the Government affirmed that the holder of the new office would be appointed/dismissed by the King and would be constitutionally responsible and subordinate to the King.[50] Thus Mussolini had built his personal position upon an inherently insecure foundation in opting to emphasize the state rather than Party component of his regime. There was a superior source of constitutional/state authority that could be used to remove him from his most powerful office without the need for coups or revolutions.

Mussolini's personal position was also formally overshadowed by the post-1928 Grand Council of Fascism. With a constitutional authority second only to the King's, the Grand Council clearly possessed a legal authority over state organizations – including the state-serving Fascist Party – which was greater than that of the Chief of the Government. So it may have been partly wariness, a concern for what might happen if he ever lost control of a Grand Council meeting, that led Mussolini to convene the Grand Council with decreasing frequency – as early as 1934 it met only once in the year.[51] The Grand Council met very rarely in the later 1930s and was not convened at all in the early 1940s, not even to approve Italy's entry into the war.

Therefore it is surprising that in the face of the crisis caused by the Allies' invasion of Sicily in July 1943 Mussolini decided to call a meeting of the virtually defunct Grand Council. After the meeting had gone on long into the night, he also allowed an implicit vote of no confidence to be put and carried against him.[52] The following afternoon the King replaced him with a military man, Marshal Badoglio, as Chief of the Government, and Mussolini was taken into police custody.[53] Thus Mussolini's personal rule was ended by the two sources of authority that were theoretically and legally superior to him, the Grand Council and the King. The most obvious reason why the public, the Party, and the Militia did not then rally to his support was because of his disastrous handling of the war that he had foisted upon Italy. But another reason was that Mussolini, his Fascist ideology and his regime had for many years emphasized the statist/legal aspect of the Fascist regime. By 1943 it was too late to change tack from the course set as far back as October 1922 when the violent, lawless Fascist movement had not carried out a real political revolution but instead seen its leader constitutionally appointed Prime Minister by the King and then follow a largely legal path to personal rule.

However, the fundamental weakness of Mussolini's Fascist party-state regime was not so much his attempt to establish personal rule upon legal/state foundations; it was the fact that the personal rule was built upon such a *weak* legal/state foundation. As Hitler pointed out, Mussolini 'had failed to erect a Fuehrerstaat [leader state] in which the leader had "absolute authority"'.[54] Hitler would not make the same mistake.

2 HITLER'S REGIME IN GERMANY

The coming to power of Hitler and his Nazi Party, the National Socialist German Workers Party, is one of the most written about topics in modern history. Even if the Nazis had not gone on to become a byword for evil, their spectacular rise to power through the ballot box rather than revolution or coup would have attracted much academic attention. A party which had won less than 3 per cent of the vote in the elections of 1928 saw its leader become the head of government in 1933 in accordance with the constitutional proprieties and, unlike the Fascist Party in Italy, because it held the largest number of seats in parliament.

It is often pointed out that Hitler and the Nazi Party did not come to power in truly democratic fashion. The Nazis and their Nationalist allies could not command a majority in the German parliament (the Reichstag) when Hitler became head of government (Reich Chancellor) on 30 January 1933. For the Nazi Party had won less than 33 per cent of the vote in the November 1932 elections to the Reichstag. As this had marked a significant decline from the more than 37 per cent of the vote that the Nazis had won a few months earlier in the July elections, there was also reason to believe that the Nazi phenomenon had lost its momentum. (In particular the Nazis had been unable to break into the unionized working-class constituencies of the Social Democratic and Communist parties or into the Catholic constituency of the Centre Party.) Furthermore, the actual decline in voting support between July and November seems to confirm that the earlier, 1930–2 massive rise in the Nazi vote was largely a protest vote produced by the cataclysmic economic crisis, known as the Great Depression, that had begun in 1929 and by late 1932 was beginning to ease.

Nevertheless, when President Hindenburg appointed Hitler to the office of Chancellor and head of a new government, the President was acting in a comparatively democratic manner. Since 1930 President Hindenburg had been using his emergency powers, given him by Article 48 of the Constitution, to appoint and support Chancellors and governments that could not command a majority in the Reichstag. When these governments were unable to pass legislation, the President would use his emergency decree powers to implement their policy. In 1932 the President resorted to appointing as Chancellor first a minor conservative politician, Papen, and then an unknown military man, General Schleicher. In comparison to his appointment of these two figures, the President's reluctant decision to turn to Hitler was a relatively democratic move and produced a government that could credibly claim to have major, albeit not majority, support from the public.

Nazi Ideology

The Nazis' radically rightist, fascist ideology of National Socialism differed in several ways from its Fascist counterpart in Italy. For example, National Socialism did not espouse a corporativist ideal like the Corporative State and instead was committed to a form of 'socialism' and to the fraternal/populist ideal of a '*Volk* community'.[55] However, the most significant difference between the two fascist ideologies was that National Socialism was based not on nationalism and statism but on racism.

The most famous or notorious element of National Socialism

was its racial *Weltanschauung* (world view) of a perpetual conflict between the 'culture-creating' Aryan race and the parasitical but cunning Jewish race. The cunning of the Jews was supposedly to be seen in their being behind such outwardly opposed forces as Bolshevism in Russia and international financial capitalism in New York. Nazi racial doctrines also included a Social Darwinist belief in the 'survival of the fittest', both in the deadly struggle between the races and in the social forms of struggle that existed within a race. An accompanying eugenic belief in the need to maintain the purity and health of the race would be used to legitimate not only the Nazis' eugenic policies, including the sterilization of 'defectives', but also the anti-Semitic 'Nuremburg' Laws for the Protection of German Blood. Yet although the racial doctrines of Nazi ideology were used to legitimate many aspects of the regime's persecution of German Jews, these anti-Semitic doctrines were not used to legitimate publicly the ultimate, genocidal 'Final Solution', which was kept secret from the German people and even from the ordinary membership of the Party.

National Socialism's conception of a racial clash of good and evil between Aryans and Jews was complicated by the existence of 'sub-human' races, such as the Negroes and Slavs, and by the existence of national or ethnic subdivisions within the Aryan race. But as the German subdivision of the Aryan race was supposedly the purest and most valuable, German nationalism could be accommodated within the racial ideological framework. The Nazis could exploit the already long-established doctrines of German nationalism by presenting their National Socialist ideology and propaganda in nationalist as well as racist guise.

However, neither nationalism nor racism was publicly used to support National Socialism's imperialist doctrine, for this *Lebensraum* doctrine was not propagated among the German people as part of the regime's official ideology. The Nazis were reticent about presenting the doctrine, let alone the actual policy implications, of the German Aryans' supposed need for more *Lebensraum* (living space) in the east, in the territories inhabited by the Slavs. Not surprisingly, the policy implications of this doctrine – a war of conquest against Eastern Europe and the Soviet Union

– were not spelled out in public.[56] Instead Hitler portrayed himself as seeking to use peaceful means to attain Germany's limited and nationalist, not imperialist, foreign policy goals. Even the rearmament policy that would culminate in the autarkic Four Year Plan of 1936 was portrayed as helping to attain Germany's international goals peacefully, by allowing Germany to negotiate from a position of strength. Outwardly National Socialism had little in common with the open, almost bombastic imperialism and bellicoseness of Fascist ideology.

In contrast to the reticence shown in espousing the imperialist *Lebensraum* doctrine, great publicity was given to the Nazis' social ideal of the *Volksgemeinschaft* (*Volk* community), of establishing a fraternal and populist community of Aryan Germans free of class divisions and selfishness. The *Volksgemeinschaft* ideal was one of the key elements of National Socialist ideology and was used to legitimate much of the regime's social policy – not to mention providing support for the Nazis' opposition to liberal individualism and Marxist class antagonism. It was also linked to the socialist component of National Socialism, which was a social-welfarist 'German' socialism or 'socialism of the deed' that was expressed in such measures as the Winter Relief fund-raising campaign to help the poor through the winter months.

The leader principle (*Führerprinzip*) was National Socialism's highly publicized and pervasive authority principle. It sought an end to collective (committees and parliaments) and rule-governed (bureaucratic) forms of authority and to have them replaced by a personal form of authority exercised by individual leaders. As Hitler himself put it, such leaders were 'to receive unconditional authority and freedom of action downward, but to be charged with unlimited responsibility upward'.[57] Throughout German society and even in the civil service there was an attempt to conform to the Nazi regime's leader principle. It was also used to legitimate the regime's production-oriented policy of increasing employers' power to direct their work-force – the 1934 Law for the Ordering of National Labour transformed employers into authoritarian 'leaders' of their employees.[58] Furthermore, the leader principle legitimated the regime itself (or at least the form the regime took) by legitimating Hitler's absolutist leader position over the regime and the German people.

Therefore, not surprisingly, the Nazis were as ideologically opposed to democracy as the Fascists were in Italy. In his writings of the 1920s Hitler referred to majority rule as being 'mass rule' and made his opposition to parliamentary democracy very clear.[59] Later in his political career he used the concept of 'German democracy' to describe the system of absolutist leaders chosen by the people, but nothing was said by him or other ideologists about how the people could remove or replace a leader.[60]

The Nazi Party

Within a few months of becoming head of government Hitler had established a legally recognized monopoly for the Nazi Party. The repressive, 'anti-Communist' Reichstag Fire Decree of 28 February 1933 eliminated the Communist Party. The Social Democratic Party was outlawed in June, the two liberal parties dissolved themselves only a few days later, and the Catholic Centre Party followed suit in early July. As even the Nazis' Nationalist allies had dissolved their DNVP party in June, the Nazi Party was left with a clear monopoly. Finally, the Law Against the New Formation of Parties promulgated on 14 July enshrined in law the existence of a literal one-party state in Germany.

The Party's membership stood at about 1 million at the beginning of 1933 but had reached 2.5 million by the end of 1934, nearly 5 per cent of the population and proportionately more than twice as extensive as the Fascist Party's membership had been several years after the March on Rome.[61] In reaction to the flood of new, opportunist and careerist members the Party followed the Fascist approach and virtually closed its membership rolls in March 1933 to anyone except worthy graduates of its youth organization. In 1937 a more liberal attitude was adopted towards adult applications for membership and within a year membership had reached no less than 5 million, albeit in a territorially enlarged population of now over 80 million.[62] The Party was also meant to be assisted by a very extensive set of Nazi functional or sectional organizations, such as those aimed at labour (the Labour Front), at youth (the Hitler Youth) and at women (the NSF and DSW).[63] But, like its Fascist counterpart, the Nazi Party was unable to maintain or acquire control over some of these auxiliary organizations. In particular, the Labour Front, the Hitler Youth, and the SS bodyguard/security organization were autonomous entities that were attached in name only to the Party.

The multi-million member Party was both administered and led by its very extensive Politische Organisation (PO), a hierarchical apparatus of Party leaders and their staff which numbered in all some 373 000 men in 1934.[64] (Although women were allowed to join the Party and comprised more than 5 per cent of the membership, they were not allowed to be members of the PO.[65]) Hitler was the ultimate leader and the head of the PO but after becoming head of government he found he could not spare the time to administer the Party. Therefore in April 1933 he appointed his personal secretary, Rudolf Hess, to the new post of Deputy Führer (for Party affairs) to deputize for him in all matters relating to Party administration.[66] Under the title of Office of the Deputy Führer, the headquarters of the PO grew into a substantial institution which was renamed the Party Chancellery in 1941 when Bormann took over Hess's post but was not given the title of Deputy Führer. At the regional level the PO leader-officials were the 32 Gauleiter (leader of a Gau region) and beneath them were more than 800 district leaders (Kreisleiter), the some 20 000 local-branch leaders, and about 250 000 cell or block leaders.

Like the Fascist Party, the Nazi Party was hierarchical and disciplined in both theory and practice and had a militarist view of politics. Party members wore a brown-shirted uniform, and the PO saw themselves as 'political soldiers'.[67] The military analogy also influenced the development in the 1920s of the earlier-mentioned *Führerprinzip* element of Nazi ideology. In accordance with the 'leader principle' the Party eschewed any form of political committee or collective body, as well as Party elections, and each leader at each level of the PO apparatus was given an absolutist authority over his subordinates or 'followers'.

Nevertheless, the chain of command often fell far short of what would be expected of such an apparently hierarchical, disciplined, and virtually militarized party. The most obvious weakness was in the central-to-regional link, which was to prove a weak link in several other regime parties' chains of command. The problem in Nazi Germany was that while the regional Gauleiter proclaimed their personal loyalty and obedience to Hitler, they were by no means obedient to his official representatives at Party headquarters.[68] Hess and Bormann were never able to use the threat of dismissal in dealing with troublesome Gauleiter because Hitler was very loath to dismiss a Gauleiter who was apparently still personally loyal to him. So it is not surprising that Hess and Bormann were never able to enforce any semblance of bureaucratic, let alone quasi-military, discipline upon the political soldiers of the PO. As will be seen when describing the Party's governing role, this lack of discipline was one reason why the Nazi Party was almost as weak a multi-role regime party as its more disciplined Fascist counterpart.

The Nazi Party's political role lost its significance more quickly than had the Fascist Party's. The last multi-party elections in Nazi Germany were held less than two months after Hitler became head of government. Only a few months later Germany became a literal one-party state in law, meaning that any further elections would be of the referendum-like, 'single list' type seen in Fascist Italy in 1929. (Moreover, the German parliament was stripped of all political and even legal significance as early as March 1933 when it passed an Enabling Law that transferred to the government the parliament's right to legislate.) The Party's political role was reduced to mobilizing the voters in the series of uncontested referendums – in 1933, 1934, 1936 and 1938 – that Hitler used to provide evidence of the overwhelming popular support for him and his policies.[69]

In performing its indoctrinating, solidarity-strengthening social role the Party had a distinct organizational advantage over its Fascist counterpart. The Party boasted a more balanced geographical coverage of the country and a more comprehensive grassroots presence in society, with each neighbourhood and apartment block having its own Party 'block leader'. Nevertheless, the available evidence suggests that the Party was an ineffective instiller of Nazi ideology in the hearts and minds of the German people. Although large sections of the population appear to have accepted the 'Hitler cult', the Party converted few non-Nazis into believers in such key tenets of Nazi ideology as its racist anti-Semitism.[70]

As for the Party's governing role, the commitment to the *Führerprinzip* meant that the Party had no form of political committee and therefore did not perform a policy-making governing role. But the question of whether it performed a supervisory governing role is much more difficult to answer. The Nazi regime was quite ambiguous or vague when it came to specifying the relationship between Party and state. There was never any suggestion of the Party's being subordinate to the state, in the manner of the Fascist Party and the Italian state. Neither, though, was the PO's wishful slogan that 'the Party commands the state' given any legal or official recognition; the December 1933 Law for Ensuring the Unity of Party and State declared only that the Party was 'the bearer of the concept of the German state' and was 'inseparably tied to the state'.[71]

No significant supervisory powers were acquired by the Party's central organs.[72] Hitler did confer on Hess the right to be consulted, as the administrative head of the PO, about appointments and promotions within the civil service, but the state affairs division of Hess's Office of the Deputy Führer was never able to transform this right into any real influence over the civil service's activities. Nor was there any prospect of the Party's exploiting the presence of Party members within the civil service. Few senior civil servants were or became Party members, and from the outset Hitler's government Ministers refused to allow the Party to exert any influence over how the Party members in their departments carried out their duties as civil servants. The Nazi regime's own 1937 Law on the German Civil Service explicitly declared that Party members in the civil service were to obey their state rather than Party superiors when carrying out their official duties.

At the regional level, though, Party officials acquired a position from which they could do more than just monitor the activities of the civil service. For many of the Party's Gauleiter were appointed to the newly created state post of regional Reich Governor – in fact all but one of the Reich Governors was also a Gauleiter.[73] Such a combining of Party and state posts (known in Nazi Germany as 'personal union'[74]) at the regional level was a significant innovation of the Nazi regime and it was never copied by any other party-state regime. But the Gauleiter corps's apparently powerful position did not provide the Party with a powerful supervisory role in the regions. The Reich Governors were themselves placed under the 'administrative supervision' of the Reich Minister of the Interior, who sought to limit and control their powers of state office.[75] More importantly, any control over the state exercised by a Gauleiter/Governor was in practice exercised by him as an individual rather than as an agent of the Party.[76] The weakness in the chain of command from Hess and Bormann to the Gauleiter (combined with Hitler's reluctance to intervene and personally order a Gauleiter to carry out a particular action) meant that the various Gauleiter tended to indulge in a personal and parochial form of administration.[77] In dealing with them, the central Party organs as well as the government Ministries were plagued by 'not only this defense of personal and local power but a difference in policy implementation occasioned by personal and local circumstance and the values of the holder of power'; he would choose 'on occasion to implement an order vigorously, moderately, or not at all, assuming correctly that whatever he did, very few of those who issued the orders could get Hitler to throw him out' or to convert their orders into personal orders from Hitler himself.[78]

One thing the Office of the Deputy Führer and the Gauleiter corps agreed upon was the inadvisability of combining Party and state offices (of personal union) below the regional level, because of the likelihood of divided energies and loyalties.[79] Only a minority of the Kreisleiter (district Party leaders) became state Landräte (district Governors) or mayors, and in 1937 the personal union of Party and state offices at the district level was actually banned by law.[80] The Kreisleiter were included in any important discussions by the civil servants of their districts and shared in the Interior Ministry's supervision and appointment of the mayors in their districts. But it was not until the war years that the Kreisleiter began to direct the mayors and to intervene in the work of the local civil servants.

The Second World War brought a marked increase in the power of Party officials. Bormann, the Gauleiter corps, and the Kreisleiter corps all eventually acquired a degree of control over the state apparatus at their respective levels of administration.[81] However, the weaknesses in the chain of command from Bormann's Party Chancellery to the Party officials in the regions were not removed – and were actually increased by the wartime weakening in the link between Gauleiter and Kreisleiter. Consequently, the wartime expansion of the Party officials' power over the state was not translated into the Party as an organization acquiring a markedly more powerful supervisory role.

The Party never acquired any sort of supervisory role in relation to the military arm of the state apparatus. In fact the Party had virtually no contacts of any kind with the military.[82] The Nazi regime did not remove the long-established ban on active-service members of the German armed forces belonging to a political party. (With the introduction of conscription in 1935 many existing Party members were conscripted into the army and its officer corps but a conscript's Party membership was suspended during his period of military service.) This is not to say that there was no Nazification of the German army. By 1934 fortnightly bulletins of Nazi propaganda prepared by the War Ministry were being used to provide 'political instruction' in the army. By 1937 weekly political instruction, based upon the army's own textbook, was being given to enlisted men. However, this indoctrination programme was carried out by regular army officers, not Party officials or members, and even the content of the indoctrination programme was prepared by the military rather than by the Party.

The official theory of civil–military relations depicted the Nazi regime or state as resting on two separate pillars – the Nazi Party (the political) and the army (the military).[83] That conception had been violently affirmed on 30 June

1934 when Hitler had liquidated the high command of the Party's massive paramilitary wing, the Storm Troopers (SA), and eliminated their ambition to transform the SA into a 'people's army' that would supplement or even replace the regular army. Yet within a few years of Hitler's elimination of the SA's ambitions the SS, the Party's bodyguard/security force, was allowed to create its own small military force, known as the Waffen(armed)-SS.[84] This was the thin end of the wedge that would be driven home during the Second World War as the Waffen-SS was expanded to comprise hundreds of thousands of men and some of the élite units of Germany's armed forces. Although developed much later in the history of its regime than was the Militia in Fascist Italy, the Waffen-SS eventually provided a separate, political army that provided a much more effective counterbalance to the military arm of the state than the Militia ever did in Italy. However, the SS as a whole was so independent from the Party and played such an important role in the regime that it must be viewed as a separate component of the Nazi regime rather than just as a supplier of military and other services to the Party.

The SS (Schutzstaffel)

The black-shirted Schutzstaffel (protection units) of the Nazi movement had been formed in the mid-1920s to provide bodyguards for Hitler and other prominent Nazis. The bodyguard role would remain throughout the SS's history and was the basis for the personal bond between the SS and Hitler. On induction into the SS the new member swore an oath of personal loyalty to Hitler, and the SS motto 'my honour is called loyalty' referred to this undertaking. However, the SS had also seen itself as the Party's internal police or security organ and this policing or security role became the primary basis for the peacetime expansion of the power and size of the SS, which in early 1933 was some 50 000 strong.[85]

Himmler, the head of the SS, had by the end of 1933 won control over all the political police in Germany, including the dreaded Gestapo (Secret State Police). Then, in 1936, Hitler gave Himmler the specially created post of Chief of the German Police. The new head of all Germany's police declared that the state's police force would be 'fused with the Order of the SS', and from then on 'members of the police were brought under more or less severe pressure to join the SS'.[86] Thanks to its fusion with the police, by the end of 1938 the SS had increased in size to 162 000 members and had become a very powerful component of the Nazi regime.[87]

The SS had won its formal independence from the Party in 1934 and seems to have had ambitions of replacing the Party as the leading political component of the Nazi regime.[88] In 1937 Himmler officially expanded the SS and police's policing responsibility to include the creating, not just protecting, of the National Socialist political order. This was an obvious pretext for the SS to intrude into the Party's political realm, and a 'political administration' was established at SS headquarters with the aim of developing 'SS departments for all political areas'.[89] Furthermore, during the war the SS experimented in the occupied territories with an SS-dominated political system.

During the war the SS also seemed to be replacing or rivalling the army as the leading military component of the regime. The military arm of the SS, the Waffen-SS, grew from less than 23 000 men at the beginning of 1939 to almost 600 000 by mid-1944 and perhaps as many as 900 000 by the end of 1944.[90] But as a supposedly volunteer force the Waffen-SS had been able to meet its recruiting needs only by accepting non-German volunteers, so that by 1945 as much as 60 per cent of the Waffen-SS had been born outside Germany.[91]

That the SS should have ended up as a multinational entity was only one more incongruous feature of a very unorthodox organization.[92] The SS was a wholly unique institution and was the Nazi regime's most striking innovation, a bodyguard/security/military organ that belonged to neither Party nor state. More than anything else it was an instrument of Hitler's personal rule – the implementer of his key policies of domestic control, foreign conquest, and international genocide.

Hitler's Personal Rule

Hitler's use of the SS as his personal instrument of rule was just one of the ways in which he established perhaps the most secure, absolutist and explicit position of personal rule seen this century. Even before becoming Chancellor he had sought to be more than just an agent of the Party, and he became a personal ruler in much quicker time than his Fascist counterpart. By the end of 1934 – less than two years after becoming Chancellor – Hitler had achieved a much more secure personal position than Mussolini would ever attain.

In addition to enjoying a strong personal relationship with the increasingly powerful SS, Hitler had established himself as the official Führer of the leader-principled Nazi Party years before he came to power. After leading it from relative obscurity to political monopoly, he had little difficulty in converting the Party into an agent or instrument of his personal rule. However, he was reluctant to bestow much power on the Party, and the weaknesses in the Party's chain of command reduced its effectiveness as an instrument of rule. As in Fascist Italy the personal ruler would derive more of his power from his constitutional or other state offices than from his leadership of the Party.

Where Hitler differed from Mussolini, though, was in establishing a much more secure and powerful legal/state foundation for his personal rule. For he eventually acquired the post and powers of head of state in addition to his original post of head of government. After the Enabling Law of March 1933 Hitler's office of Chancellor was comparable in power to Mussolini's office of Chief of the Government. For while the Enabling Law gave the Chancellor control over the drafting of the government's laws,[93] Hitler's power was still restricted by the extensive constitutional powers available to President Hindenburg as head of state, including being able to dismiss Hitler and rule by emergency decree. The death of Hindenburg in August 1934 provided Hitler with the opportunity to eliminate this threat to his position. A new law, quickly confirmed by a referendum, abolished the title of President and conferred the office and powers of head of state upon Hitler by giving him the new, combined post of 'Führer and Reich Chancellor'. Thus unlike Mussolini, from then on Hitler could never be legally deposed from his now virtually absolutist state office.

By the end of 1934 Führer and Reich Chancellor Hitler had received personal oaths of loyalty and obedience from his Ministers, the civil service, and even the judiciary.[94] Indeed German legal theorists depicted the Führer as the supreme judge as well as supreme legislator of the German people. His word was quite literally taken as law, with civil servants deeming his speeches to be binding bases for legislation.[95] Hitler and his legal theorists referred to this modern form of absolutism as a *Führerstaat* (leader state); more recently it has been described as 'the Hitler state'.[96]

Hitler was able to establish a degree of personal authority over even the military arm of the state. In acquiring Hindenburg's powers and role as head of state, Hitler automatically became titular Commander-in-Chief of the armed forces. He followed this up by quickly having all members of the military swear a personal oath of loyalty and obedience to him: 'I swear by God this holy oath, that I will render to Adolf Hitler, Leader of the German nation and people, Supreme Commander of the armed forces, unconditional obedience, and I am ready as a brave soldier to risk my life at any time for this oath.'[97] In 1938 Hitler also abolished the post of Defence Minister and converted part of the former Defence Ministry into a High Command of the Armed Forces (OKW) whose head, General Keitel, was directly subordinate to him.[98] At the end of 1941 Hitler actually took over operational command of the army and from then on exercised a close, if not stifling, control over the military's conduct of the war.[99]

In addition to acquiring all these various posts and powers, Hitler became the focus of what has been called a 'Hitler cult' or 'Hitler myth', which matched in extravagance the cult of the Duce and *mussolinismo* in Fascist Italy. The Hitler cult and its trappings, such as the 'Heil Hitler' salute, have become so familiar to the modern reader and viewer that they need no description.[100] In terms of its actual acceptance by the people the Hitler cult easily surpassed the cult of the Duce. Not only were Nazi propaganda agencies

more comprehensive and effective but also they could point
to Hitler's apparently miraculous economic and foreign
policy successes in the middle and late 1930s. There seems
little doubt that Hitler enjoyed great prestige and support
among wide sections of the population. To an even greater
degree than in Fascist Italy there was a tendency for the
public to use the Party as a scapegoat and to give the
personal ruler all the credit for the regime's apparent
successes.[101]

Hitler's public standing evaporated in 1943–4 as the
German people came to realize that Germany was losing
the war, but he could not be removed from power in the
same legal and bloodless manner in which Mussolini had
been deposed in July 1943. Hitler's position was legally
invulnerable and was buttressed by more and stronger sources
of personal power than Mussolini's position had been in
Italy. For example, the military's 1934 oath of personal
loyalty to Hitler made some disaffected members of the
officer corps unwilling to move against him, while his personally loyal SS bodyguard/security/military force was a
very powerful guardian of his rule. It is little wonder that
the military and civilian plotters who staged the attempted
coup of July 1944 believed that their only hope of depos-
ing Hitler was to assassinate him. And indeed once their
assassination attempt was shown to have failed, their attempted coup quickly collapsed. Hitler had created such
a secure position of personal rule that only his death or
Germany's defeat in war could put an end to it. He himself chose the former alternative when he committed suicide in his bunker under the Reich Chancellery in April
1945.

4 The Communist Regime in the Soviet Union from 1917 to 1945

By 1917 the military disasters and home-front privations suffered by the Russian Empire in the First World War had brought the autocratic monarchy of the reigning Tsar, Nicholas II, to the point of destruction. But at the beginning of 1917 few observers would have predicted that the successors to the Tsars would be the Marxists of the 'Russian Social Democratic Labour Party (Bolsheviks)'. Since the Social Democratic Party's split into separate Bolshevik (majority) and Menshevik (minority) factions in 1903, the Bolsheviks had not enjoyed great success politically or numerically. The Tsarist regime's effective repression of the Bolshevik party had forced its leader, Lenin, to live in exile in Europe. He and his party continued to be on the sidelines when in February 1917 the Tsarist regime was overthrown and a Provisional Government was established to govern the country until a Constituent Assembly could be elected.

But on Lenin's return to Russia he led the Bolshevik party to increasing popularity in the capital city, Petrograd (St Petersburg), and in other urban areas of what was still, though, a predominantly rural country. By October the Bolsheviks had emerged as a major political force through their popularity among factory workers and their ability to secure the benevolent neutrality or active support of key military units. With the help of detachments of sailors and garrison troops, the Bolsheviks and their bands of armed workers staged a coup on 25 October in Petrograd which overthrew the Provisional Government and seized power on behalf of the proletariat, the working class. However, what would become known as the October Revolution had in reality given the Bolsheviks power over not much more than Petrograd, Moscow, and the central part of European Russia.

51

The political and military struggle to extend this power
into the remainder of the former Russian Empire would
occupy all the energies of the new regime in the next few
years. But during the Civil War of 1918–20, fought between the Bolshevik 'Reds' and their counter-revolutionary
'White' opponents, the new regime would develop into a
party-state type of ideological one-party state. As in March
1918 the Bolsheviks had renamed their party the Communist Party, the title of 'Communist' would be applied to
this variety of party-state regime and to the many similar
regimes which would follow in its footsteps in other parts
of the world.

1   COMMUNIST IDEOLOGY

The ideology of the Communist regime would prove to be
the most influential developed this century, becoming eventually the basis of dozens of other regimes' ideologies. But
the original Communist ideology was itself the product of
three generations of ideologists – Marx (and Engels), Lenin
and Stalin. Marx had died thirty-four years before the establishment of the first regime to call itself Marxist, Lenin
would die less than seven years after the regime was established, and Stalin would preside over the ideology of
'Marxism–Leninism' until his death in 1953.

As the leader of the Party Lenin encouraged and was
associated with the new Communist regime's sanctification
of Marx. In addition to the reverence that Lenin and other
Communists felt for the originator of Marxism, there was
another motive: 'Marx was to help provide legitimation for
the new regime.'[1] Both before and after the October Revolution, Lenin always saw and depicted himself as only the
interpreter of Marx's doctrines.[2] Some of these 'interpretations' were actually examples of the manipulation of ideology to fit the needs or policies of the ideologist's party or
regime. However, the very fact that Lenin saw a need to
provide such ideological legitimation indicates how significant ideology was to the regime and, beforehand, to the
revolutionary Bolshevik party.

Perhaps the most famous example of Lenin's ideological

creativity was his work *What Is To Be Done?*, published in 1902, in which he first stated what was to become the very influential doctrine of the vanguard party. He argued that there was a need for a party of dedicated Marxist revolutionaries to act as the vanguard of the proletariat, the working class. Otherwise that class would prove to be incapable of staging the anti-capitalist revolution envisaged by Marx as the prelude to the creation of a classless, communist society. Lenin argued that without the leadership provided by such a party the proletariat would fall under the influence of the predominant bourgeois, capitalist ideology and never develop more than a 'trade union consciousness' – not a revolutionary consciousness which sought to overthrow the bourgeoisie and their whole capitalist system.

Lenin's emphasis on the need for the Marxist Russian Social Democrats to become such a vanguard party, comprising only highly committed and ideologically knowledgeable revolutionaries, was one of the reasons for the Social Democrats' split in 1903 into Bolshevik and Menshevik factions which later became separate parties. However, Lenin soon toned down this elitism and he also showed a new enthusiasm for intra-party democracy in his promotion of the principle of 'democratic centralism'. Democratic centralism essentially meant (a) the election of all party bodies and officials from below, the making of party policy by elected bodies, the free discussion of any issues not already decided upon by the party, and (b) the authority of central party organs to demand strict obedience to their directives on how members should implement the party's policies. In 1906 Lenin had the Bolsheviks adopt the principle of democratic centralism as the basic principle of their party's internal organization and activities. He was enthusiastic about the democratic component of the principle and its protection of minority opinion.[3]

However, after the October 1917 revolution the centralist component of the principle became more evident as the Communist regime fought for survival in the Civil War and demanded extra commitment and discipline from Communist Party members. The emphasis on centralism at the expense of democracy was formalized at the 1921 Party Congress, during which Lenin successfully introduced a

'Party Unity' resolution which prohibited the existence within
the Party of groups having their own policy platforms.[4]
This new, 'anti-factionalism' rule removed whatever protection democratic centralism had provided for minority
opinion.[5]

The 1921 Party Congress also saw the formal acceptance of Lenin's new doctrine that the vanguard party would
continue to lead the proletariat *after* the proletarian revolution had taken place. By 1919 he had acknowledged that
the temporary post-revolutionary 'dictatorship of the proletariat' envisaged by Marx had become in reality the dictatorship of the proletariat's vanguard, the Communist
Party.[6] At the 1921 Party Congress he successfully introduced a resolution on 'The Syndicalist and Anarchist Deviation in our Party' which implicitly confirmed that the
leadership exercised by the proletariat's party over the
proletariat was to continue on into the post-revolutionary
era. In introducing this resolution Lenin had declared:

> Marxism teaches us that only the political party of the
> working class, the communist party, is capable of unit-
> ing, educating and organizing such a vanguard of the
> proletariat of the working masses as is capable of resist-
> ing the inevitable petty-bourgeois waverings of these
> masses... [and] their trade union prejudices.[7]

Marxism did not teach such a doctrine; it was Lenin
himself who was ideologically confirming the post-revolutionary (and authoritarian) leadership of the Communist
Party over the proletariat. As in Marxist theory the proletariat was supposed to be implementing a class dictatorship over the rest of society, Lenin had also provided the
Communist Party with an ideological justification for maintaining a party dictatorship over the whole of Russian society.
He had provided the first ever ideological legitimation of
a party-state regime.

Lenin's two Congress resolutions, which were soon to be
viewed as part of his ideological legacy of 'Leninism', were
indirectly linked to a shift in the regime's economic and
social policy. Lenin had won the 1921 Party Congress's
approval for the first steps of the radical New Economic
Policy (NEP). The new policy saw an end to the economi-

cally disastrous War Communism of the Civil War period, when the Communist state had taken over industry and commerce and forcibly requisitioned food from the peasantry.[8] The NEP instead introduced a mixed, partly market economy in which the state would own only the 'commanding heights' of the economy, such as heavy industry, and would use taxation (in kind) rather than requisitions to procure food from the peasantry. Lenin referred to the NEP as a retreat and apparently expected that in the capitalist environment reintroduced by the NEP the Communists were likely to lose their political unity and sense of direction – and thus required the ideological and institutional 'stiffening' provided by his two Congress resolutions.[9]

As for Lenin's attitude to democracy, he followed Marx in opposing what he termed 'bourgeois' democracy and in espousing its proletarian form. In fact in his *State and Revolution*, written in the third quarter of 1917, Lenin offered an almost anarchic vision of the amount of direct democracy and popular participation in administration that would occur in the post-revolutionary era of, first, the dictatorship of the proletariat and then the period of socialism. (Socialism was the first and lower phase of what Marx had seen as the two successive phases of communist society.) After the October Revolution, though, the role of the Party as vanguard of the proletariat returned to the forefront of Lenin's thinking on the post-revolutionary situation. In later years he would argue that the political and social system of Communist Russia 'was the most democratic and the most free in the world' because the membership of the parliamentary assemblies and municipal councils was drawn largely from the proletariat and the peasantry.[10]

It was not until 1923, when Lenin was incapacitated by his fatal illness, that his followers began to acknowledge publicly that his 'interpretations' of Marx constituted a distinct new generation or layer of ideology that ought to be identified as Lenin's own contribution – as Leninism.[11] Indeed the 1923 Party Congress pledged that from now on his writings would take Lenin's place as the Party's guide. To this end a Lenin Institute was established and began publishing what would eventually be no fewer than forty-five volumes of his collected works.[12] But already a new official ideologist, Stalin, was emerging and would add a new set of doctrines to what was now officially the Marxist–Leninist ideology of the regime.[13]

The need to justify ideologically a drastic shift in policy arose in 1928–9, when Lenin's New Economic Policy was abandoned and replaced by the radically socialist Five Year Plan.[14] The Plan involved not only the state's expropriation and ownership of the whole urban economy but also the forced collectivization of agriculture. Collectivization meant that the peasants and their land were to be amalgamated into very large collectively owned (rather than state-owned) farms, where each family would be allowed only a small plot of land for its own use and would be remunerated according to its contribution to the collective effort at farming the collectively owned land. The collectivization programme of the Five Year Plan originally included only 20 per cent of farming but was dramatically retargeted at the end of 1929 to include the destruction of the wealthier or more politically and socially prominent peasants, the so-called 'kulaks'.[15] In fact by the middle of 1933 65 per cent of peasant households and 70 per cent of peasant crop land had been collectivized.[16]

The new policy of collectivization was given an ideological gloss by Stalin in his supposedly Leninist thesis that the class war becomes more intense in post-revolutionary society as it approaches socialism, the lower phase of communism.[17] Later he would provide a more memorable and accurate ideological interpretation of collectivization when he coined the term 'revolution from above'. The new concept was included in the main text or summation of Stalinist theory, the *History of the Communist Party of the Soviet Union (Bolshevik): Short Course*:

> This was a profound revolution... equivalent in its consequences to the revolution of October 1917. The distinguishing feature of this revolution is that it was accomplished *from above*, on the initiative of the state, and directly supported *from below*, by the millions of peasants, who were fighting to throw off kulak bondage and to live in freedom on collective farms.[18]

By the 1930s such drastically new interpretations of Marxist-Leninist ideology had acquired official status. Stalin's writings were accorded quite comparable status to those of Marx and Lenin, and the Central Committee of the Party told the Marx-Engels-Lenin Institute to begin publishing his collective works.[19] Among his writings could be found the new doctrine that the socialist society being built in the Soviet Union still contained classes – the intelligentsia 'stratum', the proletariat, and the peasantry – but that these were 'non-antagonistic' classes because they did not exploit one another. This doctrine provided ideological legitimation for Stalin's policy of favouring the new, Communist-trained technical intelligentsia (of managers, engineers, and the like) by giving them high incomes and other material privileges as well as encouraging them to join the Party. Moreover, Stalin justified ideologically his favourable attitude towards the state apparatus by explaining that the state would not wither away, not even when full communism was attained, until the external threat of attack by the encircling capitalist states had been removed. His most useful doctrine, though, from the point of view of ideology as policy-legitimator was his theory that 'the correctness of Marxist doctrines was limited to the period in which they were expressed'.[20] There was no need for a loyal Communist to be disturbed if Stalin's pronouncements or policies seemed to contradict Marx's or Lenin's doctrine – the present period might require a different approach from what was appropriate in their time.

2   THE COMMUNIST PARTY

Although the Communist Party did not establish a clear monopoly until the early 1920s, soon after the October Revolution the Bolsheviks/Communists displayed their monopolistic attitude by their behaviour towards the democratically elected Constituent Assembly. In elections for the Assembly that were held only a few weeks after the October Revolution, the Bolsheviks had won only 24 per cent of the vote.[21] Their reaction was to allow the Assembly to meet for a day and then dissolve it. The Bolsheviks continued to

base their government's claim to legitimacy on their command of a majority within the national Congress of Soviets.
The delegates comprising this supposedly parliamentary
body were drawn from soviets (elected councils) that had
been set up in cities, towns, factories and military units
but rarely in rural areas – where the Bolsheviks had only
weak support but where the great majority of the population lived.

There were also early signs of the Bolsheviks/Communists' repressive attitude towards other parties. The several monarchist parties had already disappeared before the
October Revolution but the liberal Constitutional-Democratic
Party (the Kadets) was actually outlawed by the Bolshevik
government in November 1917.[22] In June 1918 the now
renamed Communists also decreed that both their fellow
Marxist party, the Mensheviks, and the peasantry's favourite party, the Socialist Revolutionaries, were to be expelled
from the soviets.[23] After the Civil War, in 1921–2, the remnants of these parties were destroyed and a literal one-party
state was established. The Communist Party's monopoly
was never formally declared in law,[24] but it did not need to
be when the state's political police, the GPU or OGPU,
was so tightly controlled by the Party that it seemed to be
nothing more than 'an agency of the party'.[25]

The Party had also become quite extensive.[26] At the
beginning of 1917 the Bolsheviks had been a small party
of less than 24 000 members operating in the underground,
conspiratorial fashion forced upon them by the Tsarist
regime's repression. After the February Revolution's overthrow of the Tsarist regime the Bolsheviks had been able
to operate in the open, and as they made no effort to enforce their elitist policy of restricting membership to dedicated Marxist revolutionaries, by August the Bolsheviks could
credibly claim an estimated 200 000 members. The October Revolution and the following Civil War brought a further expansion in membership – by March 1920 the now
renamed Communist Party had reached a membership of
over 600 000. During the 1920s membership increased at
a slower rate to reach the still impressive total of 1.3 million by the beginning of 1928. Yet for all its extensiveness
the Party's size seems quite inadequate when measured

against the size of this vast country and its population of almost 150 million. In particular, the Party's presence in the countryside was still very weak – there were only 200 000 Party members among a rural population of 120 million.

However, the Party possessed several attached organizations that supplemented its mass membership.[27] In addition to the trade unions and other Party-controlled organizations, the Party was developing two very large youth organizations. The revival in 1922 of the Party's youth movement, Komsomol, led to this elitist League of Young Communists reaching a membership of 2 million in 1927. In the same year that Komsomol was revived the Party established the Young Pioneers youth organization, aimed at a younger age group and having a less elitist orientation than Komsomol.

To organize its extensive membership the Party obviously needed an extensive administrative apparatus – by 1925 the Party employed some 25 000 full-time officials.[28] The core of the administrative apparatus comprised the full- or part-time Party secretaries elected at each level of the Party, from the Central Committee down to the smallest 'cell' unit of as few as three members. During the Civil War there was a tendency for key Party secretaries to be appointed from above rather than elected from below.[29] What was originally an emergency measure became accepted as the standard practice in the post-Civil War era, with mandatory 'recommendations' by higher organs to Party meetings 'electing' a secretary.[30] (In any case, according to Party rules the election of a secretary had to be 'confirmed' by a higher organ, which gave the higher organ at least the power of veto.) The Party's thousands of secretaries were transformed into an appointive, hierarchical, administrative apparatus that stretched from the central Party organs down to the local units.

The growth and consolidation of the Party's administrative apparatus allowed the Communists to revive their elitist aspirations for the Party – one of the Party's most innovative features. They reinstituted an elitist approach to recruiting new members, such as requiring them to undergo a period of probationary or 'candidate' membership, and the Party was prepared to expel even full members for not only indiscipline but also 'careerism' and such personal failings as drunkenness.[31] In fact there were several wholesale purges in the 1920s when a concerted effort was made to expel unworthy elements from the Party.[32]

The Party was also becoming more disciplined as its centralist aspect predominated over what remained of its democratic aspect. By 1922 the Party's pyramid of directly or indirectly elected executive committees, from the Central Committee down to the regional, district and local committees, now 'stood in a hierarchical relation of subordination', and 'every lower committee when elected required the confirmation of the next higher committee'.[33] In fact the new Party Rules adopted in 1922 were interpreted to mean that the higher Party organs could actually sack and replace the members of a lower committee. What is more, in the crisis conditions of the Civil War there was a shift from collective to individual decision-making at the lower levels of the Party's structure, and this tendency was formally confirmed and reinforced by a Central Committee decree that made the secretaries of (lower-level) Party executive committees personally responsible for – and thus implicitly having authority over – the actions of their committees.[34] As these secretaries were members of an already centralised and hierarchical administrative apparatus, their dominance over the executive committees meant that the Party in the regions was bound to take on some of the bureaucratic attitudes and discipline to be found in its administrative apparatus.

The Communist Party was also becoming one of the best examples of a multi-role regime party. In carrying out its political role the Party selected appropriate candidates (quite often not actual Party members) for election to the soviets and congresses of soviets and then mobilized voters to provide a gloss of mass participation on what by the 1920s had become one-candidate elections. The Party's political role was complicated by the fact that the regime's 1918 Constitution opted for indirect elections to its constitutionally supreme parliament, the All-Russia Congress of Soviets. This was elected by urban soviets and provincial congresses of soviets, with the distribution of votes heavily weighted

towards the urban soviets in order to inflate the influence
of the proletariat within a predominantly peasant voting
population.[35] Eventually the 1936 Constitution simplified
matters by introducing direct parliamentary elections to what
was now the Supreme Soviet of the Union of Soviet Socialist Republics.[36]

As for the Party's social role, the Bolsheviks had become famous in 1917 for the effectiveness of their 'propaganda and agitation' among workers and soldiers. But in
performing its social role of instilling Communist ideology
in the hearts and minds of the population, the Communist
Party was severely handicapped by its very weak presence
in the countryside. Moreover, the onset of the Five Year
Plan in 1929 seems to have led to an emphasis on economic matters and goals – 'fulfilling the Plan' – in the
Party's agitation in the work-place, where its lowest-level
units, the Party cells, were based.[37] Therefore, the Party's
performance of its social role, despite the assistance it received from its attached organizations, had major flaws in
execution and design which greatly reduced its effectiveness. It was the governing, not social, role of the Party
which would be its real claim to fame as a regime party.

Just as the Communists did not legally recognize the
political monopoly enjoyed by their party, neither did they
include the doctrine of Party 'leadership' in their first two
Constitutions. In fact neither in the 1918 Constitution nor
in the 1924 Constitution that renamed the Russian state
as the Union of Soviet Socialist Republics was there any
mention at all of the Communist Party. Not until the 1936
Constitution, in Article 126, was some reference made to
the Party and its leadership role.[38] But as Lenin pointed
out at the 1921 Party Congress, 'Our party is the governmental party and the resolution which the Party Congress
adopts will be obligatory for the entire republic.'[39]

At the centre the Party had consolidated its hold over
the state and ensured that its central Party organs and
officials had the ultimate say in determining state policy.
The official governing body established after the October
Revolution, the Council of People's Commissars, was chaired
by Lenin and stacked with trusted Party members who individually headed the various state departments, now known

as Commissariats rather than Ministries. The presence of these Party members ensured not only that the Council governed in accordance with the Party's interests but also that it implemented any policy decisions made by members of the Party's Central Committee.[40] However, the Eighth Party Congress of March 1919 established a small political (sub-)committee, the Political Bureau, to make urgent political and policy decisions on behalf of the full, twenty-seven-member Central Committee.[41] This 'Politburo' comprised Lenin and other leading or key members of the Party: Trotsky, Stalin, Kamenev, and Krestinskii, who was replaced by Zinoviev two years later. During the remainder of 1919 the new body met on average almost twice a week (in contrast the Central Committee met on average about once a month) and was engaged in the detailed policy-making decisions typical of a government.[42] The Council of People's Commissars was left to deal with only questions of policy implementation and of administration. It is true that as all but one member of the Politburo was also an important member of the Council of People's Commissars, the Politburo was in a sense acting as an 'inner Cabinet' in Party garb. But the key point is that now a Party organ, the Party's political committee, had become the *de facto* government – and would be recognized as such throughout the regime. By 1921 the Politburo and Central Committee were 'operating as the focal center of political authority for the governmental [state] bureaucracy'.[43] This novel process of governmental policy making by a party's political committee constituted the first example of a party performing a policy-making governing role.

What is more, by having Communist Party officials supervise the state apparatus's implementation of the regime's policies, the Communists gave their party a supervisory as well as policy-making governing role. In doing so the Communists again dramatically displayed their innovative capacities. For not only were they the first to give a party a supervisory governing role but also they developed different structures and types of party supervision to fit each of the two very different arms – the civilian and the military – of the state apparatus.

The fact that the military rather than civilian arm of

the state apparatus was the first to be placed under Party supervision resulted from the immediate military threat posed to the regime by the Civil War.[44] The People's Commissar for War, Leon Trotsky, dealt with the many weaknesses of the Communists' newly formed Red Army by introducing conscription, establishing greater central control, instilling military discipline, and employing former officers of the defunct Tsarist army. (In fact in 1918 former Tsarist officers comprised more than three-quarters of the officer corps of the Red Army.) It was because of well-founded doubts about the loyalty of these ex-Tsarist officers that the Communists introduced a new system of having the officer corps supervised by political officials attached to military units. By the end of 1918 there were nearly 7000 of these 'political commissars' in a Red Army of 800000 men.

Trotsky described the political commissars' duties as being to 'direct Party work in the army, to carry on political propaganda among the raw peasant and worker recruits, and to control the activity of the commanding personnel'.[45] In performing the duty of controlling 'commanding personnel', the commissar could veto any orders given by the commanding officer of the unit to which the commissar was attached. For now all the officer's orders required the signature of the political commissar to certify that the order was not counter-revolutionary in intent.

In addition to keeping a watchful eye on the officer corps, the commissars directed the activities of Party cells and other Party units that had been established within the Red Army. (Party members comprised as much as 15 per cent and as little as 4 per cent of the personnel in the various military units, with 6–8 per cent being about the average.[46]) In 1919 the military Party units and the commissars were placed under the control of the 'political departments' established in each division and separate army of the Red Army.[47] The political departments were themselves placed under the direction of the new Political Administration of the Red Army, which in turn was placed under the direction of the Central Committee of the Party.[48] Thus a structure of Party supervision of the military had been created which stretched from the Party's Central

Committee to the Political Administration of the Red Army, to the political departments, to the thousands and later tens of thousands of political commissars, and finally to the multitude of Party units within the military.

After the Civil War many of the ex-Tsarist officers retired and were replaced by militarily competent Communists or reliable Communist supporters. As if in recognition of this change, in the mid-1920s 'unity of command' (as opposed to the existing officer/commissar 'dual command') was introduced by removing the need for officers to have their orders approved by commissars.[49] Although the commissars obviously could still perform at least a monitoring supervisory role on behalf of Party and regime, it was officially acknowledged that they were being transformed from (political) controllers into (military) administrators whose efforts would be concentrated on political work (indoctrination) aimed basically at improving the battle-readiness of the Red Army.[50]

The Party was distinctly slower to establish some form of supervision over the civilian state apparatus than over the military. During 1918 the Communists ruled the territory under their control through the executive committees of the pyramid of soviets and congresses of soviets that extended from the localities upwards to the constitutionally supreme All-Russia Congress of Soviets. The key Communist figure at the local level was the chairman of the executive committee of the local soviet, who wielded the same sort of governmental power over state organs at the local level that Lenin wielded at the central level as the Chairman of the Council of People's Commissars.[51] The local Party units and committees were confined largely to propaganda activities and became little more than, in one leading Communist's words, 'the agitation department of the local soviet'.[52] There were even suggestions within the Party that perhaps it should be abolished.[53]

The Eighth Party Congress in March 1919 put a stop to any such ideas and actually reversed the tendency towards lower-level Party units and committees fading into the background. The change in approach was not caused by the same problem of potential disloyalty that had virtually demanded Party supervision of the officer corps. It is true

(a) that the civil service and other white-collar workers had greeted the October Revolution by staging an effective strike which the Bolsheviks did not finally break until January 1918,[54] and (b) that the new regime was in such need of the ex-Tsarist civil servants' professional skills and experience that it continued to employ many of them.[55] But Party supervision was not introduced until more than a year after the strike, and the Party established a much stronger form of supervision than the countersigning commissar system it had introduced earlier in the military.

The introduction of this Party supervision began when the Eighth Party Congress decided that lower-level Party organs should exercise some control over the soviets.[56] The local Party committees – that is, in reality their secretaries – were told not to get involved in the detailed administrative work of the soviets but to 'guide' and 'control' them by issuing directives to the group, the 'fraction', of Party members within each soviet.[57] 'The meaning of the word *kontrol'* is perhaps closer in meaning to "supervision" or "verification" than "control".'[58] But the word 'guide' obviously meant an active form of supervision in which directives would be issued providing 'guidance' on *how* the regime's policies should be implemented. It is not surprising that by 1921 the local Party secretary had replaced the chairman of the local soviet's executive committee as the regime's most important local official.[59]

Such Party supervision was soon extended to encompass the whole civilian state apparatus. A Party statute of December 1919 required that a fraction or cell unit of Party members be established in not only all the soviets but also every non-Party organization, including state departments, to facilitate their control by the Party.[60] This Party fraction or cell unit would pass information to and also receive *instructions* from an appropriate Party committee and secretary – according to Party statute the fraction or cell was 'completely subordinate' to the Party.[61] Although not until 1927 were more than 20 per cent of state officials also members of the Party,[62] the Party cells possessed sufficient influence within state organs to allow the 'guiding' and 'controlling' Party officials to exercise a strong, directive form of supervision over the civilian state apparatus. Lenin's vanguard party of the proletariat had thus created a supervisory as well as policy-making role for itself that still sets the standard for what a regime party's governing role involves. Therefore it would not be surprising to find that Lenin himself had acquired a powerful governing role.

3 LENIN'S LEADERSHIP OF THE REGIME

As is often pointed out, Lenin never held a formal leadership position over the Party and was only one of the theoretically equal members of the Party's collective leadership organ – the Central Committee and later the Politburo. In 1917 Lenin's standing among the Bolsheviks as their main spokesman and informal leader could not prevent the views of the more moderate Bolshevik figures from often winning majority support and therefore taking precedence over Lenin's views. 'Although he was the acknowledged head of the party, in practice this meant little because his positions were judged largely on their merits with no special weight given to his status.'[63] In the first year of the regime's existence he continued to have to struggle and persuade to have his views accepted by the Party's Central Committee, sometimes having to threaten to resign and on occasions having to acquiesce to policies he did not support. But by the end of 1918 he had been proved right so many times that even Party figures who had often opposed his policies in the past had come to believe in his political infallibility. Lenin's authority 'had grown to the point where no one would oppose him'.[64] For virtually all intents and purposes he held a leadership position over the Party.

From the beginning of the Communist regime Lenin also held the most powerful state office, Chairman of the Council of People's Commissars, which meant he was the head of the government and in a sense also the head of state.[65] (As this post was recognized in the 1918 Constitution, from then on he was holding constitutionally recognized powers of office.) In practice he held appointment powers over the Council and dominated its proceedings, as well as intervening in and co-ordinating the activities of the individual Commissars' departments.[66] Moreover, he controlled

the legislative powers that the Council had given itself –
his signature on a Council decree was both necessary and
sufficient for the decree to be viewed as having the force
of law.

Lenin therefore seems to have held a strong personal
position, becoming an increasingly more authoritative informal leader of the ruling Party and being from the outset the holder of the key state office of head of government.
It is true that he was not even the informal leader of the
military. He never claimed any sort of leadership over the
Red Army and was content to leave Trotsky in charge of
conducting the military side of the Civil War.[67] Nor did
Lenin at first seem to enjoy any popularity among the ordinary, non-Communist public. For at least the first ten months
of the regime's life the public were hardly aware of his
existence.[68] However, these two weaknesses were either
unimportant or only temporary. The Party's supervision of
the Red Army through the Political Administration and
the network of political commissars reduced the need for
a leader of the Party to have military backing for his personal rule. And as for Lenin's lack of public standing, by
the later months of 1918 a propaganda campaign to boost
his popular prestige was under way.

The assassination attempt that badly wounded Lenin in
August 1918 began the development of what has been called
the 'Lenin cult'.[69] There was an outpouring of public and
extravagant, often quasi-religious, praise of Lenin by leading Communists and the Party's propagandists – until he
recovered from his wounds and put a stop to the incipient
cult. His fiftieth birthday in April 1920 brought forth a
revival of the cult activities of 1918, despite Lenin's publicly expressed annoyance at the praise being heaped upon
him. The continuation, at a lower pitch, of the cult of the
personally modest but politically infallible Lenin meant that
he became known to the public as the undisputed leader
of the Communist Party and as the personification of the
regime it had established.[70] What is more, 'Lenin was the
first political figure of modern times to be addressed as
"leader" (*vozhd'*)'.[71]

Nevertheless, there are some unusual features of Lenin's
position which make it difficult to describe him as a personal

ruler. He appears to have viewed himself as being only the
agent of 'the Party' as a historical force.[72] This impression that he was more concerned with the fate of the Party
and its regime than with his personal power is confirmed
by his willingness in 1919–21 to allow the Lenin-headed
Council of People's Commissars and its attendant soviets/
state apparatus to be subordinated to the Party's Politburo and administrative apparatus of secretaries. (The
contrast with Mussolini's attitude is very striking.) Again,
when he became too ill to perform his duties for the Party
and the regime properly, he was prepared to relinquish
his hold on policy making and leave the week-to-week rule
of the country to his Politburo colleagues. During 1922
he was no longer capable of full-time work and in May
suffered the first of the series of strokes which would lead
to his death in 1924.[73] But contrary to what would be expected of a personal ruler, he allowed the weekly governmental Politburo meetings and decisions to be held and
made in his absence – and certainly not at his rural conva-
lescent retreat in Gorki.[74]

Therefore it was not only because of his illness but also
because of his willingness to relinquish some of his power
– for the good of the Party and the regime – that in the
last years of his life he held a much weaker position than
in 1919–21. (Or than the position he still appeared to hold
in the eyes of ordinary Party members and the public, who
were never told how serious and debilitating his illness was.)
Lenin had in reality 'ceased active political leadership in
1922'; his 'authority was still great, but his advice could
be, and was, disregarded' by his fellow members of the
Politburo.[75] Without public fanfare, almost surreptitiously,
Lenin's role of informal Party and regime leader had come
to an end and been replaced by truly collective leadership
by the Politburo.

4   STALIN'S RISE TO PERSONAL RULE

After Lenin's death the Party continued on for a time with
the same collective leadership, centred on the Politburo,
that had assumed control during Lenin's illness. The lead-

ing figures of the Party presented themselves to the public as Lenin's disciples, and in their individual jockeying for power each depicted himself as having been Lenin's close and devoted colleague.[76] But apart from this emphasis on Lenin and the continuation of a now posthumous Lenin cult, the Party itself rather than any individual figure would hold the political centre stage for the next few years. In the mid-1920s the Party's Central Committee and annual Party Congress not only made key policy decisions but also slowly, almost inadvertently, chose one of the rivals for power within the Politburo to be Lenin's successor as individual leader of the Party and the regime. However, that chosen individual, Josef Stalin, would differ from Lenin in eventually becoming a truly personal ruler and in no sense an agent of the Party.

Stalin's position as head of the Party's administrative apparatus was the key to his rise to pre-eminence within the post-Lenin collective leadership. Although he had been a member of the Politburo since its inception in 1919, he was one of the lesser-known and seemingly less gifted of Lenin's colleagues. However, by 1921 Stalin was the only member of the Politburo who was also a member of the Organization Bureau (Orgburo), the Party's organizational or administrative equivalent of the Politburo. He became the Orgburo's unofficial head and the Party's most prominent organizational specialist and spokesman.[77] He was also directing the work of the Central Committee's Secretariat, the committee of three elected Secretaries who collectively and individually ran the central administrative organs of the Party.[78] His role of directing the work of the Secretariat was formally recognized and institutionalized in April 1922 when he acquired the post of General Secretary of the Central Committee.

As General Secretary and head of the Central Committee's Secretariat Stalin was in effect head of the Party's whole administrative apparatus. This included not only the hundreds of officials employed in the Secretariat's departments in Moscow but also the huge hierarchical structure of Party secretaries that extended down into the regions, districts and localities. And as the Party secretaries had become the dominant figures in the Party at the regional

and district levels, Stalin was very well placed to win political support from these levels of the Party, including
the support of their delegates to the annual Party Congress. In fact the Party administrators themselves often took
on the role of Congress delegate. By 1923 they comprised
more than half the membership of the Party Congress and
by 1925 more than two-thirds.[79] There was an understand-
able tendency for these secretary-delegates (and delegates
chosen or approved by secretaries) to back Stalin in any
conflicts among the Party leaders and to elect a Central
Committee that was also likely to support him.[80] The process
by which Stalin's administrative subordinates provided him
with overwhelming support in the Party Congress and Central
Committee has been described as a 'circular flow of power',
flowing down through the hierarchical administrative apparatus and back up through the elected Party Congress
and Central Committee.[81] But in addition to the coercive,
hierarchical aspect of these administrators' support for their
bureaucratic 'boss', there must also have often been a degree
of emotional identification with him as the holder of the
same administrative position at the central level that they
held in their own region or district back home. Moreover,
in the public debates on Party ideology and policy Stalin
presented a political programme and a style of leadership
that were attractive to them and other influential members of the Party.[82]

From his strong position as General Secretary Stalin was
able to defeat and politically eliminate the other leading
Party figures, albeit one individual or group at a time and
over a period of several years. The first to be politically
defeated was his most dangerous rival, the famous Trotsky
– the brilliant intellectual, orator and revolutionary who
was also the Commissar for War and the virtual founder
of the Red Army. In 1925 Zinoviev and Kamenev established what became known as the 'Left Opposition' and
eventually allied themselves with the weakened Trotsky. But
Stalin was able to defeat them and in 1926 had all three
of these leaders dropped from the Politburo. Then Stalin
politically eliminated the Party leaders loosely grouped into
what was dubbed the 'Right Opposition', so called because
of their opposition to his new, left-wing economic policy

contained in the Five Year Plan. By the end of 1930 the Politburo was almost entirely in the hands of Stalin and his cronies, henchmen or strong supporters.[83]

As early as the 1929 Party Congress Stalin was being publicly referred to as the Party's *vozhd'* (leader) and within the Party he was known as 'the boss'.[84] He would continue to maintain a public image of collective leadership but by the time of the 1934 Party Congress there were semi-official indications of his special standing within the Politburo and Central Committee. In newspaper coverage of the Congress his name was placed at the head of an otherwise alphabetical listing of the members of the Politburo and Central Committee, and his photograph was given greater prominence than those of his Politburo colleagues.[85]

Like Lenin, though, he still held no formal leader position over the Party. Even as the informal Party leader he lacked Lenin's prestige as not only the founding leader of the Party (and indeed of the Communist regime) but also the great ideologist who had provided ideological legitimacy for the Party's rule. Furthermore, Stalin did not hold any powerful constitutional/state offices, such as Lenin's former post of Chairman of the Council of People's Commissars. Nor did Stalin have the sort of military following and support that Trotsky had enjoyed in the early 1920s. On the other hand, the post of Chairman of the Council of People's Commissars was by 1930 in the safe and obedient hands of Molotov, soon to be the most famous of Stalin's henchmen. And Stalin's military crony, General Voroshilov, had been made Commissar for War in 1925.[86]

What is more, Stalin wielded as General Secretary some special Party powers that Lenin had not possessed when he was leader of the Party. The Party's central administrative apparatus in Moscow had acquired during the Civil War the right to make or confirm (veto) appointments to key Party and non-Party posts, and it was allowed to continue exercising this control over appointments after the Civil War ended.[87] By 1926 appointments to more than 5 000 top positions in the Party, state apparatus and public organizations fell within the personnel jurisdiction (*nomenklatura*) of the Secretariat of the Central Committee.[88] What became known as the *nomenklatura* powers to make or veto appointments were another means by which the Party performed its strong supervisory governing role. (Such powers were also given to regional and district secretaries to use within their territories, so that all significant Party, state and public posts came to be included in the *nomenklatura* of a Party official at some level.[89]) But these appointment powers were also a source of personal power for the head of the Secretariat, General-Secretary Stalin. He could place personal supporters in important posts and also win the support of those who sought such posts and knew that he controlled access to them.

The other source of personal power which arose from Stalin's position as head of the Secretariat was more of a 'power multiplier'. It took the form of a small department of the Secretariat that acted as Stalin's personal secretariat and helped him deploy his powers to his best advantage. Officially known as the Secretariat's Special Section, it was known informally as 'Comrade Stalin's secretariat' and by Party insiders as 'Stalin's Cabinet'.[90] Some of its officials were responsible for keeping a watching brief on particular areas of policy or fields of activity administered by state or Party departments. Others assisted Stalin in the use of his *nomenklatura* powers and in maintaining direct, personal contact with regional and even district-level Party secretaries. Moreover, this department of the Secretariat included among its official duties that of liaising with the political police, officially on behalf of the Party but in reality on behalf of the Party's new leader.

Stalin also had his personal position strengthened during the 1930s by a Stalin cult which was markedly more extravagant than the Lenin cult had been. (The posthumous Lenin cult was continued into the 1930s but was combined with the Stalin cult to form a composite Lenin–Stalin cult in which the image of Lenin was shaped to fit the needs of the Stalin cult.[91]) The Sixteenth Party Congress in 1930 brought forth not only ridiculously extravagant praise of Stalin but also the naming after him of a multitude of villages, collective farms, factories, schools and the like.[92] By the mid-1930s there were 'relentless calls to heed the teachings of the "Great and Wise Teacher" Comrade Stalin' and it was the practice 'to attribute every initiative and policy to the Great Teacher'.[93] The press was also constantly pointing to evidence of the country and the Party being united behind or around Stalin, the leader. The Seventeenth Party Congress in 1934 saw Stalin proclaimed to be not just the Communists' *vozhd'* but the Greatest Leader of all Ages and all Lands.[94]

Stalin's unwillingness to curb the cult's excesses was partly due to his political, not just psychological, needs and weaknesses. His popularity had 'plummeted' with the onset of the forced collectivization programme in the countryside in 1930.[95] This is hardly surprising considering that, according to conservative estimates, collectivization directly or indirectly (through the resulting rural famine) cost some 3.5 million lives.[96] Apparently Stalin sought to revive his popularity through the Stalin cult. In particular he sought to win a mass following for himself as a people's *vozhd'*, as a paternal, friendly, and almost populist figure.[97] Thus in the mid-1930s the normally reclusive Stalin made an effort to be seen mingling with the people, even if only in hosting Kremlin receptions for deserving groups. The effort that he and many others put into propagating the Stalin cult seems to have succeeded in producing an often unfeigned enthusiasm and support for Stalin among some sections of the population.[98]

In 1956 Khrushchev, his successor as Party and regime leader, would denounce Stalin in what became a famous speech, 'On the Personality Cult and its Consequences', for having encouraged a 'cult of the individual' – the Stalin cult.[99] As Khrushchev pointed out, a cult focused upon an individual was quite contrary to Marxism–Leninism's emphasis on class and party, not on individual leaders. But a (successful) personality cult was an important basis for the modern form of personal rule. Both the fascist dictators had developed a personality cult – the cult of the Duce and the Hitler cult – and so would many other personal rulers.

His successful personality cult helped Stalin reach the powerful personal position from which he could complete his transformation into an absolutist personal ruler by initiating, in June 1937, a violent and wide-ranging purge of the Party's élite. (After Stalin's death one of the excuses offered by high-ranking Party members for their passive reaction to his 1937–8 purge was that any action taken against Stalin would have lacked popular support.[100]) He could never have instituted such a drastic attack upon the Party élite unless he had already attained some degree of personal rule – he was certainly no longer just the agent of the Party.[101] But this purge actually reversed the former principal–agent relationship between the Party and Stalin, converting the Party into nothing more than his agent or instrument of personal rule.

The purge of 1937–8 was the first occasion on which the state organs of repression were used to carry out a full-scale purge of the Party. The purge was carried out by the political police of the NKVD, the People's Commissariat of Internal Affairs, which also controlled the ordinary police and all penal institutions.[102] In contrast, the long-established form of internal Party purge, such as those that had recently taken place in 1933 and 1935–6, did not use the state organs of repression and their weapons of execution or incarceration in prison or in a labour camp. The 'quality-control' internal Party purges of pre-1937 sought to maintain the Party's élite status as the vanguard of the proletariat by expelling members for personal defects, political passivity, being a socially alien element, or lack of Party discipline.[103] In the 1937–8 purge the victims were charged with 'traitorous' offences against the state as well as the Party: economic sabotage ('wrecking'), spying for a foreign power (usually Nazi Germany), and working with or for the exiled arch-traitor, Trotsky. Anyone accused of such crimes obviously faced much stiffer punishments than being expelled from the Party.

Another distinctive feature of the 1937–8 purge was that its victims included so many prestigious and powerful Communists. The upper ranks of the Party were so drastically purged that 90 of the 139 members of the Central Committee were incarcerated or executed, and 1 108 of the 1 966 delegates to the most recent (1934) Party Congress were arrested and usually incarcerated or executed.[104] It is true that a huge mass of ordinary Communists and non-Communists were also being caught up in the flood of arrests and denunciations that had been let loose and that seems

to have got out of control. Recent estimates suggest that
4.5 to 5.5 million people were arrested in 1937–8, of whom
over 800 000 were executed and most of the remainder sent
to prison or, more often, to one of the many labour camps.[105]
Nevertheless, the 1937–8 purge differed from earlier, internal Party purges not so much in its extensiveness as in
falling so heavily upon the Party élite.

The purge began in mid-1937 with the arrest of members of the military's (thoroughly Communist) high command.[106] No fewer than 80 of the 101 members of the high
command were eventually executed, including the Commander-in-Chief of Land Forces, Marshal Tukhachevsky,
who was also the deputy War Commissar. In addition about
140 of the 187 divisional commanders were purged, as were
many other, less senior, members of the officer corps – by
the end of 1938 over 38 000 army and 3 000 naval personnel had been executed. Not surprisingly, seven of the ten
members of the high command who were not arrested were
men who had long-established personal ties with Stalin and
have been described as Stalin's 'military clients'.[107] One of
them was War Commissar Voroshilov, and another,
Timoshenko, would succeed him in 1940 as Commissar for
War. Similarly, a former member of Stalin's personal secretariat, Mekhlis, became the new head of the Political
Administration within the Red Army. He carried out an
extensive purge which led to the advancement within the
Political Administration of thousands of what he termed
the 'Leninist–Stalinist breed' of Communist.[108]

The purge very quickly expanded to take in leading civilian as well as military Communists. As early as 1936
Stalin had begun a series of carefully staged and publicized show trials that physically eliminated the former Party
leaders who had belonged to the Left Opposition and Right
Opposition. But his attack on the Party's administrative
apparatus in later 1937 was harder to understand, because
here Stalin seemed to be attacking and destroying his own
supporters. As in the case of the military purge, though,
Stalin excluded his closest supporters and his political clients
from the list of victims. His cronies, henchmen, and protégés
in the Secretariat and its departments survived the purge
and indeed sometimes helped to carry it out. In contrast,

the Party apparatus in the regions – as will be seen later – was devastated by a flood of arrests.

The 1937–8 purge in fact devastated the whole Party as a political organization and destroyed what remained of its independence from Stalin. From then on it was 'merely one of the several instruments of personal despotic rule'.[109] (The Party was not even the dominant or leading instrument of Stalin's rule; after 1938 he used the political police and other state officials as a no less important, indeed rival, instrument of his personal rule.[110]) The Party was now officially described as a Party 'of Lenin–*Stalin* followers', a description which came close to identifying the Party as only the organized personal following of Stalin.[111] He hardly bothered to maintain the image of the Party as an independent organization. As his successor, Khrushchev, would complain, there was a thirteen-year gap between the Eighteenth Party Congress in 1939 and the Nineteenth in 1952, meetings of the Central Committee 'were hardly ever called', and even the Politburo met 'only occasionally'.[112]

During the 1940s Stalin further strengthened his personal position by assuming in May 1941 the post of Chairman of the Council of People's Commissars. The wartime emergency caused by the Nazi invasion in June 1941 led to an apparent re-emphasizing of collective leadership with the establishment of a small State Committee of Defence (GOKO) that exercised ultimate and absolute authority over the Party, as well as the military and civilian arms of the state.[113] However, Stalin was chairman of GOKO and there was never any doubt that he was in command of the war effort. He took on the posts of Commissar for Defence and Supreme Commander-in-Chief of the armed forces, holding the military rank of Marshal until in June 1945 he acquired the newly created rank of Generalissimo of the Soviet Union.[114] At the end of the war GOKO was dissolved and the regime returned to its pre-war political structure. The glorification of Stalin's wartime 'military genius' and the propaganda portrayal of him as the saviour of his country added to his prestige and made 'his personal position even more impregnable than before'.[115]

One of the distinctive features of Stalin's rise to such a position is that not until the 1940s did he acquire the sorts of state post – head of government, Commander-in-Chief of the armed forces, and the like – which most other personal rulers have used as the 'normal' route to personal rule. The main reason why his Party post and personality cult had proved sufficient to take him to a position of personal rule by mid-1937 was that he was able to exploit the powerful governing role that the Party had given itself in the 1920s. But, somewhat paradoxically, after going on to attain an absolutist and secure degree of personal rule in 1937–8, Stalin then largely abolished the Party's governing role. It has already been noted that the Politburo became virtually defunct as a political committee, let alone a *de facto* government. In addition, the Party suffered a major reduction in its supervisory governing role as part of the series of dramatic events it experienced under Stalin's leadership and then personal rule.

5   THE PARTY UNDER STALIN'S LEADERSHIP AND THEN PERSONAL RULE

Under Stalin's leadership and then personal rule the Communist Party experienced several major developments: (a) it underwent a massive expansion in membership and in its supervisory governing role, (b) it showed signs of a breakdown in its chain of command from the centre to the regions, (c) it suffered a violent and devastating purge, and (d) it experienced a weakening in its supervisory governing role in relation to the civilian state apparatus. These developments followed one another chronologically and, to differing degrees, each contributed to bringing about the next event in the series.

The second revolution (albeit 'from above') involved in implementing the Five Year Plan produced a massive expansion in Party membership similar to that produced by the October Revolution. In 1929–31 the Party more than doubled in size as some 1.8 million new members joined it.[116] In an attempt to rectify its failure, or rather inability, to process and evaluate these new members properly, the Party carried out an internal purge in 1933 and followed it up with the Verification of Party Documents campaign of 1935 and the Exchange of Party Documents campaign of 1936.[117]

The Five Year Plan also greatly expanded the Party's supervisory governing role by thrusting new and very extensive economic responsibilities upon the Party's officials. In the cities they had to supervise the state's expropriation of industry and commerce and then the attempt of this now wholly state-owned urban economy to implement a very ambitious industrialization programme. In the countryside Party officials had to supervise the forced collectivization of farming and then the attempt to extract the required amount of production from a demoralized or downright hostile rural population. The central Party officials obviously had to devolve a large part of these new responsibilities to the Party officials in the regions.[118] The regional and district secretaries thus became 'industrial and agricultural executives' as well as Party leaders and *de facto* Governors of their territories.[119] In fact they became the most powerful regional and district officials ever employed by any form of one-party state.[120] Considering the extent of their responsibilities and power, it is not surprising that the regional secretaries developed an independent attitude that greatly weakened the Party's chain of command from Moscow to the regions.

The problems in the Party's chain of command emerged publicly at the 1934 Party Congress. Stalin and other central Party administrators 'complained bitterly' about the Party's administrative apparatus in the regions not fulfilling central Party decisions across the whole range of issues and activities, from economic matters to Party work.[121] The next few years were to confirm this picture of, if not insubordinate, at least unresponsive Party officials in the regions. 'Important Central Committee instructions – "the fulfilment of decisions" – were simply not carried out in the provinces', and in fact the 'chain of command often broke down altogether'.[122] Clearly the Party's administrative apparatus – and thus the Party as whole – was displaying very little bureaucratic or 'Leninist' discipline.

However, at the February 1937 meeting of the Central Committee Stalin implicitly levelled the more serious charge that the secretaries in the regions were transforming themselves into personal rulers rather than agents of the Party (and Stalin's rule). He criticized the way in which the regional secretaries used their *nomenklatura* appointment powers to build up a personal following among the top Party and state officials in their regions. He went on to suggest that 'when selecting personally devoted people as workers, these comrades evidently have wanted to create for themselves conditions which give them a certain independence both of the local people and of the Central Committee of the party'.[123] Unless Stalin could reverse the secretaries' moves towards establishing a degree of independent, personal rule, he would be left presiding over a collection of quasi-feudal Party 'barons' rather than a political party.

It appears that Stalin first attempted to deal with the problem through the quite radical and non-bureaucratic measure of re-emphasizing the democratic component of the Party's organizational principle of democratic centralism. For in March–April 1937 all Party posts in the regions, from the lowest level up to the regional level, were included in a set of sweeping Party elections that were backed up by a major press campaign in favour of free elections and the accountability of Party leaders to the ordinary members.[124] But the regional secretaries were able to use their local power and prestige to protect themselves and their personal followings from this democratic attack from below launched at them from above.[125] Only a month after the failure of the Party elections became clear, Stalin resorted to a new and more drastic measure to break the power of his overly independent subordinates.

The Party's regional secretaries became one of the most prominent targets of the violent purge that began in June 1937. By the end of the year virtually all of them had been removed from their posts and most of them had been executed or incarcerated.[126] Their fate was shared by many of their personal followers, such as their district secretaries, as the purge cut a huge swathe through the Party's administrative apparatus – and the rest of the Party élite – in the regions. Yet even after the purge the central Party officials would continue to be plagued by the 'non-fulfilment of decisions' in the regions, albeit now more because of laziness and incompetence than any attempt at personal independence.[127] Although it had become only an agent or instrument of Stalin's personal rule, the Party was still not operating like a well-oiled bureaucratic machine.

Apart from the further strengthening of Stalin's personal position, the main structural effect of the 1937–8 purge was the weakening of the Party's supervisory governing role. A 1939 restructuring abolished all but one (Agriculture) of the Secretariat's four economic departments in a deliberate move to reduce the Party's control of state economic enterprises.[128] In the regions and districts the Party apparatus seems to have lost some of its authority to direct the state apparatus.[129] In particular, secretaries were not allowed to supervise in any way the NKVD personnel operating in their territory.[130] Thus from top to bottom of the Party apparatus there had been a reduction in the extent or strength of its supervision of the state apparatus. In fact the 'Stalin period has often been treated in the West as one in which the state apparatus came to dominate the party apparatus'.[131] Although this view was too extreme, in the 1940s the state's bureaucracy of administrative officials 'became at least as important as, if not more than, the party apparatus of secretaries'.[132]

There were several obvious indications of the increased importance of the state apparatus, if only in Stalin's estimation and use of it as an instrument of personal rule. He ideologically boosted the prestige of the state apparatus and its administrative and technical employees, who were also encouraged to join the Party.[133] (The Party was inundated by intelligentsia in the post-purge doubling of its membership from 1.9 million to 3.9 million, and by 1941 they constituted a third of the total Party membership.[134]) Stalin's assumption of the state office of head of the government in May 1941 also indicated the new importance of the state apparatus in his eyes, and even the emergency war directorate was called the *State* Committee of Defence. Finally, in 1946 the Council of People's Commissars was renamed the Council of Ministers and the Commissariats were renamed Ministries, providing them with more international prestige and with formal recognition that they were permanent state institutions.

On the other hand, the 1937–8 purge brought an actual

strengthening, albeit only temporarily, of the Party's supervision of the *military* arm of the state. For the beginning of
the purge was preceded in May 1937 by the reintroduction of
dual command, with the joint signing of orders by officer and
political commissar.[135] So although the Political Administration within the Red Army would suffer from the disruptive
effects of a major purge, its extensive network of over 30 000
political commissars and other officials would enjoy a newly
enhanced power to supervise the military arm of the state.[136]

By August 1940, though, Stalin felt confident enough
about the loyalty of the military to remove the political
commissars' power of veto and thus return to the militarily
much more efficient unity-of-command system.[137] He also
renamed the political commissars as Assistant Commanders for Political Affairs (Zampolity). The German invasion
and Soviet military disasters of 1941 brought a reintroduction of the title of political commissar and of the system
of dual command. But in October 1942 there was a return
to the title of Zampolit and to unity of command, leaving
the military professionals with a free hand in waging the
war – under Stalin's central control. After the war there
would be a reduction in pro-military propaganda and a
return to the pre-war emphasis on ideological indoctrination within the military, but never again would the regime
return to the title of commissar and to the system of dual
command.[138] The political officers would become militarized auxiliaries of the military officers. From 1942 onwards
they would have the same rank structure, uniforms and
insignia as the military officers and would evolve into professional soldiers specializing in political education but
having such additional duties as improving the morale,
discipline, and even technical competence of their military
unit.[139] They would become just as integrated/subordinated
within the military hierarchy as were the Party units in
the military. (The members of a Party unit were forbidden
to criticize the commands and official activities of their
military unit's commander, while he had the right and duty
to direct the activity of the Party unit to which he belonged.[140])
Like several other innovations of the first Communist regime,
the commissars and military Party units would be extinct
or irrelevant in the post-war years of the Stalin era.

5 A Survey of the Communist Regimes from the 1940s to 1980s

1 THE SOVIET UNION AFTER STALIN

On Stalin's death in 1953 there began another period of collective leadership by the Politburo (temporarily renamed the Presidium) similar to that which had occurred in the 1920s after Lenin's death. There was also a reassertion of Party supremacy over the state. One of the most obvious symbols of this was the transferral of the political police from the control of the very powerful Ministry of Internal Affairs (MVD) to the newly created Committee for State Security (KGB), which was under the direct control of the Politburo. More generally, the Secretariat and the Party apparatus as a whole recovered the supervisory powers over the Ministries and other state organs that had been lost under Stalin. As such a reassertion of the Party's governing role in turn strengthened the position of the head of the Secretariat and Party apparatus as a whole, it is not surprising that the holder of this post, Khrushchev, emerged as the individual leader of the Party and the regime.

Stalin's position as head of the Secretariat had been taken over by Khrushchev through his acquisition of the renamed post of First (rather than General) Secretary of the Central Committee. Khrushchev was able to use the same sort of administrative authority and powers available to Stalin in the 1920s to strengthen his political following, politically eliminate his rivals, and achieve a degree of informal leadership over the Party. In fact by 1956 Khrushchev felt confident enough about his political position to launch an attack on Stalin and the Stalinist legacy. The secret speech in which he denounced Stalin to the Central Committee was only the beginning of what became an official and very public campaign to denigrate Stalin and in particular his personal rule.

When a trial of strength occurred in 1957 between Khrushchev and the Stalinist old guard among the Party's still formally collective leadership, Khrushchev was unable to command a majority within the Politburo. However, he met his opponents' attempt to remove him from the post of First Secretary by appealing to the Central Committee, where he did enjoy majority support. He was actually able to turn the tables on his opponents by having the ringleaders, such as Molotov, removed from office by the Central Committee. All of this may seem somewhat reminiscent of Stalin's use of 'the circular flow of power' but Khrushchev did not go on to establish a Stalin-like personal rule. His de-Stalinization programme included several major changes to Stalin's authoritarian and personalist policies: the ending of 'terror' methods by the political police, a liberalizing 'thaw' in artistic and intellectual censorship, and an attack on the very idea of a personality cult.

Khrushchev also attempted to rectify the problems of a Stalinist centrally planned economy by decentralizing planning to the regions. In an attempt to reform the Party apparatus, too, he split the regional and district Party administration into separate industrial–urban and agricultural–rural apparatuses and instituted a system of limited tenure and regular turnovers for the holders of Party office. He also introduced the populist policy of involving the general populace in grassroots local government and even in policing and judicial duties. Such populist, participatory policies were legitimated by Khrushchev's ideological interpretations of Marxism–Leninism. These included the notion of the 'all people's' state and the somewhat utopian belief that even this form of state would soon wither away – leaving the people to administer themselves – because the material base for full (the higher phase of) communism would be attained as early as 1980. However, while the state might wither away as communism was attained, Khrushchev believed that the Party would continue to exist and would play an important role within the new, fully communist, society.

Khrushchev's radical reforms, the failure of his agricultural and foreign policies, and the impulsive manner in which he made policy eventually aroused strong opposition to him among the Party hierarchy. Therefore when his own protégés within the Politburo moved against him in 1964, they were able to secure majority support in the Central Committee and force Khrushchev's resignation, ostensibly for health reasons. The new, collective leadership undid most of his reforms and adopted a conservative approach that later Communists would blame for producing an 'era of stagnation'. Brezhnev, the First and later General Secretary, gradually became the pre-eminent figure in the Politburo, confirming that the post of head of the Secretariat sooner or later bestowed an informal Party and regime leadership on its holder.

After Brezhnev's death in November 1982 the new General Secretary, Andropov, a former head of the KGB, instituted a campaign against corruption and labour indiscipline. However, he did not live long enough to make much of an impact, dying in February 1984 after a debilitating illness. His successor as General Secretary, the elderly and Brezhnev-like Chernenko, also suffered from serious health problems and was little more than a figurehead. His death in March 1985 brought a relatively young man, Gorbachev, to the post of General Secretary and he began a radical, Khrushchev-like reform of the Soviet Union's stultified political and economic systems.

Gorbachev's reform programme was summed up in the concepts or slogans of *glasnost* (openness) and *perestroika* (restructuring or reconstructing). It differed from Khrushchev's in that it was less utopian and ideological – and sought to reduce the role of the Party rather than of the state. The new emphasis upon the state was apparent in Gorbachev's creating for himself a powerful state office of 'executive' President, in his aim of returning real power to the elected soviets, and in his emphasis upon the rule of law. In contrast, there was a reduction in the Party's governing role, especially its supervision of the economy, and the social role of the Party was at least implicitly abandoned with the introduction of the *glasnost* policy.

However, the political role of the Party seemed set to take on a new importance as political *perestroika* sought to introduce some real democracy by returning power to the pyramid of soviets and by allowing multi-candidate and competitive, rather than Party-controlled, elections to the soviets. The 1990 Law on Public Associations actually recognized and formalized the development of a genuine multiparty system, which had emerged in practice during the 1989 elections with the founding of a number of albeit small or tiny parties. As for the economic aspect of *perestroika*, the main features included giving individual state enterprises more autonomy, allowing privately owned 'co-operatives' to be established and compete with state-owned enterprises, and allowing farmers to lease land and other resources from collective farms and the state. Just how far *perestroika* would have gone towards introducing market mechanisms in the economy and 'restructuring' the collective farms would never be known because the events of late 1991 – the failed coup, the closing down of the Communist Party, and the replacement of the Soviet Union by the Commonwealth of Independent States – brought an end to the Communist regime.

The obvious lack of public support for Marxism–Leninism even before 1991 confirmed that the Party had been very ineffective in performing its social role of instilling the official ideology in the hearts and minds of the people. The actual break-up of the Soviet Union itself was also, if in a different way, a confirmation of this failure to instil the solidarity-building ideology in society. Ethnic and historical nationalism proved a much more potent force than the class-based solidarity (or even the Soviet patriotism) that had been espoused by the Party.

2 THE EAST EUROPEAN COMMUNIST REGIMES

The opportunity for the massive expansion of Communism into Eastern Europe after the Second World War was created by the 1944–5 destruction of Nazi Germany's armies and its allied/collaborating regimes in Eastern Europe by the Red Army or local Communist guerrilla forces. The actual transformation of the states of Eastern Europe into Communist one-party states was produced by a combination of electoral-coalition politics and the military power embodied in the Red Army and/or local Communist military forces, such as the Yugoslav partisan army. The mixture of the two elements varied from case to case, from strongly military in Poland to almost entirely political in Czechoslovakia.

The innovative political tactic developed by the Communists in post-war Eastern Europe was to use coalition 'popular front' politics as either a democratic weapon or a democratic disguise in their seizure of power. In several Eastern European countries both the popular front and a multiparty façade were preserved by the Communists even after they gained complete power and established a Communist regime. In Czechoslovakia several parties – socialist, populist and Slovak – were preserved as puppet parties along with the National Front. In Communist Poland there was a United Front (later the National Unity Front) and the preserved puppet parties were peasant and liberal parties, with small Catholic parties or associations also acquiring some recognition. In East Germany there was a National Front and farmer, liberal and Catholic puppet parties, while in Bulgaria there was a Fatherland Front and a peasant puppet party. In Hungary there was a People's Front for Independence (later the Patriotic Front) and until 1956 two puppet peasant parties. Elsewhere the Communists eliminated their former coalition parties and preserved only the popular front: in Albania the Democratic Front, in Yugoslavia the People's Front (later renamed the Socialist Alliance), and in Romania the People's Democratic Front (later renamed the Socialist Unity Front).[1]

Several of the Eastern European Communist regimes did not even call their Marxist–Leninist regime party a 'Communist' party. In Albania the Communists' party was called the Party of Labour, in Hungary the Hungarian Workers' Party, in Romania the Romanian Workers' Party (later renamed the Romanian Communist Party), in Poland the Polish United Workers' Party, and in East Germany the Socialist Unity Party. In East Germany, Poland and Hungary there had also been a 'merger' with the local socialists or social-democrat parties.

Nevertheless, whatever the outward differences from the Soviet model of establishing a *de facto* literal one-party state, the result was basically the same. The Fronts and non-Communist parties were closely controlled shells or puppets whose only role was to provide a farcical multi-party decoration for these Communist party-state regimes. The political role of the Communist parties was complicated by the presence of the Fronts and the puppet coalition parties. Yet basically it did not differ much from the political role performed by the Soviet Communist Party – ensuring that a reliable set of candidates were given a resounding vote of confidence in the one-candidate elections. (However, Poland (in 1957), Hungary (in 1968), and Romania (in 1974) introduced multi-candidate elections in which the voters could choose between two or more Party-approved candidates for the same public office.[2]) The performance of social and governing roles was no different at all in Soviet-dominated Eastern Europe than it was in the Soviet Union itself, and the very structure and terminology of these East European Communist parties closely followed the Soviet model.

Ideologically the Soviet-dominated Communist regimes had nothing new to offer apart from designating themselves 'people's democracies', signifying that they had not reached the more advanced, socialist stage of development attained by the Soviet Union. The satellite states had to conform to whatever interpretation of Communist ideology was currently the officially orthodox one in the Soviet Union. When Czechoslovakia developed an increasingly liberal version of Communist rule, the Soviet Union invaded the country to stop any further development of such an 'un-Leninist' approach. Romania was able to inject a large dose of nationalism into its ideology without Soviet intervention but probably only because the Romanian regime remained so rigidly orthodox in the remainder of its ideological interpretations. There were few examples in Eastern Europe of even deviations in policy from the norm or model of a Communist regime provided by the Soviet Union. Hungary would provide a new form of state-owned economy in the late 1960s when it shifted from a Stalinist, centrally planned, command economy towards a market economy – or 'market socialism'. Poland would decide not to go ahead with the usual collectivization of agriculture, and in 1980–1 would permit the development of an independent trade union movement, Solidarity.

Only the Albanian and Yugoslavian regimes were able to

show any real ideological independence from the Soviet Union. Albania broke its military and economic ties with the Soviet Union in the 1960s because of the too liberal, de-Stalinizing version of Marxism–Leninism being espoused and practised by Khrushchev. In the case of Yugoslavia the political separation from the Soviet Union preceded the ideological differences – and they became much more pronounced than in the Albanian case. A 1948 dispute between Stalin and the Yugoslavian Communist leader, Tito, led to an irreversible split between the two countries and the creation of 'Titoism' as a new interpretation of Marxism–Leninism. The seriousness of the split was reflected in Tito's foreign policy, as Yugoslavia was forced to find friends outside the Soviet-dominated, Communist bloc of states. This in turn was legitimated by Titoism's opposition to the division of the world into ideological blocs and its espousal of a neutralist or 'non-aligned' approach. However, the rift with the Soviet Union also cleared the way for the introduction of some radically new domestic policies that were soon viewed as characteristic of the Titoist approach. The most famous of these was the switch from a Stalinist centrally planned, command economy to a form of socialist market economy in which elected workers' councils ran the factories and other enterprises – eventually being given the right to hire and fire managers and determine the level of wages. Titoism justified this 'self-management' system ideologically by emphasizing the withering-away-of-the-state element in Marxist-Leninist thought.[3] Titoist ideology also presented a revised view of the role of the Communist Party, which was depicted as truly leading and guiding, not directing and controlling, the people of Yugoslavia. (In practice this meant relinquishing much of its governing role, especially in economic matters.) To distinguish it from the Soviet model of a Communist Party the Yugoslav version was renamed the League of Communists, the Politburo was renamed the Execburo, and the Central Committee renamed the Presidium.

But the most distinctive feature of the Yugoslav regime's political structure was the establishment of personal rule by Tito. As the leader of the Party since the late 1930s he naturally assumed the new post of President of the League of Communists and thus head of the Execburo – one of the few cases of a Communist regime party having an explicit, formal individual leadership position. He also acquired the quite powerful state office of President, which in very personalist style was constitutionally declared to be his for life because of his 'historic merits'.[4] Being President meant Tito was titular Commander-in-Chief of the armed forces, and he also had a notable personal military background as the former leader of the Yugoslavian Communists' guerrilla army in the Second World War. (Although originally a civilian party leader, he valued and cultivated this wartime military background, bestowing on himself the rank of Marshal and often being seen in uniform.) Furthermore, Tito was the object of a personality cult as not only a wartime hero and the founder of the regime but also the political and ideological defender of its independence.

When provision was made for the eventual post-Tito era, he opted for an institutional successor – a collective Presidency with equal representation from all the republics of the Yugoslav federation. Another unique innovation was the introduction of a system of short tenure for leading party and state posts – in the case of the head of the collective Presidency it was to be only an annual tenure. After Tito's death in 1980 the system operated quite well for a time but fell apart at the end of the decade. As Yugoslavia itself fell apart in the 1990s and saw civil war break out within the former republics, it became apparent that Tito's personal rule had held together the state of Yugoslavia as well as its Communist regime.

In all East European countries there was a tendency for an individual to become the Party and regime leader. But the ultimate political control exercised by the Soviet Union over nearly all these countries meant that their individual leaders were more agents of Soviet rule than personal rulers. (The client and dependent status of the Soviet Union's East European satellite states was vividly revealed when Soviet troops were used to intervene in their internal affairs: in 1953 in East Germany to put down popular unrest, in 1956 in Hungary to suppress an anti-Soviet uprising, and in 1968 in Czechoslovakia to replace a liberalizing Communist regime with a more orthodox form of Communism.) In contrast

Albania's independence from the Soviet Union means that its all-powerful Party leader, Hoxha, can be viewed as having acquired a position of personal rule as the guardian of Stalinist ideological orthodoxy, the object of a personality cult, and the frequent purger of the Party. Another example was the Party leader of Romania from 1965 onwards, Ceauşescu, who seems to have been allowed a degree of independence by the Soviet Union, notably in foreign policy. He accumulated Party and state posts, instigated an extravagant personality cult, and even bestowed power on his wife, his son, and other close family members.[5] He also modified the structure of the Romanian Communist regime in a way that seems very typical of a personal ruler, transforming his police and paramilitary security force, the Securitate, into the regime's most powerful organization.

However, the most significant structural deviation from the Soviet model occurred not in Romania, or even Yugoslavia, but in Poland in 1981. The head of the armed forces, General Jaruzelski, had taken on the posts of head of government (February) and head of the Party (October) before in December 1981 placing the country under martial law and the authority of a junta, the Military Council of National Salvation. Poland had clearly shifted from being a party-state to a military-party type of ideological one-party state. The regime was apparently returned to Communist normality only a year later, with the military going back to the barracks and Jaruzelski staying on as an outwardly civilian ruler. But the Polish case is a very interesting one and deserves the much more detailed investigation that it will receive in Part III.

In 1989 the East European regimes began falling apart. Their collapse was in part caused by their unpopularity, which was itself the result of their corruption, economic failure and lack of democratic legitimacy. But the other vital factor was the realization on all sides that Gorbachev's Soviet Union would not intervene and prop up such unpopular regimes with military force. The collapse of these Communist regimes was remarkably bloodless and sudden; by June 1991 the last remaining Communist government in Eastern Europe, the Albanian, had succumbed. The Communist regimes in Asia would prove much more resilient.

3   COMMUNISM IN ASIA: CHINA, VIETNAM AND NORTH KOREA

The three post-war Communist successes in Asia were all based on military power, with electoral-coalition politics playing at most a supporting role. In the case of North Korea the military power was that of the Soviet Union's Red Army, which had occupied the north of Korea after the defeat of Japan, the country's colonial ruler. As Korea was divided into Soviet and American zones of occupation, this case seems particularly comparable to the establishment of a Communist regime in the Soviet, eastern zone of occupation in Germany. However, unlike East Germany the new state of North Korea did not remain for long under Soviet control, for during the Korean war of 1950–3 it became dependent upon Chinese military assistance for its very survival. With the deterioration in Sino-Soviet relations in the late 1950s, the North Korean regime was able to play its two powerful northern neighbours off against each other and achieve a degree of independence from both.

The establishment of a Communist regime in Vietnam was based upon a quite different sort of military power and involved a unique, two-stage victory – in 1954 in the north and 1975 in the south. During the early 1940s the local Communists' Viet Minh movement fought a guerrilla war against the Japanese army of occupation that had been accepted by the country's French colonial rulers. The Viet Minh actually took control of the country for a time when the Japanese surrendered to the Allies in August 1945. However, France's attempt to regain Vietnam and other parts of its colony of French Indo-China meant that the Viet Minh was soon at war again. After a long guerrilla war against the French the Communists were eventually, in 1954, able to establish an internationally recognized state and regime in the northern half of Vietnam. But not until the second and last wave of world-wide Communist expansion, in the 1970s, was the southern part of Vietnam conquered by the Communist north's armies.

Although the establishment of a Communist regime in China also took a unique form, there were some similarities with the origins of other post-Second World War

Communist regimes, notably in the waging of a guerrilla war against a foreign invader. The 1937–45 war against the Japanese invader gave the Communists a great opportunity to increase their military strength and the size of their political and territorial base. By the end of the war against Japan the Communists had acquired extensive territory in north-west China, had greatly increased their political support, and were developing the conventional military forces that would enable them to defeat opposing armies on the battlefield as well as through guerrilla warfare. This military strength was vital because after the Japanese surrender the Communists had to go on and fight the Kuomintang regime which nominally controlled much of China. When full-scale civil war eventually broke out between the Communists and the weak Kuomintang regime, the Communists unleashed a powerful military campaign that in 1948–9 drove the Kuomintang out of mainland China and onto the island of Taiwan.

Despite the vital role played by military power in their origins, all three of these Asian Communist regimes established a 'people's democracy' with a multi-party façade. Similarly, neither the Vietnamese nor the Korean Communists called their parties 'Communist', preferring to name them the Vietnam Workers' Party and the Korean Workers' Party. (The Vietnamese party eventually took the name of Communist in 1976, after its conquest of the south.) All three Asian Communist regimes also adopted much the same ideology and policies as those adopted by the Soviet-dominated Eastern European regimes. The Asian regime parties were given the same roles, political, social and governing, as in the Soviet Union and performed them in much the same way.

By the later 1950s, though, the Chinese regime was secure and confident enough to begin showing signs of deviation from the Soviet model of a Communist regime. The 'Great Leap Forward' of 1958–60 involved much more than simply proclaiming unrealistically high production targets in agriculture and industry. It also included herding the peasants into massive and radically, perhaps uniquely, collectivist 'people's communes' – extremely communal administrative-farming units that incorporated tens of thousands of people. Even more innovatory was the accompanying attempt at a rural form of industrialization through small-scale production within the communes, most famously through the 'backyard' blast furnaces that supposedly would produce a great leap forward in China's steel production.

The Great Leap Forward showed that the Chinese regime was developing as radical a new interpretation of Communist ideology as Titoism had in Yugoslavia. The leader of the Chinese Communist Party, Mao Zedong (Mao Tsetung), had put forward new doctrines that glorified the peasantry – and the people as a whole – rather than just the working class. Instead of emphasizing the need for a Soviet-style programme of urban industrialization to transform much of the overwhelmingly large rural population of China into a (socialist) working class, Mao believed that a socialist consciousness could be instilled in the peasantry through indoctrination and an appropriately collectivist restructuring of rural economy and society.[6] This 'Maoist' ideology legitimated the Great Leap Forward's creation of the radically collectivist people's communes and their attempts at small-scale industrialization. In fact official pronouncements in 1958 spoke of the commune policy as not only accelerating the building of socialism but also carrying out the gradual transition to (full or the higher phase of) communism.[7]

Although the Great Leap Forward was a recognized failure, Mao's utopianism and emphasis on consciousness would emerge again in the Cultural Revolution that he instigated in 1966. Mao here stressed the strongly egalitarian and antibureaucratic strain in his thought, and his commitment to changing the consciousness of the 'bureaucratic bourgeoisie' and other deviants became very obvious. The Great Proletarian Cultural Revolution was therefore only partly about culture in the narrower sense of the term; it also included a populist attack on material inequalities and on bureaucratic/technocratic authority and attitudes. This in turn involved a purge of not only state but also Party bureaucrats from their privileged positions. The purge did not take on a Stalinist hue of mass executions and a huge network of labour camps – the characteristic fate of its victims was public humiliation, forced 'self-criticism', and

being made to do menial manual work, often in the countryside. Nevertheless, the official figures produced in the
early 1980s, when victims and opponents of the Cultural
Revolution were ruling China, indicate that some 34000
people died as a result of persecution during the Revolution.[8] And the number who lost their careers and otherwise had their lives destroyed ran into the millions.

The fact that the purge extended into the ranks of the
Party apparatus – the Central Committee Secretariat was
actually abolished as part of the drive against bureaucracy – meant that the Cultural Revolution had a major
political effect. The Revolutionary purge was not carried
out by state organs of repression like Stalin's NKVD but
instead often by militant youths organized into the notorious Red Guards. Yet, as with Stalin's 1937–8 purge, the
Revolutionary purge weakened the Party apparatus's hold
on the state. Indeed in China the purge so weakened the
Party's hold on the country as a whole that the military,
the People's Liberation Army, had to be brought into the
political arena as guarantor of a modicum of order and
central control. Military men were given important governmental responsibilities at the provincial level and acquired
a stronger presence in the Party's central bodies. The official disbanding of the Red Guards in 1968 marked the
beginning of the end of the Cultural Revolution as a revolutionary political and social event, but its political ramifications, such as the increased political role of the military,
would continue on into the 1970s.

The most obvious of these political ramifications was that
Mao appears to have become a personal ruler. After the
failure of the Mao-initiated Great Leap Forward of 1958–60
his prestige and political prominence had declined significantly, though he retained his formal leadership post of
Chairman of the Party. His initiation of the Cultural Revolution produced the opposite effect and left him as the
publicly idolized leader of Communist China. The personality cult which grew up around him during the Cultural
Revolution is not surprising considering that the Revolution was ideologically based upon 'Mao Zedong Thought'
and led to Maoism's being officially included alongside
Marxism–Leninism as the regime's official ideology. Until

his death in 1976 Mao was an absolutist personal ruler, although in his final years, with his health and mental faculties failing, he may have been manipulated by those close to him.

When Mao died, the succession problem was temporarily solved by having the head of government, Hua Guofeng (Hua Kuo-feng), succeed to Mao's post of Chairman of the Communist Party. One of the distinctive features of the Chinese Communist Party had been the adoption of this title of Party Chairman, which conferred some sort of formal leadership position upon its holder, and the post had been given yet greater authority by its association with the idolized 'Chairman Mao'. Yet despite being Chairman of the Party and the head of government, Hua Guofeng was pushed into the background in the late 1970s and early 1980s by a group of pragmatists and modernizers led by Deng Xiaoping (Teng Hsiao-p'ing), a former General Secretary of the Party who had been purged in the Cultural Revolution. Hua relinquished his post of head of government in 1980 and saw his Party post of Chairman abolished in 1982. The new regime leader, or leader of the regime's ruling group, did not take on such key Party or state posts as General Secretary or head of government. Deng was prepared to leave such posts to his supporters and be content with being an ordinary member of the Standing Committee of the Politburo and with holding the important military-related post of head of the Military Affairs Committee. In 1987 the ageing Deng retired from the Politburo and became one of the few examples of a regime leader relying solely on his personal prestige and influence to maintain his pre-eminence and see his policies put into effect. In this case the key policies were those involved in his radical economic reform programme of the 1980s, described in the mid-1980s as 'socialism with Chinese characteristics' but later more accurately described as the establishment of a 'socialist market economy'. Although more radical than Gorbachev's economic *perestroika*, these reforms were not accompanied by an equivalent of *glasnost* – as was emphasized by the brutal use of the military against the demonstrators in Tiananmen Square in 1989.

The other two Asian Communist regimes showed, until

recently, less divergence than China from the orthodox Soviet model. In the case of North Korea the regime has claimed great ideological gifts and originality for its personal ruler, Kim Il Sung. However, his much vaunted addition to Marxism–Leninism, his concept of Juche (*chuch'e*), does not really constitute a new interpretation of Communist ideology in the manner of Titoism and Maoism.[9] Juche appears to mean national self-reliance in both the economic and political sense, and also in the ideological sense of the Korean Workers' Party making its own ideological interpretations and political evaluations rather than copying what has been done in other Communist countries. The most distinctive feature of the regime was not the unequalled extravagance of the personality cult surrounding Kim Il Sung but the fact that in recent years he has clearly been preparing the way for the first Communist example of hereditary personal rule. For by the end of the 1980s his son, Kim Jong Il, was the officially designated successor and had taken over some of the important posts, notably supreme command of the armed forces, that would position him to succeed to the personal rule enjoyed by his father.

In contrast the North Vietnamese regime's unique feature was that of having experienced two different types of *non*-personal rule. Ho Chi Minh appears to have enjoyed all the trappings of personal rule in the 1950s and 1960s. Not only was he the (founding) Chairman of the Party and (founding) head of state until his death in 1969 but also he was the object of widespread veneration inside and outside the Party – as was exemplified in the 1970s by the decision to rename Saigon as Ho Chi Minh City. However, he was very similar to Lenin in viewing himself as no more than the agent of the Party, in using persuasion rather than command, and in not encouraging a personality cult. On his death the Party abolished the title of Chairman of the Party and began a period of collective leadership by the Politburo which lasted into the 1990s. This was the longest period of collective leadership experienced by any one-party state in the twentieth century. What is more, the collective leadership was rejuvenated in an orderly fashion in 1986, with almost half of the Politburo being replaced, as the Party committed itself to a liberalizing economic policy of *doi moi* (economic renovation).

After the post-Second World War wave of expansion the international spread of Communism lost momentum. During the period of stagnation in the 1950s and 1960s the only major Communist victory or advance – apart from North Vietnam – was the establishment of a Communist regime in Castro's Cuba. Even this victory was a far from typical or straightforward Communist take-over. Only after the 1961 abortive Bay of Pigs invasion by US-backed Cuban exiles did Castro officially link his 2-year-old regime to the Soviet Union, commit himself to a full-fledged revolution, and declare himself to be a Marxist–Leninist. Moreover, the regime continued for years to come to be heavily influenced by its military element, especially by the members of Castro's former guerrilla army, and despite civilianization in the 1970s and 1980s it was still strictly speaking a military-party rather than a party-state regime. The Cuban Communist regime will receive much greater attention later, in Part III, as an example of an only partially completed transformation from military to party type of ideological one-party state.

The Cuban regime was a forerunner of the several military-party Marxist–Leninist regimes that arose in the 1970s, most notably in Ethiopia. Apart from them the second wave of Communist expansion showed few distinctive features. There was a general abandonment of the popular front and electoral-coalition tactic of the first wave of Communist expansion, but many regimes continued with the practice of not calling the party 'Communist'. Geographically, the new examples of Communist regime were confined to Asia and Africa. The vintage year for Communism in Asia was 1975, with South Vietnam being conquered by the North, Laos falling to the Pathet Lao movement of the Lao People's Revolutionary Party, and Cambodia falling to the Khmer Rouge movement of the Communist Party of Kampuchea. However, the only other Communist gain in Asia was in Afghanistan in 1978, and it would later result in the Soviet military intervention which contributed to the weakening of the Soviet regime in the 1980s.

The majority of the new Communist, or at least avowedly Marxist–Leninist, regimes were established in Africa. But in these African cases it is often doubtful whether a regime should really be classified as Communist. Although they all officially espoused Marxism–Leninism, most did not attempt to implement typically Communist policies, such as collectivization. Ethiopia's attempt at pushing through such a massive and inappropriate restructuring of agriculture and rural society was the exception rather than the rule among Africa's Marxist–Leninist regimes. Even such apparently solid examples of Communist regime as Mozambique seem closer to the 'African socialist' versions of party-state regime that had appeared in Africa in the late 1950s and the 1960s. For example, Touré's Guinea during its Socialist Cultural Revolution was at least as radically leftist as Mozambique. And it is this Guinean regime and Nkrumah's less radically socialist regime in Ghana that will be used in the next chapter as case studies of Third World party-state regimes.

6 Third World Case Studies

1 NKRUMAH'S GHANA

Ghana was one of the first states to be created by the decolonization of Africa. In 1957 the British colony of the Gold Coast gained its independence as the new state of Ghana. The Gold Coast had been the most advanced British colony in West Africa, not only being the wealthiest (thanks to cocoa exports) but also having the largest Western-educated African intelligentsia of secondary-school and university graduates. After the Second World War the British had envisaged a gradual transition in Ghana from their colonial rule to a Western form of self-government. In 1946 they began this transition by bestowing a Constitution and a powerless, unrepresentative legislative council upon the colony. However, the following year the United Gold Coast Convention was founded by some of the intelligentsia in order to press for a speedier transition to self-government – for self-government 'as soon as possible'. The Chairman of the UGCC decided to appoint as its full-time General Secretary a young Ghanaian, by the name of Nkrumah, who had earned a reputation as an organizer of African students living in London. As General Secretary of the UGCC, the energetic and militant Nkrumah soon made himself the most well-known politician in the colony and developed a personal political following of his own. When he formed his own political party in 1949, he was able to bring into it many of the UGCC's young activists and many recruits from the various Gold Coast youth associations. The slogan of his new party was 'Self-Government Now' but the party was not simply a militantly nationalist movement. As its name, the Convention People's Party, suggested, it was also in part a populist movement – appealing to the ordinary people as distinct from the intelligentsia and the chiefs.[1]

Nkrumah's popular standing was further increased when

he was imprisoned for his campaign of civil disobedience, of 'Positive Action', against the colonial administration. His CPP won a clear-cut victory in the 1951 elections for a more representative and powerful Gold Coast legislative assembly, and Nkrumah became 'leader of government business' in the new legislature.[2] Soon afterwards he became the first Prime Minister of the colony, if still with only limited powers and under the supervision of the colonial Governor. In 1954 a revamped Constitution allowing a large measure of self-government was granted by the British and in the accompanying elections the CPP won a large majority of the seats in the new parliament. In the 1956 elections the CPP was vigorously opposed by an alliance of regional, ethnic and religious parties or groups yet still managed to win 57 per cent of the vote and, more importantly, 72 of the 104 seats in parliament.[3]

The opponents of the CPP had little chance of making a political impact after Britain granted full independence in March 1957. A number of the members of the opposition, including twelve members of parliament, recognized this political fact of life and defected to the CPP during the next few years.[4] The last opportunity for the opposition, grouped together as the United Party, came in the 1960 combined referendum/election for the creation of a Republic and election of a President. But the result of the referendum/election was an almost 90 per cent vote (on a low turnout) for the Republic and for Nkrumah as President.[5] Now holding the extensive powers of the new Presidency, Nkrumah had reached a virtually unassailable constitutional position of power over Ghana. A few years later he moved to give the CPP a completely unassailable legal position by enshrining in law its status as the regime party. But well before then it was already very clear that a party type of ideological one-party state had been established in Ghana.

Nkrumaist Ideology

The development of an official ideology had been delayed until the 1960s, when Nkrumaism 'emerged as a full-fledged ideology' – the early 1960s have been termed Ghana's 'Age of Ideology'.[6] Nkrumah had already written several works in which he had propounded his views on imperialism, Marxism and Africa, becoming known internationally as a self-proclaimed Christian Marxist socialist who was a leading exponent of anti-imperialism and Pan-Africanism. Then in 1961 he began espousing a socialist ideology that was defined by a leading member of the regime 'as a nonatheistic socialist philosophy' that had been 'adapted to suit the conditions and circumstances of Africa'.[7] Nkrumah initially preferred a technocratic emphasis when expounding this Africanized form of socialism. 'It is not socialism for the sake of socialism, but a practical solution of the country's problems.'[8] Thus the 1962 Work and Happiness development programme emphasized that, because of the pernicious colonial heritage, socialism was the only means of bringing about the economic and social progress sought by the programme.

The same apparently technocratic, developmental justification of socialism was evident in the promulgation of a socialist Seven Year Plan to speed up Ghana's economic and social development. In fact the introduction of the Seven Year Plan was the ultimate expression of the technocratic aspect of Nkrumah's belief in 'scientific socialism'.[9] The Plan was not a very radical document and envisaged a long transitional period, lasting twenty years, during which a mixed economy would continue to exist and a vigorous private sector would have its own assigned tasks. Not surprisingly, the Plan did not include any attempt to collectivize Ghana's agriculture, though the regime did use state controls to extract resources from the lucrative cocoa-farming industry.

In 1963 Nkrumah published *Africa Must Unite*, which emphasized his 1950s theme of Pan-Africanism and the need for African political unity. The renewed emphasis on Pan-Africanism was displayed in the formal definition of Nkrumaism constructed by the Kwame Nkrumah Institute of Ideology in 1964 and approved by him:

> Nkrumaism is the ideology of the New Africa, independent and absolutely free from imperialism, organized on a continental scale, founded upon the conception of one and united Africa, drawing its strength from modern

science and technology and from the traditional African belief that the free development of each is the condition for the free development of all.[10]

Although such an ideology could readily legitimate Nkrumah's foreign policies, its comparative lack of political, social and economic content restricted its ability to legitimate his regime's domestic policies.

However, in 1964 Nkrumah also published his definitive ideological work, *Consciencism*, which shifted Nkrumaism's emphasis back to domestic matters.[11] In this work he also provided a social and African basis for the socialist content of his new ideology of Consciencism. He argued that this socialism was but the modern expression of the communalism and classlessness of African traditional society. Centralized control of the economy by a socialist government was needed in a modern, technically developed African society to ensure that the principles underlying the traditional communalism were maintained and that class cleavages were prevented from developing. However, there was no need for a socialist social revolution in the communal African context – socialism could be achieved through reform rather than revolution.

Consciencism also described the political means by which newly independent Africa could achieve this reformist transition to socialism. Apparently Africa required a continent-wide mass party, presumably a Pan-African version of the CPP, that would have Consciencism as its ideology. More realistically, Nkrumah described the main tasks of African socialists within even the existing political boundaries as being: to eliminate the colonial–capitalist development of class cleavages; to eliminate the colonial mentality from the people's psychology and make contact with the classless pre-colonial past; to adopt those elements of the colonialists' methods of production and organization which would be beneficial to society; and to maintain the people's independence and security.

Throughout the development of Nkrumaism as an ideology, little attention was paid to the question of democracy or to justifying the imposition in law of a one-party state. However, in 1961, one of the regime's leading ideologists advanced some of the soon-to-be-standard justifications for the African one-party state: 'As Nkrumaists, we believe that a monolithic party is necessary in an ex-colonial state which... cannot afford to dissipate its national efforts through the senseless wranglings and obstructive and destructive tactics that organized political opposition encourages.'[12] But he also reassured his readers that the CPP and the Constitution would ensure 'freedom of opinion, freedom of speech, and freedom of individual activity in public life', and he argued that it was these sorts of things, not organized opposition, which were necessary for democracy.

The Convention People's Party

Although in 1962 the CPP's eleventh Party Congress called for the establishment of a one-party state, it was not until 1964 that a referendum was held on the issue. Over 96 per cent of the electorate voted in favour – thanks to widespread vote-rigging and intimidation – and the Constitution was duly amended to enshrine the CPP's monopoly in law.[13] However, several years earlier the regime had already taken steps to ensure a monopoly in effectiveness for the CPP. In particular, the 1958 Preventive Detention Law had enabled the CPP regime to silence its opponents in quite legal fashion. All but one of the twelve opposition members of parliament were to fall victim to the new law within a few years. By the end of the regime's life in 1966 more than 900 people were being held under the Preventive Detention Law, and an additional several hundred were thought to have been arbitrarily imprisoned by the regime.[14]

As early as 1952 the CPP had a membership of 700 000, some 15 per cent of a population of less than 4.5 million, and after independence was (quite unrealistically) claimed to incorporate the overwhelming majority of the people.[15] The CPP also possessed an extensive range of supplementary organizations, known as integral wings or organizations of the Party. Among them were the National Council of Ghana Women, the Young Pioneers youth organization, the TUC trade union movement, and the United Ghana Farmers' Council. (The least extensive but most interesting wing of the Party was the parliamentary wing, for while the CPP-monopolized National Assembly always passed the government's legislation, on occasion the bills provoked contentious and vigorous debate.[16]) Moreover, the Party possessed an extensive administrative apparatus. The central Party headquarters included no fewer than fifteen different bureaux and committees by 1964. Beneath the central organs and officials of the Party was the familiar structure of regional, district and local units, with their own executive organs and administrative secretaries.

In addition to the usual Party officials there were the unique Regional and District Commissioners, whose possession of 'dual', Party/state powers was an important innovation of the CPP regime.[17] The leading Party figures (usually from the parliamentary wing) appointed by Nkrumah to the eight offices of Regional Commissioner officially enjoyed the status (but not title) of a Minister, and indeed this was the only basis in law for the state authority which they wielded over their own regional state officials. But, unlike Ministers, the Regional Commissioners (RCs) also wielded authority over the Party structure in their regions. Their increasing concentration on political and Party matters was formally acknowledged in 1961 when they were given the additional post of regional Party secretary. The District Commissioners (DCs), too, exercised dual, Party/state powers but from the outset the Party aspect of their office and responsibilities was more obvious than the state aspect. Although the RCs had an important say in the appointment of District Commissioners within their regions, the DCs theoretically were elected by the Party's district conferences and then endorsed by the Central Committee. The DCs were told by Nkrumah to view themselves as primarily Party workers and they certainly performed many Party functions within their districts, eventually becoming head of the Party's district executive organ. The DCs exercised tight control over the local Party branches, and the average DC 'wielded enormous, almost unlimited, *actual* power in his locality'.[18]

Since an apparently hierarchical structure of officials controlled the CPP from top to bottom, the Party as a whole appeared to be subject to an at least bureaucratic degree of discipline. The chain of command stretched down from the centre to the RCs and DCs and then to the local leaders. At the head of the Party was its Chairman for Life, President Nkrumah. As the permanent chairman of the Central Committee he appointed the Party's General Secretary and in 1961 actually appointed himself to that post. Although the annual Conference or Congress of the Party theoretically wielded the supreme authority within the CPP, in reality it simply rubber-stamped the Chairman's policies and proposals.

However, Nkrumah discovered that his Regional Commissioners were by no means reliable links in the chain of command. They were publicly depicted as being 'personally and directly responsible' to President Nkrumah, but the RCs' tendency 'to act without reference to the president and, at times, in opposition to presidential instructions', meant that there was 'a serious breach in the chain of command' between the centre and the regions.[19] What is more, there was a further weakness in the chain of command as it passed from the regional to the district level. For although the RCs were usually able to have their nominees appointed as District Commissioner, once a nominee had been installed in his new office (from which he could be removed only by the President) he could prove very difficult for a Regional Commissioner to control.

Instead of acting as disciplined bureaucratic officials, the Regional and District Commissioners behaved like virtually independent political bosses, in a fashion reminiscent of the regional Communist Party bosses of the Soviet Union in the mid-1930s. In the final years of the regime's life 'one of the day-to-day problems of the CPP and the government was the many decisions and policy statements issued at the regional and local levels, most of which seriously contradicted presidential policy pronouncements'.[20] All that Nkrumah did in response was to warn against any repetition of previous cases of disobedience; there would be no Stalin-like purge of the Party bosses.

As a multi-role regime party the CPP fell well short of the Communist standard and was little, if at all, superior to the Nazi Party. The usual verdict on the CPP is that while the Party was an effective mobilizer of voters at election or referendum time or of crowds for political rallies, it was not at all effective at propagating the regime's ideology – even within its own ranks.[21] In other words, the Party performed a significant political role but was ineffective in performing its social role of instilling the regime's solidarity-building ideology in the hearts and minds of the people. However, even the Party's political role of selecting candidates and mobilizing voters for the informally and later legally one-candidate elections (and the two referendums) was greatly reduced in 1965, when Nkrumah dispensed with the charade of a parliamentary election and simply declared that all CPP parliamentary candidates were returned unopposed.

The Party never performed a significant governing role. Not until the 1964 legal recognition of a one-party state was there an explicit and clear-cut commitment to the idea of Party supremacy.[22] The CPP was declared in law to be the 'vanguard of the people' and 'the leading core of all organizations of the people'.[23] Yet despite the obvious similarities here with the Communist language of Party rule, there was still no move to introduce the 'Politburo system' of having a political committee of the Party act as the *de facto* government of the country. Government was still centred on the Presidency and the Cabinet of Ministers, and the Party was still excluded from a policy-making governing role.

Nor did the Party take on the supervisory governing role of supervising the Ministries' implementation of the regime's policies. The British ideal of a politically neutral civil service, loyal to the state rather than to a particular political party, remained the official principle and practice in Ghana during the early years of the regime. In 1962 Nkrumah appeared to change tack, declaring that the Party was assuming the 'central leadership' of the civil service.[24] He announced that all civil servants, like any other citizens, should have the right of participating fully in political affairs and that therefore the Party was supporting the establishment of CPP branches in the civil service. However, this apparent drive to Party-ize the civil service lacked momentum.[25] And, anyway, the new Party branches were prevented from effectively monitoring, let alone vetoing or directing, the work of the higher civil service.[26] The Party militants continued to protest against the 'unpolitical' and thus 'disloyal' civil service but without much to show for their attacks until the Civil Service Commission (which supervised all but the highest rank of the civil service) was replaced by the Party's civil service committee in late 1965, only a few months before the regime's demise.[27]

At first glance the Party does seem to have acquired a supervisory role at the regional, district and local levels.[28] The Regional Commissioners directed the work of their regional state officials and at the regional level the civil servants of several of the central Ministries were in practice subject to the political control of the RCs and regional Party officials. In addition the Party enjoyed an extensive control over local government, exercised largely through the District Commissioners. The DCs tended to dominate the local councils, which often ended up simply rubber-stamping the DC's personal decisions. But the fact that this regional- and district- level control over parts of the state apparatus was exercised largely by RCs and DCs means that it was not really Party supervision at all. For the control the RCs and DCs exercised was more an example of personal rule by Party bosses than of supervision by the Party as an organization.[29] The breakdown of Party discipline in the chain of command from Nkrumah to the RCs and from them to the DCs meant that the Party as an organization could not perform a supervisory governing role.

Nor did the Party ever perform a supervisory role in relation to the military arm of the state apparatus.[30] Ghana's military establishment had been inherited from the colonial regime and in fact until the 1961 Africanization of the officer corps most officers were of British origin, either on post-retirement contract or active-service secondment. As in the case of the civil service, during the regime's early years no steps were taken to Party-ize the military. The apolitical, professionalist ethos that the British had sought to instil in the military was not threatened until 1963, when it was announced that all officer cadets had to apply for Party membership. Then in 1964 came the dispatch of application forms for Party membership to all army units and the announcement of plans for the introduction of political commissars. Many officers, though, refused to apply for CPP

membership, and bureaucratic stalling held up the plans
for commissars until the army coup of February 1966 permanently put an end to any ideas of Party supervision of
the military.

Although the idea of Party-izing the military had been
unpopular with the officer corps, Nkrumah had reason to
believe that he was in a stronger position in 1964–5 than
ever before to push through such a move.[31] For by then
he had created a presidential military force, separate from
the regular army, to protect the President and the regime
from any armed opposition. Known as the President's Own
Guard Regiment, this force differed in its uniforms, equipment and officer-training (all of which were largely of Soviet origin) from the regular army and was officially detached
from the army's chain of command in 1965.[32] With plans
having been drawn up for the further expansion of the POGR
to three or five battalions, it could soon have rivalled the
regular army in size – and was already being given preference over the army in the purchase of military equipment.
Thus the POGR seems quite similar to the Waffen-SS of
wartime Nazi Germany. For here in Ghana was another case
of a regime's establishing a full-time military force that
was quite distinct from the regular army and of sufficient
size and effectiveness to challenge the army's military pre-
eminence.

   Another similarity with the Waffen-SS was that the POGR
was part of a wider bodyguard/security organization, the
National Security Service.[33] The NSS was established in 1963,
after the second attempt on Nkrumah's life, as a new security service that would be directly responsible to and at
the disposal of the President. It immediately acquired the
Military Intelligence section of the army, established a civilian Special Intelligence unit, and in 1964 acquired the
police's Special Branch. The bodyguard element of the NSS
was provided by the Presidential Detail Department, comprising a civilian bodyguard unit, internal counter-intelli-
gence section, and the President's Own Guard Regiment.

   Yet the Ghanaian NSS was never really an organizational
equivalent of Hitler's SS. The members of the NSS were
still solely members of the Ghanaian state apparatus, not

of a Party or political organization, and they were attached to the governing office of state, the Presidency, not to Nkrumah personally. Like the dual Party/state powers of the Regional and District Commissioners, the NSS and its POGR was a unique innovation. But it was also another unsuccessful innovation. The existence of the POGR seems to have provoked more than deterred military intervention: 'it was resentment against . . . the Guard Regiment, which contributed most to the growing chasm between Nkrumah and his regular military forces'.[34] And when the military eventually did intervene, the POGR and the rest of the NSS proved ineffective guardians of President Nkrumah's rule. In the the final analysis, the development of the POGR may have actually weakened rather than strengthened Nkrumah's attempt to establish a secure position of personal rule.

Nkrumah's Personal Rule

By the 1960s Nkrumah was clearly not just an agent of the Party and could be said to have reversed any former principal–agent relationship. But his apparently authoritative leadership position over the Party was not a great source of strength for him as a personal ruler. He was the founder and formal leader, in fact Life Chairman, of the Party and its central organs deferred completely to him and his wishes.[35] However, in light of the Party's indiscipline and other deficiencies it is difficult to portray the CPP as being an 'agent or instrument' of his rule – certainly it was not an effective agent or instrument. Perhaps the greatest benefit Nkrumah received from his leadership of the Party arose from its constitutionally prescribed role, after 1964, of nominating presidential candidates. As only the CPP could nominate candidates for the Presidency, Nkrumah could in theory be re-elected President for as many five year terms as he wished – life Chairmanship of the Party gave him the option of also being life President of Ghana.

As President he was head of state and government and enjoyed the unusually strong constitutional powers to alter any legislation as well as to appoint and dismiss civil servants, military officers, judges and even tribal chiefs.[36] The power of the Presidency was further increased by Nkrumah's expansion of its administrative unit, the Office of the President, into an administrative empire rivalling in size the whole set of government Ministries.[37] Eventually nearly half of all the state's central administrative organs had been placed under the umbrella of the Office of the President. (Moreover, in an administrative equivalent of the relationship between a Communist Politburo and Council of Ministers, the organs grouped within the Office of the President tended to be policy formulators and the Ministries to be policy implementers.) So Nkrumah's creation of the presidential NSS and POGR was only one expression of his policy of expanding the Presidency's role and power.

In addition to his post of President and his leadership of the Party, Nkrumah enjoyed considerable public standing and personal authority as the founding father of Ghana, as the explicit source of the regime's ideology, and as one of Africa's leading spokesmen in world forums, such as the Non-Aligned Movement. Furthermore, he was the subject of an extravagant personality cult propagated by the CPP and the Ghanaian mass media.[38] His name was bestowed on streets, markets, public buildings, state farms, and even the university. His likeness was displayed on Ghana's postage stamps and currency, and his birthplace was declared to be sacred. Sacredness or divinity also seemed to be ascribed to his own person, with such religious terminology as 'Messiah', 'redeemer', and 'miracle' being applied to him and his works.

The best symbol of the personality cult, and of the purely personal authority claimed by Nkrumah, was the traditional chiefly title of Osagyefo that was officially bestowed upon him in 1960. It was often used instead of President or Chairman when his political supporters were referring to him in public meetings or in the press.[39] However, it was only one of a number of titles he had acquired.

Among the titles Nkrumah acquired or arrogated to himself were: *Osagyefo* (victorious in war), *Kantamanto* (one never guilty, one who never goes back on his word), Teacher and Author of the Revolution, *Oyeadeeyie* (one who puts things right), Man of Destiny, Star of Africa,

Deliverer of Ghana, Iron Boy, the Messiah, His High Dedication.[40]

There were two obvious weaknesses in Nkrumah's position as a personal ruler. They were (a) his lack of control over the regions – thanks to his RCs and DCs having themselves become virtually personal rulers – and (b) his lack of any leadership position over the military. The former limited his power to impress his policies upon the largest part of the population, but the latter was more significant because it left him potentially vulnerable to being removed from all power by a military coup. Although as Ghana's President he was also titular Commander-in-Chief of the armed forces, this was a constitutional rather than military position and was held by a professional politician who had never served in the military. His lack of a leadership position over the military might not have mattered so much if the military had been placed under Party supervision or if a Party militia or alternative military force had been created to balance the army's armed might. But Nkrumah's moves in the direction of Party-izing the army and building up the President's Own Guard Regiment had alienated the officer corps, while still not being far enough advanced in 1966 to provide him with much security against being deposed by the military.

By then he had actually become more vulnerable to military intervention. For he had lost that apparently great support among the civilian population which in earlier years would have deterred the military from moving against him – for fear of having to deal with massive civilian opposition to their attack on Nkrumah's regime. His own popularity as well as that of the CPP fell away in the middle 1960s with the onset of economic crisis, food shortages, and an increasing discontent with the amount of corruption associated with the regime.[41]

The officer corps not only shared these civilian grievances, such as seeing high inflation erode the purchasing power of their fixed salaries, but also had several new grievances of their own to add to their fear of imminent Party-ization and their resentment at the growth of the POGR.[42] Therefore the coup of 23–4 February 1966 had at least the tacit support of a majority of the officer corps, even though the leaders of the coup were a small number of middle-ranking officers allied with the senior commanders of the police, not with their own high command.[43]

They staged the coup when Nkrumah was out of the country and thus unable to deploy against them what remained of his personal popularity and prestige. Yet even if he had been able to do so, the coup would probably still have been successful. For far from showing any sign of support for the Osagyefo, crowds acclaimed the victorious soldiers and tore down or smashed signs and images of Nkrumah as well as of the unpopular CPP. 'Foreign correspondents' reports and numerous other oral evidence from a wide variety of sources confirm that the coup was a genuinely popular one.'[44]

2   TOURÉS GUINEA

The West African state of Guinea, a close neighbour of Ghana's, went through a similar process of decolonization in the 1950s, but as a French rather than British colony – in fact it was known simply as 'French Guinea'. In 1946 each of the colonies comprising French West Africa was granted a degree of self-government, with an elected assembly having powers over the territory's budget. The following year saw the founding in French Guinea of the leftist Parti Démocratique de Guinée (PDG), which was radically opposed to – and was strongly opposed by – the French colonial administration.[45] Ahmed Sékou Touré, the Secretary-General of the colony's small trade union movement, also became Secretary-General of the PDG in 1952. He led both organizations into the long and legendary strike of 1953 that was to make him and the PDG a major political force within the colony. After the strike the party expanded from its urban base into the rural hinterland and soon the rural villagers became the main basis of the PDG's popular support.[46] The growth of support for the PDG was evident in the increase of its popular vote in assembly elections from less than 15 per cent in 1951 to nearly 35 per cent in 1954 and then to 62 per cent in 1956.

By 1956 the PDG and the French colonial administration had become more accommodating to each other (as the CPP and the British had in Ghana from the 1951 election onwards) and the PDG became the obvious inheritor of power from the French. In 1957 it won an overwhelming victory in the elections, taking 56 of the 60 seats, and so could take full advantage of the 1956 reforms allowing the assembly to elect a government of Ministers presided over by the colonial Governor. As leader of the PDG Touré became first the Vice-President of this council of government and then, in July 1958, its President.

The PDG appeared to be content for the moment with the degree of self-government that had been achieved within the colonial framework. However, in 1958 France's new President, General de Gaulle, offered the colonies of French West Africa either a greater degree of self-government within what would become the French 'Community' or complete independence as separate and sovereign states. Faced with this choice, Touré and the PDG proved true to their past reputation for radicalism. Unlike the other leaders and parties of French West African colonies Touré and the PDG committed themselves to supporting a 'No' vote in the French-organized referendum of September 1958 on the question of joining the Community. As a result French Guinea became the completely independent state of Guinea, with Touré as its first President.

It also soon became one of the first African examples of an ideological one-party state – and it would be perhaps the most extreme example that has yet been seen in Africa. The Guinean regime would be much more repressive than its counterpart in Ghana. There would be much less ideological and political tolerance, many more political prisoners and much harsher treatment of prisoners. As early as 1962 the regime had laid the foundations of what would become a 'full-blown apparatus of secret police, prisons, and modern forms of torture' that was used by the Ministry of Defence and Security to ensure ideological conformity and defend the regime from the succession of real or imaginary plots which would bedevil its history.[47] Guinea would frequently be labelled a police state and, because of its emphasis upon ideological conformity and commitment, would be described as 'the most deeply politicized nation in West Africa'.[48]

Touré's Ideology

From early on in the regime's history Touré placed great emphasis on ideology as the means of mobilizing the masses for the transformation of Guinean society. Despite lacking even a secondary-school education, he ensured an appropriate ideology would be available by producing a mass of articles, speeches, and other pronouncements which by 1970 already filled seventeen published volumes of collected works.[49] He did not present his ideas as 'Touréism' but rather as the Party's ideology – his volumes of collected works were officially titled *The Works of the PDG*. However, it is difficult to describe this ideology as anything else than 'Touréism' because it is such an individual collection, or rather progression, of ideas.

In the initial, post-independence stage of his ideological development the most prominent strands in Touré's ideological pronouncements were nationalism and radical populism. The independence struggle was depicted as having been a nationalist revolution whose foes were the French and other imperialist powers.[50] Touré would describe the newly independent state as an example of 'national democracy', a form of democracy 'designed to suppress ethnic and social contradictions, and to lead the people in the struggle against neo-colonialism, underdevelopment and injustice'.[51] He distinguished Guinean-style national democracy from the 'people's democracy' of East European Communist regimes by emphasizing Guinean democracy's broader social base and greater concern with national unity.

Nevertheless, Guinean national democracy was similar to Communist 'people's democracy' in looking to a particular party for leadership and thus legitimating the rule of that party and the existence of a party-state regime. Touré viewed the PDG as 'the definer of this general interest, the custodian of the popular will, and the incarnation of the collective thought of the whole Guinean people'.[52] As in the Communist case, the emphasis on leadership by the

Party was accompanied by a belief in Party rule and control of the state. (Within the Party itself the familiar Communist principle of democratic centralism was supposed in theory to ensure that the people retained supreme power and that the leaders would be only agents of the people.[53]) However, as Touré hoped to build social solidarity among the people through their common membership in the Party, the PDG would have a very different approach to Party membership from the Communists' elitist approach of allowing only worthy candidates to join their vanguard party.

The second stage in Touré's and the regime's ideological development began in 1964 with the pronouncement of a socialist revolution and the call to struggle against Guinea's emergent bourgeoisie. Touré expressed publicly some doubts about whether it was possible to 'build socialism in a still agricultural economy' but described the decision to adopt socialism as being based on a commitment to social justice and to a social consciousness, where each was concerned with the good of all.[54] Although the emphasis on social consciousness is reminiscent of his earlier theme of national social solidarity, the 1964 shift to socialism was also marked by an implicit abandonment of his earlier, nationalist–populist pronouncements about the lack of social classes and class struggle in African society. He now argued that antagonistic social classes would develop unless the embryo national bourgeoisie – comprising merchants, rural landowners and the like – could be crushed as it emerged.

The shift in ideology legitimated a major shift in the direction of economic policy. The new ideological commitment to socialism was used to justify the extensive commerce-regulating laws of November 1964 and the socialist direction taken by the Seven Year Plan of 1964–71. The November laws gave the state a monopoly over foreign trade and wholesale commerce as well as tight control over retailing. The Seven Year Plan sought to industrialize Guinea through state-owned enterprises, and by 1971 had strangled private-sector industries into oblivion.[55] (However, the vital bauxite mining industry, which produced much of Guinea's export revenue, was left in the hands of ideologically suspect but technically proficient foreign companies.) The Plan did not, though, attempt to collectivize agriculture, being content with state controls and encouraging agricultural co-operatives.

A third stage in Touré's and the regime's ideological development came in 1967 when Touré announced Guinea's commitment to a Socialist Cultural Revolution. It came a year after Mao's launching of China's Great Proletarian Cultural Revolution and was heavily influenced by its Chinese forerunner.[56] As in China the Cultural Revolution unleashed a political and social assault (supposedly by the masses) upon the bureaucrats, not just the civil servants but also the Party officials.[57] Thus the commitment to a Cultural Revolution legitimated a populist, anti-bureaucratic reform of the Party and state administration as well as a radicalizing of the regime's cultural policy. The Cultural Revolution's specifically cultural aim of complete decolonization and 'de-occidentalisation' led to such extreme measures as publicly undressing supposed hippies and miniskirted young women.[58] The more positive aspect of this cultural aim was the effort to restore African culture through a renewal of indigenous art forms and a shift in emphasis away from French to the indigenous languages.

A separate ideological development that belongs to the Cultural Revolution era was Touré's justification for the repressive climate of his regime. He argued that revolutionary Guinea was faced with a state of permanent conspiracy, the 'permanent plot', by its various domestic and foreign enemies. Considering the number of supposed plots that had already been unearthed in Guinea's short history, such an idea might not have seemed too far-fetched. However, in November 1970 a very real plot took the regime by surprise when an abortive sea-borne invasion by Portuguese soldiers and Guinean political exiles caught the regime's forces unprepared. The subsequent almost panic-stricken punishment of the invaders and those accused of being their secret supporters brought forth from Touré new ideological pronouncements to legitimate the form of 'revolutionary justice' meted out.

The invasion also recharged the intolerant and extreme aspect of the regime's use of ideology. Public speakers would be careful to include quotes from Touré in their speeches, students would learn and cite lengthy quotations from his works, and there would continue to be 'a situation in which hardly anyone in any position can feel safe from denunciation for ideological crimes such as the harbouring of counter-revolutionary sentiments'.[59] There was a clear contrast with the more ideologically tolerant and pragmatic CPP regime in Ghana.

However, in the late 1970s Touré shifted towards a more pragmatic position, perhaps because of the riots in 1977 which had revealed the people's discontent with the regime's economic policies and repressiveness.[60] In 1978 Touré set a new course by publicly declaring the Party's desire for co-operation with capitalist states, by personally making a massive diplomatic effort at presenting an outward-looking and moderate image to the world, and by encouraging investment by foreign business in exploiting Guinea's natural resources. At the 1978 Party Congress Touré denied that his effort to strengthen ties with the capitalist world marked an ideological turning-point. But the impression of a watershed in policy, if not yet in ideological justification, was reinforced by the degree of economic and (less obviously) political liberalization he was allowing on the domestic front. In the area of religious policy, too, a new pragmatism was evident as the regime changed its approach from controlling and persecuting to one of fervently supporting Islam – the religion of more than two-thirds of Guinea's people.[61] By the end of 1980 Touré was even prepared to admit publicly that applying the doctrine of Party rule had its dangers, such as 'egoism, incompetence or treachery', but he still saw no advantages in a multi-party system which often represented a 'hypocritical dispersion of the organization of the ruling class'.[62]

The Parti Démocratique de Guinée

Soon after Guinea became an independent state, the PDG acquired a clear monopoly when its political opponents decided to join it. However, unlike in Ghana, this monopoly was never enshrined in law. The Constitution continued to recognize the principle of multi-party democracy, and dissidents' plans in 1965 to establish a rival political party had to be quashed as a supposedly counter-revolutionary plot, rather than as an infringement of any legal provision banning other parties.[63]

Even before independence the PDG had possessed a truly mass membership and by 1962 this had increased to a claimed 1.65 million members out of a total population of little more than 3 million. Yet the Party was not satisfied with this very extensive level of membership and decided, in 1962, to make Party membership automatic and universal – for taxpayers at least. From then on Party dues were integrated into the state tax paid by all adult Guineans.[64] Such universality of membership was demanded by the PDG's ideological commitment to building national social solidarity through the Guinean people's common membership and participation in the Party. The 1967 Party Statutes actually listed as the first object of the PDG: 'to group *all* the citizens of the Republic of Guinea and to organize them within the national territory into a united, strong, democratic and socialist nation'.[65] In addition to this comprehensively extensive membership the PDG was equipped with several attached organizations – a women's section, a youth section, an attached trade union movement, and so forth. A feature of the PDG in the 1950s had been the large and very active Women's Section but by the 1960s it was overshadowed by the Party's massive youth organization, the JRDA.[66] During the Cultural Revolution the JRDA militants seemed to overshadow the Party itself in carrying out their allotted duties in the areas of culture, revolutionary morale and defence.

To organize such an extensive party the PDG had to develop an accompanying administrative apparatus.[67] Beneath the central administration directed by Touré and the other Party secretaries was a layer of twenty-nine regional Party federations, each having a federal secretary – the key Party official in the regions. Beneath them were the district-level Party units, with their own secretaries, and then the thousands of local Party units and officials, with a unit in each village and urban quarter.

In its formative years the PDG had copied some of the structural features of the French Communist Party and had become 'the best example in former French West Africa of the tightly organized, highly disciplined hierarchic party'.[68] As was noted earlier, the PDG adopted the Communists' organizational principle of democratic centralism, and the centralist element, as usual, predominated in practice over the democratic element. The Party Statutes demanded 'rigorous discipline' in the Party and strict adherence by lower Party bodies to the decisions of higher bodies.[69] The Party's central and highest-ranking executive organ was the National Political Bureau, which also constituted the theoretically collective leadership of the Party. But the Political Bureau was itself dominated by the Party's Secretary-General, Touré, who headed the hierarchical administrative apparatus of secretaries that, again in standard Communist fashion, controlled the Party in the regions and localities.

This administrative apparatus displayed an at least bureaucratic degree of discipline. Touré was not plagued by that remarkable indiscipline in the chain of command which in effect removed Ghana's regions from Nkrumah's rule. Yet Touré had such unrealistically high expectations that he was bound to be dissatisfied with his middle-level officials.[70] His dissatisfaction was made abundantly clear in the Cultural Revolution's populist attack on (middle-ranking) Party and state officialdom. Touré and his militants encouraged the people, the virtuous revolutionary masses, to denounce all those officials 'whose loss of touch with the people was evidenced by corruption, inefficiency or lack of revolutionary zeal'.[71] Not surprisingly, the Cultural Revolution demoralized the Party's regional and district officials, leaving them 'unwilling to act or take responsibility', and was in a sense administratively counter-productive.[72] Touré won only a temporary respite from his sense of frustration about what he saw as his lack of central control over Guinea.

As might be expected, the PDG was a stronger multi-role party than was the Ghanaian CPP, and came close to Communist standards in overall performance. The Party performed its political role in the one-candidate elections for the Presidency and the rubber-stamping parliament – which considered and passed the country's budget in less than an hour.[73] President Touré's re-election campaigns in 1968, 1974 and 1982 were such triumphs that on the last two occasions he apparently won no less than 100 per cent of the votes. As for its social role, the Party not only was supposed to instil the official ideology in the hearts and minds of the people, but also was supposed to act as a directly social means of building social solidarity by means of the nation's common membership and participation in the Party. (It is little wonder that a Guinean writer used the term 'party-nation' to describe his country under the PDG.[74]) After the regime's demise in 1984 the people displayed little attachment to the PDG ideology but did reveal a significant degree of national solidarity – indicating that the Party may have quite effectively performed its social role.

When it came to the governing role of the Party, Touré's regime followed the Communist approach but added its own idiosyncratic innovations. Touré repeatedly declared, as a fundamental principle, the Party's supremacy over the state apparatus, which was referred to as the 'instrument' of the Party.[75] The PDG's Political Bureau became the country's *de facto* government and the Cabinet of Ministers was relegated to a policy-advising and policy-implementing role. But performing this policy-making governing role was easier for the Party than performing a Communist-style supervisory role. For the central administration of the Party lacked the technically skilled staff needed to supervise the Ministries competently, and at the regional level the thirty federal secretaries were the Party's only full-time officials.[76] Touré had to allow 'the better-staffed state administrative machinery to exercise more powers than those permitted by the party ideology'.[77]

The relationship between the federal Party secretary and the state Governor of his region was left as a balance of power described by a foreign administrative expert as 'Compulsory co-operation and collaboration; *mutual* control and supervision.'[78] The same relationship of compulsory collaboration and mutual supervision between equivalent Party and state officials also existed at the district level. Therefore the Party's supervisory governing role at the crucial regional and district levels was significantly weaker than would be expected in a regime ideologically committed to Party supremacy over the state.

In contrast, at the local level the Party's governing role eventually became so strong that the Party actually replaced rather than supervised the state apparatus.[79] For in the mid-1960s the Party's omnipotence at the local level was officially recognized when the state's local government organ, the village council, was 'merged' with the Party's local village committee. What is more, during the Cultural Revolution each village and urban-quarter Party unit was converted into an all-powerful Pouvoir Révolutionnaire Locale (Local Revolutionary Authority). To these PRLs were devolved the duties of administering and safeguarding the Revolution (which included record-keeping, tax-collecting, judicial and policing responsibilities) and at least a portion of the taxes that a PRL collected was allocated to fulfilling its own local development plan. The Guinean regime had transformed its local Party units into perhaps the most powerful 'local government' institutions to be found in any modern regime.[80]

The PDG adopted a more, but still not completely, orthodox approach in its supervision of the military arm of the state.[81] As in Ghana, the new regime inherited a colonial-trained army that had little or no contact with the Party. Unlike Nkrumah, though, Touré disbanded his colonial-trained armed forces and built a new, 'popular' army supposedly coming from, and at the service of, the people. Perhaps for this reason Touré did not feel any need to institute Party supervision of the military until in 1968 a coup in the neighbouring state of Mali aroused concerns about the political reliability of the Guinean army. Elected Party committees were established within the military to monitor political opinion and to increase the role of political reliability as a criterion for promotion. The military were supposed to be so integrated into the Party, organizationally and ideologically, that they were referred to as 'militants in uniform'. Nevertheless, the regime continued to harbour suspicions about the military's loyalty, and it is surprising that Touré waited until 1977 before announcing the introduction of political commissars.[82] (After all, following the 1970 invasion the Chief of Staff and seven other senior officers had been sentenced to death for disloyalty.) However, Touré was probably waiting until a powerful counterforce was available to deter or deal with any military opposition to the introduction of political commissars.

Such a counterforce or balance to the military was taking shape in the 1970s in the form of a huge Party militia.[83] In 1966 Touré had established an 8000-strong militia drawn from the élite of the Party's JRDA youth organization. But the year after the 1970 invasion he massively expanded the militia to take in all higher-secondary and tertiary students and a large proportion of the rest of the JRDA – altogether some 300 000 recruits. When properly trained and equipped, they would provide the regime with a paramilitary force that vastly outnumbered the regular army of around 13 000 men. The military's commanders were well aware that if there was ever a confrontation between them and the Party leaders over such an issue as introducing commissars, the Party leaders could look to the militia for assistance.

But when political commissars were finally introduced into the army, it was as part of a much wider programme of introducing commissars into the Party, the JRDA, and the whole of the state apparatus.[84] In particular, at the regional level these 'all-powerful envoys' of (in theory) the Political Bureau and (in reality) Touré were to 'stand ready to correct and expose any failings of the regional party secretaries and governors'.[85] Therefore, the introduction of supervision by political commissars was more an attempt by Touré to strengthen his personal hold over the regions and over the regime as a whole than a move to strengthen the Party's supervision of the military. Yet he had long enjoyed a more secure and powerful degree of personal rule than Nkrumah ever had in Ghana.

Touré's Personal Rule

According to Touré's own ideology he was only the agent of the Party but by the end of the 1960s he had clearly reversed any such principal–agent relationship. Touré had been the Party's leader, ideologist, and Secretary-General since 1952, and in 1967 the Party Statutes formalized his leadership of the Party by conferring on his post of Secretary-General the title of Supreme Leader of the Revolution, the ultimate responsibility for 'the life of the Party', and the right to expel any Party member.[86] He had become so identified with the Party that its emblem, Sily (the elephant), was used to describe Touré himself.[87] Although he maintained a façade of collective leadership by the Political Bureau, he was the absolutist individual leader of the Party and hand-picked the members of the Political Bureau.[88] Despite his own ideological emphasis on the primacy and supremacy of the Party, the PDG became in reality an agent or instrument of Touré's personal rule.

Touré also held by far the country's most powerful constitutional office, the Presidency, from independence until his death in 1984. The President was head of state and government and enjoyed extensive appointment powers that covered all state offices and military posts. What is more, the Presidency possessed an unusually powerful legislative role, for the Constitution specified that legislation had to be 'initiated and drafted' by the President.[89] But the President was also given such extensive decree powers that most of the legal measures promulgated by Touré's regime would take the form of executive decrees rather than laws.

Touré's public standing was perhaps the highest of any African ruler and was strengthened by, not dependent upon, a quasi-official personality cult. Like Nkrumah, he enjoyed the personal prestige of having led the struggle for independence and thus being in a sense the founder of the state of Guinea. In later years he was commonly referred to as The Father of Guinea.[90] Furthermore, Touré was an inspiring orator and possessed remarkable leadership qualities – even the ageing Touré of the late 1970s seemed to a Western visitor to be 'a magnetic, awesome figure'.[91] The personality cult surrounding him was not taken to the same lengths as the Nkrumah cult in Ghana but still led to his being called 'Our Well-beloved Secretary-General', 'The Helmsman of Our Revolution', 'The Faithful and Supreme Servant of the People', 'The Great Son of Africa', 'The Liberator of Oppressed Peoples', and 'The Terror of International Imperialism, of Colonialism and Neocolonialism'.[92]

The only obvious weakness in his position as a personal ruler was that, like Nkrumah, he lacked any form of leadership over the military apart from his constitutional role of titular Commander-in-Chief. However, although Touré's regime followed the Ghanaian pattern of being eventually overthrown by a military coup led by middle-ranking officers, the coup would occur only after his death in 1984 and after a reign of more than thirty years. His success in avoiding military intervention may have been owing to the much greater progress he had made in Party-izing the military and in creating an effective counterforce (the militia) to the regular army. But as political commissars and the militia failed to protect the PDG regime after his death, the most likely reason for the passivity of the military during Touré's rule was his own public standing. The leaders of the army coup subsequently acknowledged that a successful attempt would have been impossible while Touré was alive.[93] There seems little doubt that Touré maintained his public standing more effectively than had Nkrumah and thus enjoyed a more secure basis for his personal rule.

Yet it must never be forgotten that Touré's personal rule was also supported by the repressive activities of his internal security apparatus and by his periodic purging of supposed plotters. The anti-plot purges provided a mechanism for removing any threats to his position from whole segments of state or society, as well as from politically dangerous individuals and groups. One foreign observer identified nine of the anti-plot purges as being clearly aimed at potential opposition from segments of state or society.[94] The regime itself referred to the 1961, 1965 and 1969 'plots' as respectively the Teachers, the Traders, and the Military plots.

However, the purges that followed the 1970 Portuguese-backed invasion included not only 'all remaining figures whose pasts included any history of activity in opposition parties in the 1940s and 1950s' but also 'a considerable swathe' of 'old PDG militants' and even some 'long-standing supporters of Sékou Touré who had been entrusted with posts of high responsibility'.[95] Seventeen of his twenty-four Ministers were sacked, seven former Ministers were sentenced to death in the initial trials of January 1971 and several more were arrested in the follow-up purge of mid-1971. Therefore the 1971 purges and accompanying show trials of the senior victims seem very similar to Stalin's 1937–8 purge, especially as Touré's included a drastic purge of the military high command in which 90 per cent of the top-ranking officers were put on trial for their treasonous inefficiency in combatting the invasion. On the other hand, Touré's 1971 purges were provoked by a real attack on the regime and were not as extensive, especially in relation to Party officials and other intelligentsia, as the 1937–8 purge in the Soviet Union had been.[96]

In both countries such drastic purges of the regime's élite strengthened the position of the personal ruler. Only once more, in 1976, did Touré feel the need for a major anti-plot purge. But another political effect of the continual purges was a continual narrowing of the political inner circle formed by the close associates of the leader.[97] Many of the remaining members of the inner circle were members of Touré's family, and in fact by the 1980s the political inner circle was dominated by two political 'clans' that were each centred upon his close relatives by blood or marriage.[98] Touré resorted to the time-honoured political tactic of acting as arbiter of their factional disputes and playing one faction off against the other to prevent either from becoming too powerful. But his reliance on family members rather than Party or state figures was a good illustration of how personalized Touré's rule had become. Such a degree of personalization left the Guinean ideological one-party state dependent for its continued political existence upon the continuing biological existence of its personal ruler. The weakness of the regime was revealed within a week of his death by the ease with which a very popular coup was carried out by army officers aiming to set a new political and economic course for the country.[99]

Part II
The Military-Party Type

7 The Quasi-Fascist Examples

1 PRIMO DE RIVERA'S REGIME IN SPAIN

Spain has experienced a troubled political history for most of the last two centuries. During the nineteenth century the kingdom of Spain was plagued by dynastic and party disputes that on occasions drew the military into politics without ever actually leading to the establishment of a military regime. The introduction in the 1890s of universal male franchise for parliamentary elections appeared to mark a major step forward in the progression towards a democratic form of constitutional monarchy. But in practice the expanded franchise had only a marginal effect on the making and unmaking of governments.[1] For in the countryside, where the great majority of Spaniards lived, there was a continuation of the long-established system of political control by *caciques*. These were local party or political bosses who used their patronage networks and local influence to deliver large numbers of votes to their favoured candidates at election time. The local control over elections exercised by the pragmatic and self-interested *caciques* in turn allowed the Ministry of the Interior and its politically influential provincial Governors to deliver parliamentary majorities to whichever of the two main parties, Conservatives or Liberals, was in favour in Madrid. As a result the Conservatives and Liberals alternated in power, in forming governments, until 1923. On 13 September of that year the commander of the Catalonian military region, Lieutenant-General Miguel Primo de Rivera, declared that he was rebelling against the political parties and intended to set up a Military Directory as a provisional government. The Liberal government quickly capitulated and King Alfonso appointed the General to the post of Prime Minister.

This was not a very 'military' coup. In staging the coup General Primo de Rivera was by no means acting as the

leader of the military. He was not the army's commander
or senior officer and did not enjoy any great prestige or
popularity among his fellow officers.[2] Nor did most of the
military garrisons and forces in Spain take part in the initial act of rebellion or provide it with even tacit support.
The military as a whole did not fall in behind Primo until
the King conferred royal approval on him by appointing
him Prime Minister in place of the departed civilian government. Only then was a military junta, the Military Directory, established and Spain officially placed under martial
law. And the host of decrees that would be issued by Primo
and the Military Directory were not the military's decrees
– they were directly or indirectly authorized by the King.

The role played by the monarchy seems very similar to
that played by King Victor Emmanuel of Italy in constitutionally legitimating the Fascists' October 1922 March on
Rome and the new regime that Mussolini established. King
Alfonso himself made that comparison in private, just as
Primo privately acknowledged later how much he owed at
the time to Mussolini's example of seizing power in order
to 'save' the country. However, a significant difference was
that Primo had announced during the coup that the Constitution would be suspended – that there would be 'a brief
parenthesis in the constitutional government of Spain' –
which meant that the King's acceptance of the coup and
the new government was illegal and incapable of bestowing
constitutional legitimacy upon Primo.[3]

In addition to the role of the monarchy another apparent similarity with the Fascists' coming to power was the
support Primo received from sections of the upper and
middle classes because of their fear and hatred of the 'Bolshevik threat'. Although the post-war 'red years' were less
threatening in Spain than in Italy, the psychological effect
upon the upper and middle classes seems to have been very
similar – an unreasoning fear of 'Bolshevism', which in Spain
was represented at least as much by the Anarchosyndicalists
as by the Socialists.[4] Furthermore, as Primo set about creating an ideological one-party state, his Spanish military-
party regime would also show signs of *ideological* similarity
with Italian Fascism, sufficiently for the most exhaustive
history of the regime to view it as a case of fascism (from

above), though the similarities are not great enough for Primo's regime to be classed as more than quasi-fascist.[5]

Primoderriverismo Ideology

Although Primo himself did not write any major ideological tracts or treatises, in his pronouncements, speeches, interviews, articles and official notes he stimulated and confirmed the work of 'ideologues' who 'formulated and transmitted a doctrinal message' that has been termed Primoderriverismo.[6] For example, Primo's first press statement on assuming power declared that the root of the evil afflicting Spain was to be found in rural *caciquismo* and that he would make every effort to eliminate it.[7] This was transformed into an ideological crusade against *caciquismo* which in turn legitimated the regime's policy of purging and restructuring local government in order to break the hold of the *caciques* in their local strongholds and replace them with a wave of 'new men'.

Nationalism soon became one of the most important tenets of the regime's ideology, equalled only by the doctrine of Primo's mission to lead and regenerate Spain.[8] Primoderriverismo's nationalism legitimated such foreign policies as avenging Spain's disastrous military defeat by the 'natives' of Morocco in 1921 and attempting to have Spain awarded a permanent seat on the Security Council of the League of Nations – and withdrawing from the League when the attempt failed. The ideology's centralist view of Spanish nationalism also produced a bitter antagonism towards even cultural regionalism. In March 1924 Primo gave his followers the centralist slogan of 'Spain One, Great and Indivisible', and later espoused the belief that it was 'better to have a red Spain than a broken one'.[9] Such centralism legitimated his attack on the limited degree of political and cultural autonomy that had long been enjoyed by the region of Catalonia.

Primoderriverismo 'equated nationalism with the Catholic legacy of Spain'.[10] So it is not surprising that Primo's regime was more ideologically committed to the Catholic Church than was perhaps any other regime in Europe in the 1920s.[11] Catholic social thought and its corporativist doctrines would also have a major influence on the social aspect of the regime's ideology, more so than would the ideas of radical rightists like the Italian Fascists.

There were clear similarities between the Fascists' arguments for their Corporativist State and Primo's belief in the need for a corporativist harmony between capital and labour as the only long-term alternative to Bolshevism. But his concern for a 'Christian' and 'just' balance between rich and poor, capitalists and workers, was more in tune with Catholic corporativist doctrine.[12] Furthermore, unlike in Fascist Italy, but in accordance with Catholic conceptions of corporativism, the Socialist and other varieties of trade unions were legally recognized as independent labour organizations if they were prepared to operate through the regime's corporativist institutions. The Organización Corporativa Nacional was formed in 1926 with the proclaimed goal of establishing social peace between employers and workers. It created twenty-seven different corporations, each covering a particular sphere or branch of the economy. The members of each corporation were organized into a pyramid of national, provincial, local and factory committees made up of elected representatives of employers and employees and chaired by a state-appointed president. As part of Primo's two-pronged strategy of repressing the revolutionary Anarchosyndicalists and Communists but offering a partnership to the more pragmatic Socialists, the Socialist trade unions were allowed to dominate workers' representation on the corporativist committees – and intervention by the state's representative on each committee ensured that the judgements of the committees normally favoured the workers.[13] Thus Primo claimed that 'there was no need to think of reinstituting democracy in Spain because . . . the workers' aspirations were being adequately represented in the institutions of the new regime'.[14]

Obviously Primoderriverismo did not have a positive attitude towards democracy. Primo adopted the position that parliamentary democracy was historically outmoded and was incompatible with Spain's destiny. His ideologues and other supporters were constantly inspired by what they saw as the world-wide tendency during the 1920s for dictatorship to replace parliamentary government. However, Primo would have been the first to claim a plebiscitary legitimacy for his government by pointing to not only the results of his 1926 referendum but also the displays of favourable public opinion that his regime party organized in the streets and other public places.[15]

The Patriotic Union (and the Military)

The Unión Patriótica was founded by Primo in April 1924, some six months after his coup, and acquired a monopoly in effectiveness as its birthright. The UP aimed to incorporate the large body of civilian support for what Primo termed the 'patriotic movement' of 13 September.[16] Despite his view of the UP as an 'anti-party', it came to be seen as the new regime's *partido único*.[17] As the regime's official party it was not hampered by the restrictions on the rights of assembly, association and publication of political opinion. Though the other parties had not been eliminated or legally prohibited, they were excluded from political and public life and had to watch powerlessly as the upstart UP enjoyed the fruits of its privileged position as the regime party.[18] (The only near rival to the UP was the Socialist Party, which received a degree of official recognition as the political arm of the Socialist movement that was being favoured and wooed by Primo.) When Primo 'civilianized' his regime at the end of 1925, most members of his first civilian government were prominent members of the UP, and he referred to it as a UP government. Similarly, he made sure that UP members dominated the provincial and municipal councils. In 1927 he also made membership of the UP obligatory for all civilian state officials.

By July 1927 the UP was claiming a membership of 1.7 million and had become the first mass party of the Spanish right, complete with a host of local branches and attached women's and youth sections.[19] At the central level it was also a hierarchical party. The non-elected Jefe Nacional (National Chief), General Primo de Rivera, had the right to appoint and dismiss the Secretary-General of the UP and to preside over its executive council, the Gran Junta Directiva Nacional.

But the UP was a poor example of a multi-role party. It had very little in the way of a political role to perform for the simple reason that Primo did not risk any form of elections, not even at the municipal level. The only political task left to the UP and its local leaders was that of ensuring a satisfactory result in the regime's sole referendum – the 1926 referendum held ostensibly to approve the establishment of a National Assembly to draft a new Constitution. There was no serious attempt by the UP to perform an indoctrinating, social role. And except perhaps at the municipal level the UP was never given a significant supervisory (let alone policy-making) governing role.

On the contrary, the UP was itself supervised nationally by the Ministry of the Interior.[20] In particular the provincial Governors, from the outset, exerted a deal of influence over the internal affairs as well as public activities of the UP units in their provinces. Although Primo later ordered the Governors to allow the UP more independence, in practice they continued to exert a substantial influence over the affairs of provincial and local branches. While this fell short of the officially recognized authority that the Italian Prefects would later wield over the provincial units of the Fascist Party, it was clearly a case of the state officials' being allowed to exercise some supervisory powers over the regime party – the first such case to be found in a military-party regime or indeed in any one-party state.

In contrast to the weak contribution made by the regime party, the military played a very prominent part – including a policy-making and supervisory governing role – in the early years of this military-party regime's life. The regime operated under martial law and was run by a military junta, the Military Directory, that acted as a *de facto* government and whose members liaised individually, like Ministers, with particular departments of the civil service. The regime also appointed officers to posts in the civil service departments, replaced the civilian Governors of the provinces with army officers (until May 1924), and from October 1923 onwards appointed no fewer than 1400 army officers as *delegados militares gubernativos* to supervise municipal activities.[21]

The *delegados* were the regime's greatest innovation and

would remain unique in the history of military regimes. They have been well described by one historian as 'military commissars for local government'.[22] Primo gave them a very wide-ranging set of duties in addition to their ideologically motivated anti-*cacique* crusade. Thus some *delegados* not only attempted to eradicate *caciquismo* but also made and unmade municipal councils, interfered in municipal administration and the local economy, acted as the guardians of public morality, espoused the causes of primary education, public hygiene, physical exercise and civic consciousness, and helped with the launch and activities of the UP. However, Primo became disenchanted with their efforts – or often lack of effort – to regenerate local Spain. From the end of 1924 onwards he gradually reduced their numbers to only three per province, placed them under the command and supervision of the provincial Governors, and reduced their functions until they became primarily the local organizers of the UP. In a sense this final concentration on their work with the UP was very fitting, for together with the military men holding provincial Governorships the *delegados* had provided the first example in history of the military's performing a supervisory role in relation to the regime party as well as the civilian state apparatus.

Primo's civilianization of the regime at the end of 1925 greatly reduced the part played by the military in this military-party regime. There was an end to martial law, the Military Directory junta was replaced by a civilian government of Ministers, civilian Governors were provided for the last four provinces still governed by military men, and Primo declared that the military was from then on to 'abstain absolutely' from politics.[23] Yet the military was still the most crucial (and most problematic) basis or component of the position of (insecure) personal rule that Primo was establishing.

Primo de Rivera's Personal Rule

The limited degree of personal rule that Primo established was very vulnerable in exactly the area where the personal ruler of a military-party regime would normally be expected to be strong – his relationship with the military. That Primo was more than just an agent of the military was confirmed by the composition of the Military Directory junta he appointed after becoming Prime Minister. He appointed as members of the junta – the military's political committee – an assortment of officers which was representative of the military only in the geographical sense of including an army officer from each military region and a naval officer.[24] As the eight army officers were Brigadier-Generals and the naval officer a Rear-Admiral, clearly Primo had been able to avoid sharing power with his peers, the senior Generals and Admirals, or with representatives of the middle-ranking and junior officers. But he was unable to acquire a position of personal leadership over the military.

Therefore his attempt to use the military as an instrument of personal rule proved quite disastrous in the long run – he lost much of what little support he had among the military and thus further weakened his already insecure personal position.[25] Widespread resentment was aroused within the officer corps by the use of the military for political and personal ends. The resentment was focused on such blatant measures as Primo's using military men as Governors and as *delegados* – whose failings had reduced the standing of the army in civilian eyes. Primo's frequent public assertions of unanimous military support for his regime became increasingly unrealistic as the 1920s drew to a close. By 1929, if not earlier, there was a 'psychological dissociation of the majority of officers from the dictatorship'.[26]

Primo did at least hold a very powerful state post as Prime Minister. Thanks to the suspension of the Constitution he was able to rule by decree without having to worry about a parliament or other constitutional proprieties. After the return to a form of civilian government at the end of 1925, Primo's new government acquired yet further governing and legislative powers and continued to govern without any form of Constitution.[27] But although he appeared to have at least as much state power as Mussolini enjoyed as Chief of the Government in Italy, Primo was in a significantly weaker position than his Italian counterpart. For he not only lacked Mussolini's constitutional legitimacy but also suffered from the same dependency on the monarchy which undermined

Mussolini's position. This dependency upon the King was the second major weakness in Primo's personal position. (It was also connected to his other weakness, his relations with the military, by the fact that the King was also titular Commander-in-Chief of the armed forces.) The King provided the only semblance of legitimacy, albeit not constitutional legitimacy, that Primo could claim for his state powers. Disliking any such dependency, from early on Primo 'was eager to show that his power no longer rested exclusively on royal favour' – that he had a large degree of popular support.[28]

The creation of the UP provided Primo with the independent, personal post of leader of an extensive regime party that organized and stimulated his popular support. Although the UP performed only a minor political role, it propagated among its own ranks and the wider population a personality cult which sought to boost Primo's public standing and thus his personal position.[29] Predictably, the personality cult made much of his (propagandistically overblown and exaggerated) military victory in Morocco in 1925, when he oversaw the military operation which avenged the humiliating defeat of 1921. His military genius was compared with that of El Cid – Spain's other great military leader (*caudillo*) against the Moors of a much earlier age. The military genius's administrative and political skills were emphasized, too, in a 'cult of the leader possessing an inhuman power of work, unlimited dedication and perseverance, and an intuitive, genial perception of political issues'.[30] He assisted the UP in propagating the personality cult by speeches (sometimes radio broadcast) to UP rallies, frequent tours of the provinces to meet the people face to face, and nearly daily 'official notes' addressed to the public and explaining his policies in familiar and personal terms. His personal standing with the Spanish public seems to have peaked in late 1925 in the aftermath of the Moroccan triumph. The UP-led official campaign for a 'yes' vote in the 1926 referendum focused upon Primo and depicted the referendum as a vote of confidence in him. The overwhelming vote in favour, though, was somewhat marred by the fact that not much more than half of eligible voters actually took part.

However, whatever popularity Primo could claim in 1925–6 ebbed away after the referendum and declined markedly in 1929 as he proved incapable of solving Spain's currency/financial crisis and its now chronic political crisis, most obviously expressed in the continuing student unrest and riots.[31] From a wider perspective he had lost support amongst large sectors of the upper and middle classes through his so-called 'interventionist' and mildly inflationary economic policies, more equitable taxation policies, 'pro-worker' industrial relations policy, and his general failure to meet the upper and middle classes' economic and political aspirations.[32] His last desperate throw was an appeal (actually published in the press) on 26 January 1930 to the army's Generals seeking some reassurance that he could count on the support of the armed forces. All the Generals, even his close friends among them, responded by emphasizing their loyalty to the King and to whatever government had the King's confidence. When the King pressured him to resign, he capitulated and signed his resignation on 28 January 1930.

Thus just as Mussolini in 1943 would be implicitly abandoned by the Grand Council of Fascism before being sacked by the King, so Primo was implicitly abandoned by the military before the King pressured him to resign. However, the deposed personal rulers of these two examples of a fascist or quasi-fascist one-party state experienced rather different personal fates. Mussolini was eventually captured and shot by Communist partisans in 1945 as he tried to escape to Germany. Primo left Spain immediately after resigning and settled in Paris, where he died of natural causes only a short time afterwards.

2   FRANCO'S REGIME IN SPAIN

General Primo de Rivera's resignation was followed by two military-led conservative governments, each seeking to prepare a return to constitutional, civilian rule. In 1931 the King, irreparably compromised by his connection with Primo's unconstitutional regime, was forced to abdicate by public pressure and the refusal of the army to support him. However, the new democratic Republic of Spain soon experienced an increasing polarization of public opinion as three elections were held in relatively quick succession – in 1931, 1933 and 1936.[33] The forming of an electoral alliance, the Popular Front, by the several left-wing parties gave them a landslide victory in the 1936 parliamentary elections. But it also had the effect of inspiring fear and hostility among many rightists and overconfidence among many leftists. Outside parliament there was an increasing amount of revolutionary rhetoric and 'provocation', such as strikes and land seizures, that confirmed the right's fears and, in turn, led an increasing number of rightists to adopt an extremist and violent approach. This was reflected in the expansion of the radically right-wing Falangist movement's membership from some 5000 to nearly 500 000 in the six months following the electoral victory of the Popular Front.[34] But it was a right-wing military coup, not a fascist movement, which in July 1936 drastically changed the country's political situation. Unlike Primo's coup, this one would be a partial failure and go on to produce a three-year civil war before the rebels and their right-wing civilian supporters eventually emerged victorious.

Even while controlling little more than a third of Spain, these military rebels, or Nationalists as they had soon begun calling themselves, set about establishing a new regime. In September 1936 the Nationalist military leaders decided that the commander of their southern forces, Major-General Francisco Franco, should become both military and political leader of the Nationalist movement and its new regime. The Nationalists' senior officers elected him on 21 September to the post of supreme commander of the Nationalist military forces, with the new rank of Generalísimo de los Ejércitos (Generalissimo of the Armies).[35] On 28–9 September they also gave him the new political post of Chief of the Government of the Spanish State and decreed that he would 'assume all the powers of the new State' – in fact in his first decree Franco began calling himself Chief of State.[36]

Franco soon created a politically monopolistic party to organize the right-wing civilian support for this new regime.[37] On the night of 18 April 1937 Franco announced that he intended to unite the extreme right-wing Falangist and the Traditionalist movements into one political movement and also to dissolve all the other political parties and organizations in the Nationalist part of Spain. Furthermore, he announced that he himself would assume the leadership of this new political movement, despite the fact that he had never been a member of either the Falangist or Traditionalist movements. These measures were published on 20 April in what became known as the Decree of Unification (of the Falangist and Traditionalist movements).

In promulgating this decree Franco not only established a literal one-party state with a legally recognized monopoly for the new regime party, but also provided an official ideology for the Nationalist regime. For the Decree of Unification stated that the political programme of the Nationalists' New State would be the 26 Points of the Falangist programme, and the Falangists' national syndicalism would become the official social doctrine of the New State.[38] As the Falangist ideology was a radically right-wing ideology, for a few years the new military-party regime seemed to be developing into a truly fascist regime. But external events soon forced it to adopt a less radical, only quasi-fascist ideological approach that was more like Primoderriverismo than Fascism and National Socialism.

Falangist Ideology

The Falange Española (Spanish Phalanx) had been founded in late 1933 as a fervently nationalist political movement.[39] Falangist nationalism was totally opposed to any form of regional 'separatism' and was imbued with an imperialist desire to recapture an empire to replace the one Spain had lost in the nineteenth century. The Falangists also showed an authoritarian admiration for the military ethos, going so far as to maintain that the military should be the ultimate arbitrator of Spanish politics. Combined with their willingness to use violence to achieve political ends, this placed the Falangists on the extreme right wing of Spanish politics. Their radically rightist nature was confirmed in 1934 when the Falangists had absorbed a national-syndicalist movement, Juntas de Ofensiva Nacional Sindicalista (JONS), to become the Falange Española de las JONS. The national-syndicalists provided the Falangist movement with a focused and modern social ideology which also increased the Falangists' ideological similarity to the Italian Fascists. For like the early (non-statist) corporativist strand in Fascist ideology, Falangist national syndicalism sought to organize employers and workers into employer–employee industry-based syndicates that would control the economy for the good of the whole nation.

The Falangists' national-syndicalist doctrine would later legitimate the Nationalist regime's major social policy – the establishment of the state's massive and monopolistic Syndical Organization.[40] By 1945 sixteen 'vertical', combined employer–employee syndicates had been created, each covering a sector or branch of the economy and being given some economic powers as well as control over labour relations. In 1966 such vertical syndicates were officially abandoned in favour of separate syndical units for employers and employees. (Until then employers had held the dominant positions in the syndicates at the factory level.) Furthermore, in the early 1970s workers were given more control over their syndicates, with most delegates and officials being elected from below. However, the fascist heritage of banning any other, independent forms of labour organization was maintained to the end.

As for economic policy, the Falangists' statist semi-autarkic approach to economics legitimated the import-substituting industrialization policy of the 1950s.[41] But the shift in 1959 to a more open, market economy was not accompanied by any ideological manipulation of Falangist doctrine to justify this liberalization of the economy and introduction of a 'technocratic' approach to economic policy. The high economic growth rates and rising living standards of the early 1960s provided sufficient *post hoc* justification for the new economic policies – and were probably the most effective justification for the regime's own existence.

By the 1950s the ideological influence or legacy of the Falangists had already been diluted by the regime's shift in emphasis towards its Traditionalist ideological heritage.[42] The Comunión Tradicionalista had been formed in 1932 through the merger of the different factions of the 100-year-old Carlist movement. The Carlists sought more than just a shift in the line of succession from the reigning Alfonsist branch of the royal family to the 'rightful' Carlist branch. They also sought to restore Spain to its supposedly traditional, Catholic and organic, social order and to restore the supposedly traditional form of monarchy – a king whose power was limited only by his conscience and by traditional norms, not by a legalistic Constitution. In the late nineteenth and early twentieth centuries Carlism had been formulated into a systematic monarchist-Catholic ideology that had survived into the 1930s and then become part of the ideological heritage of Franco's regime with his merger of Traditionalists and Falangists in April 1937. A decade later Traditionalism was beginning to overshadow Falangist doctrines as the main source of the regime's ideology.

After the defeat of Fascist Italy and Nazi Germany in the Second World War the Nationalist regime abandoned or downplayed much of the fascist, Falangist content of its ideology. Falangist radicalism was replaced by a façade of pseudo-democratic institutions, an indirectly monarchical claim to legitimacy, and a general shift towards Traditionalist ideology. Instead of the earlier presentation of itself as the avowedly 'totalitarian' New State, now the regime would emphasize its new principle of Organic Democracy – 'of the representation of the great interests of society rather than the selfish interests of individual voters' – as the basis for a series of quasi-constitutional measures.[43] The regime had already in 1943 convened an appointive parliament, the Cortes, and in July 1945 it promulgated the Fuero de los Españoles, a charter of liberties or Bill of Rights. In 1947 came the Law of Succession, which declared that Spain was a kingdom and would eventually see monarchy restored but that Franco, the existing Head of State and Caudillo, would be the kingdom's Regent until his death or incapacity. The Law was approved by a referendum, with purportedly an 82 per cent vote in favour, to provide an aura of plebiscitary legitimacy for the Law and implicitly for the Francoist regime itself. Together with these changes in political doctrine, there was an increasing Traditionalist-like emphasis on Catholicism as the spiritual foundation of the regime, culminating in the Concordat signed with the Vatican in 1953. The growing prominence of the Traditionalist Communion heritage in the regime's ideology would reach its apogee in the 1958 Principles of the Movement, which referred to the regime party as a 'communion' and defined the regime itself as a 'traditionalist, Catholic, social, and representative monarchy'.[44]

The FET (and the Military)

The merged political movement of Falangists and Traditionalists created in April 1937 to be the Nationalists' regime party was given the cumbersome name of Falange Española Tradicionalista y de las Juntas de Ofensiva Nacional Sindicalista, which was usually shortened to FET y de las JONS or just FET. As was mentioned earlier, the FET enjoyed a legally decreed monopoly as the official political organization (the term 'party' had negative connotations for the Nationalists) of the New State. The extensiveness of the FET was a result of not only many people joining the party for reasons of political commitment or self-interest but also the fact that FET membership was 'automatic and/or obligatory' for army officers, civilian state employees, syndicate officials and, of course, the numerous staff of the FET's own bureaucracy.[45] Thus by 1942 membership had passed 900 000, close to 4 per cent of the population.[46] The FET also possessed a Women's Section with a membership of well over 500 000, and a near million-member youth organization, the Youth Front. What is more, unlike the Fascist Party in Italy, the FET was given control of the massive structure of employer–employee syndicates. The FET's own, hierarchical structure was focused upon its Jefe (Chief) Nacional, General Franco.[47] He directly or indirectly appointed the Secretary-General, the members of the FET's central executive organs, and the provincial FET chiefs – who in turn appointed the local chiefs. The FET was clearly more hierarchical than Primo's UP, whose provincial leaders had in theory been elected, and was closer in style to the German and Italian fascist parties. It adopted their highly disciplined militaristic approach, including the use of (blue-shirted) party uniforms and a party salute.

The FET was not much of a multi-role party. It performed little more of a political role than had Primo's UP regime party; the highlights were mobilizing the voters for the referendums approving the 1947 Law of Succession and the 1966 Organic Law. The rubber-stamping, purely symbolic parliament was not filled by any form of election but by allotting seats to holders of public, civil service, municipal, FET, syndical and military posts – and to Franco's personal appointees.[48] Moreover, although the FET massively and continually bombarded the population with propaganda, its social role of indoctrinating society with the regime's solidarity-strengthening ideology was soon greatly downgraded.[49] For the regime's increasing emphasis on Catholicism, as exemplified by the 1953 Concordat, meant that the FET and its ideology had to take second place to the Church and Catholicism in the regime's programme of strengthening Spanish society's solidarity after years of social conflict and civil war.

From the outset it was clear that the FET would not be allowed a significant governing role and was to be just an umbrella organization of all the supporters of the Nationalist rebellion and regime. Thus soon after its creation Franco decreed that all army officers were automatically members of the FET, and later on all state employees were expected to join.[50] As in Fascist Italy, the civil service's obligatory membership of the party was not converted into a supervisory governing role; the most that the FET could expect at the central level was unofficial monitoring of the Ministries. The FET fared better, though, at the regional and local levels of the state apparatus. In an innovatory move the state office of Governor of a province was combined in practice with the FET office of provincial chief, which eventually led to the Interior Minister and the FET Secretary-General choosing new appointees to the post of Governor/chief by mutual agreement.[51] Further down the state apparatus the FET also took over the multitude of public offices that existed at the local or municipal level.[52]

Any possibility of the FET's achieving a more prominent position in the regime was ended by the victory of the Allied powers over Fascist Italy and Nazi Germany in the Second World War. The need for Spain to downplay its fascist trappings if it was to survive, let alone prosper, in the anti-fascist post-war world meant that the FET – like Falangist ideology – would have to be pushed into the background. In fact the regime's expedient 'defascistization' of itself was perhaps its most significant innovation. Franco himself informed the world in July 1945 that the Falange had ceased to wield any political power, and he would wear the FET uniform with decreasing frequency during the 1940s until eventually he was seen wearing it only at the annual FET rally.[53] The very name of the FET was threatened by a decree of 1945 that gave the party the innocuous title of 'the (National) Movement', though not until 1970 did this become, by law, the sole official name of the FET.[54]

Although they had been drafted into the regime party, the army's officer corps were in practice no more subject to party supervision nor less important to the regime than they had been under Primo.[55] The military was constantly called the 'backbone of the country' and until April 1947 continued to enjoy the martial law powers it had acquired during the Civil War. (Even after the official return to judicial normality in the late 1940s, all cases of political and labour opposition continued to be classified as 'military rebellion' and to be tried by military courts.) In addition the military supplied almost half of the Ministers appointed by Franco in the early years of the regime.

The military also took on a supervisory role.[56] During the 1938–45 period military men held almost a third of the senior positions in the civil service – including nearly half of those in the Ministry of the Interior. At the regional level, too, well over a third of the provincial Governors were army officers. What is more, military men held over a third of the senior posts in the FET, such as member of the Junta Politica or provincial chief. Although the prominence of the military's part in the regime declined after the 1940s, it remained the most important agent or instrument, albeit largely held in reserve, of Franco's secure and absolutist personal rule.[57]

Franco's Personal Rule

The basis of Franco's strong personal rule was his leadership over the military, which as early as the 1940s appeared
to be his agent or instrument and certainly not vice versa.
Unlike Primo, he was the highest-ranking officer and supreme commander – wielding complete and undisputed
authority at the summit of the military hierarchy. It is true
Franco was careful to 'define his sovereignty as power resting on the "choice" [in September 1936] of the military
family and of all sane, patriotic elements. His role was to
preside over the other senior generals as first among equals.'[58]
But this was a typically cautious downplaying of his hold
over the military. The middle-ranking and junior officers
of the Nationalist army supported him unreservedly.[59] To
them Franco was not only the Generalísimo but also their
supreme commander in the victorious Civil War – their
personal military leader. Thus despite the fact that the
military's share of the state budget declined from over 30
per cent in 1953 to less than 15 per cent in 1968, 'the
Spanish military remained fully identified as Franco's own
Army to the very end'.[60]

Franco also held very extensive constitutional/state powers,
comparable to Hitler's.[61] As well as continuing until 1973
to be both head of state and head of government, he kept
in reserve the legislative powers bestowed upon him in the
1939 Law of the Head of State – which were confirmed as
late as 1966 in the Organic Law of that year. The 1939
Law had permanently bestowed the powers of government
upon him, and the 1947 Law of Succession regularized
Franco's very extensive and permanent powers by making
him the kingdom's Regent for life. Only in 1973 did the
81-year-old Franco ease his administrative burden by relinquishing the post of head of government to his long-time
administrative right-hand man, Admiral Carrero Blanco.

The formally absolutist leadership that Franco exercised
over the regime party was again comparable to Hitler's.
The FET's official statutes declared that the Jefe Nacional
had 'absolute authority' over the party and that his responsibility was solely to God and History.[62] The regime
party was in turn the main propagator of the Franco per-

sonality cult.[63] As early as 1937 Franco's preferred title was the personal and historic one of the Caudillo, the (military) leader. The propaganda exaltation of Franco reached a peak in 1939–40, with a personality cult similar in degree to those of Fascist Italy and Nazi Germany but with an emphasis upon his military leadership. Thereafter Franco's personality cult was less high pitched and extravagant. It included such typical features as his photograph on the wall of public offices, his face on stamps and coins, and even the inclusion of the formula 'Francisco Franco, Caudillo of Spain by the Grace of God' on the coins. In fact the cult of the Caudillo that grew up around the Generalísimo produced a Spanish version of the *Führerprinzip*, the *Teoría del Caudillaje*, which was one of the few elements in the Francoist regime's ideology that had not been borrowed from pre-1936 Spain.

Franco's form of personal rule has been described as more like the monarchy of Philip II than a modern dictatorship.[64] Although his rule was as personal and absolutist as Hitler's, a series of quasi-constitutional laws, from the 1947 Law of Succession to the 1966 Organic Law, had 'sought to provide personal rule with a decent institutional clothing'.[65] The 1947 Law of Succession had envisaged the eventual restoration of a hereditary monarchy and, eventually, in 1969 Franco officially designated Prince Juan Carlos (the grandson of the deposed King Alfonso) as his successor and eventual King of Spain. But after Franco's death the new King skilfully presided over a process of successful democratization. This time the return to democracy was not accompanied by the political polarization that had plagued the democratic years of 1931–6 and had led to their being only a short parenthesis in nearly half a century of rule by military-party regimes.

8 Third World Socialist Case Studies

1 NASSER'S EGYPT

Although Egypt can boast one of the longest histories of civilization to be found anywhere in the world, for the last 2500 years it has usually been ruled by foreigners or dominated by a foreign power. The last in the long line of foreign empires and nationalities to control Egypt were the British, who established a *de facto* protectorate over Egypt in the late nineteenth century. During the First World War the British regularized the complex question of sovereignty over Egypt by declaring its independence from the Ottoman Empire, promoting the Khedive to the rank of Sultan of the newly independent state of Egypt, and proclaiming that Egypt was a British protectorate. However, in 1922, under intense pressure from the Egyptian nationalists, the British formally recognized Egypt's independence as a sovereign state – and the Sultan now assumed the title of King.

The King promulgated a Constitution that seemed to give power to a parliament which was to be elected by universal male suffrage. Yet in practice not only did the King often show scant regard for the parliament and its right to share in government, but also the parliament itself tended to be dominated by the large landowners, who controlled the votes of the rural lower classes employed or tenanted upon their land. Nevertheless, it was more the humiliating defeat by Israel in the 1948 war than discontent with the lack of democracy that stimulated the growth of a reformist secret society among junior and middle-ranking officers of the Egyptian army and air force. The members of this Society of Free Officers blamed the country's corrupt politicians and political system for the defeat of 1948, as well as for the long-standing failure to remove the humiliating British presence. On 22 July 1952 the Free Officers group within the military finally staged the coup which would become the self-proclaimed Egyptian Revolution.

148

After seizing power the young officers soon established an open, direct form of military rule through a junta, the Revolutionary Command Council, which was composed of the former members of the Free Officers' executive committee. The monarchy was removed in 1953 and in the following year so was the Free Officers' figurehead President and Prime Minister, General Neguib, who had developed an independent outlook and a power base of his own. The regime and country were now led by the founding leader of the Free Officers, Colonel Nasser. His position was cemented in place by his political victory over Britain and France in the 1956 Suez Crisis, which made him a popular hero in Egypt and throughout the Arab world. Therefore he was in a strong position to complete the regime's supposed civilianization (which included not just an end to martial law and the RCC junta but also his and other Ministers' resignation from the military) and to transform the regime into a military type of ideological one-party state.

The Arab Nationalist and Socialist Ideology

Already, in 1953, Nasser had put forward the very first of the few ideological justifications for military rule that have ever been attempted. What might almost be seen as the military equivalent of Lenin's theory of the vanguard party was put forward by Nasser in his booklet, *The Philosophy of the Revolution*, written in the middle of 1953.[1] There he argued that the military had performed the vanguard role in the Egyptian Revolution by sweeping away the old regime and then being 'compelled' to retain power because the people were found to be unprepared to take control of their own destiny.[2] To his and the other army officers' 'disappointment' they found, after carrying out the revolutionary coup, that in Nasser's words 'the task of the vanguard, far from being completed had only just begun'.[3] Obviously what became the official doctrine that the military was the vanguard and shield of the revolution served to legitimate the open military rule of 1953–6, and it would also legitimate the still prominent role played by the military after the 1956 supposed civilianization.

Nasser's new ideological principle of Arab or Pan-Arab nationalism rose to prominence in conjunction with – and served to legitimate – his foreign policy of 1955–6. So, too, did the accompanying principle of 'positive' neutralism, which held that the Arab world should remain neutral in the Cold War between the Western and Communist blocs but should be 'positively' committed to opposing imperialism and colonialism.[4] Nasser gave Arab nationalism a strongly emotional or psychological aspect by his emphasis on Arab dignity,[5] which was obviously addressed to the feelings of inferiority plaguing many Arabs after the Arab world's centuries-long subjection to the Turks and then the infidel Westerners. But Nasser's Arab nationalism also appealed to a specifically Egyptian national pride by depicting Egypt as the centre of the Arab world. Egypt was supposedly the 'nucleus state' around which a unified Arab nation would be built.[6]

Less than a decade later Arab nationalism was relegated to second place in the regime's ideology by the new principle or doctrine of Arab socialism. The adopting of Arab socialism in 1961 legitimated the promulgation in that year of a host of socialist laws and decrees which resulted in the state either owning or controlling virtually all sectors of industry, finance and large-scale commerce. Only agriculture was excluded from any form of take-over by the state but even here there was a further land redistribution programme that limited holdings to about 100 acres. Economic planning was also introduced in 1961 with the establishment of a Ministry of Planning and a Ten Year Plan, divided into two five-year segments.[7]

The 1962 Charter of National Action provided 'a formal ideological program for Egypt that embodied its revolutionary socialist principles'.[8] The Charter's emphasis on socialism was apparent in the way it dealt with the question of democracy by arguing that 'political democracy cannot be separated from social democracy'.[9] However, the Egyptian form of socialism was depicted as allowing for a mixed economy in which the private sector would be concentrated in light industry and small-scale commerce – and, of course, in agriculture.[10] Land reform continued to take the form of redistribution, not nationalization or collectivization.

Arab socialism as expounded by Nasser and the regime's other ideologists soon became a multi-faceted and not always coherent doctrine. For example, this socialism was justified in terms of both its supposedly scientific nature and its supposed conformity with the Islamic tradition.[11] There was agreement, though, in distinguishing Arab socialism from not only Western capitalism but also Soviet-style Communism. Both of these foreign, non-Arab doctrines were said to be overly materialist and unable to achieve the harmony between material prosperity and spiritual, Islamic values that was achieved by Arab socialism.[12] The special character of the socialism – a 'humane' socialism – being established in Egypt was said to be expressed in such measures as having elected worker directors on the boards of public-sector enterprises.[13]

Arab socialist society was envisaged as being one in which the seven classes of people that before the 1952 Revolution had been exploited by the 'national reactionaries' would co-operate to achieve prosperity and social justice.[14] These formerly exploited classes were not only the workers and small farmers but also small businessmen and 'non-exploiting' proprietors and the three occupational categories – the intellectuals, the professions and the soldiers. The new, socialist society was to be one in which all citizens would use their property, labour and knowledge for the common good of increasing the nation's production, prosperity and social justice.

The NU and the ASU (and the Military)

A distinctive feature of Nasser's regime was not only the development of two consecutive regime parties, the 1957 National Union and the 1962 Arab Socialist Union, but also the fact that both inherited a legal monopoly – thanks to the military's 1953 banning of political parties. The establishment of the National Union was actually foreshadowed and given the highest possible legal recognition in the new Constitution of 1956, which declared that the National Union would replace (the still prohibited) political parties in revolutionary Egypt.[15] In a unique departure from the usual form of membership in a political organization, the NU offered an 'inactive' form of membership to all adult citizens and an 'active' form of membership only to those who met the more strenuous admission requirements and were willing to take an active part in the NU organs or units. These were of two types – the territorial and the functional. The former comprised a pyramidal structure of layers of elected committees stretching up from the village and urban quarter level to the district, the provincial, and finally the national level, where there was a General Congress. The functional type comprised the NU units and operations established within the trade unions, student organizations, and professional and business associations. Although at first glance the NU appeared to be an internally democratic party, there was a centralized and hierarchical element in its structure. Nasser was the acknowledged but unelected leader of the NU and appointed its Higher Executive Committee, while at the provincial level his provincial state Governors become *ex officio* chairmen of the NU's provincial committees.

The NU was meant to have a significant political role. The citizens elected to the country's local, district, provincial, and national representative bodies would have to be approved by the NU and preferably would have been already elected to a position in the NU.[16] But the NU was not intended to perform much of a social or governing role, and in any case was not given the time to develop even its political role. Not until 1959 were the elections for local NU committees finally held (having been delayed by the 1958 union with Syria) and only two years later Nasser was calling for the 'reactionary ridden' NU to be replaced by a new organization, the Arab Socialist Union.[17]

Virtually all adult citizens were eligible to join the new regime party, and so many did so that by 1964 the ASU had an official membership of 4.8 million, nearly a fifth of the total Egyptian population.[18] However, the ASU included a unique form of elitism in its structure by not only following the NU approach of having specially designated 'active' members, who numbered about 500 000, but also seeking to develop a *secret*, super-élite 'political vanguard', which was intended to number about 20 000.[19] At first the

ASU's structure was otherwise quite similar to that of the NU but in 1965 it adopted an almost Communist-style structure, with a hierarchy of all-powerful secretaries stretching down from the General Secretariat through provincial and district First Secretaries to the secretary of a village, urban ward, or factory unit.[20] This gave the ASU not only an extensive administrative apparatus but also the same hierarchical and disciplined orientation as that of a Communist party.

However, the Arab Socialist Union fell short of the Communist standard of a multi-role regime party, largely because of its lack of a significant governing role. The ASU's political role was similar to the NU's in ensuring that the right sort of people were elected in the one-candidate elections to the regime's largely rubber-stamping representative bodies. (The most important of these bodies was the National Assembly, which in the 1960s was allowed some freedom of debate but was still little more than a symbolic institution.[21]) As for a social role, initially the ASU's main official duty was propagating Arab socialism, for which purpose it developed a growing propaganda apparatus,[22] yet there is little evidence that this indoctrination was effectively performed. In the ASU's early years there was also much official talk, often by Nasser himself, of the ASU's occupying a higher position than the government and civil service, suggesting that the new party would – like a Communist party – have a governing as well as social and political role. But in the event Nasser allowed the government and state apparatus to remain pre-eminent, despite the ASU Secretary-General and his leftist allies' attempts to establish the principle of ASU domination of the state.[23]

While large numbers of civil servants joined the ASU, the military arm of the state was represented in the ASU by only retired or resigned military men – who controlled the party from the top downwards.[24] The acknowledged leader of the ASU, ex-Colonel Nasser, was the Chairman of a Supreme Executive Committee that from the outset was dominated by ex-officers and after 1966 comprised six military men, all of them former Free Officers.[25] But this control of the ASU was just one example of the prominent part the military continued to play in the regime even after the removal of martial law and the RCC junta in the 1956 supposed civilianization of the regime.

In addition to the strong military presence at the highest level of the ASU, military men held the key ministerial portfolios (Defence, Interior, Local Administration) and sometimes held the number two position in Ministries headed by civilian technocrats.[26] Then there were the thousands of military men who held positions in the civil service. In particular they held 22 of the 26 provincial Governorships and more than 3000 military men had extensively colonized the powerful Ministry of the Interior, which included the police and the rest of the internal security apparatus.[27] The security apparatus was 'heavily commanded' by military men, and they also comprised a large proportion of the higher-ranking police officers.[28] Such an extensive presence obviously gave them an unrivalled ability to supervise the most powerful parts of the civilian state apparatus.

A complication, though, in assessing the Egyptian case of military penetration of the regime party and the civilian arm of the state is that these military men in civilian posts had resigned from active service in the military. The civilianization of the regime which occurred in 1956 involved not only officers holding ministerial posts having to resign from the military, but also those holding posts in the civil service having to choose between their military and civilian careers.[29] Yet while 'former officers who chose government employment in preference to military careers became progressively civilianized . . . in civilian employment they showed a high degree of solidarity'.[30]

The key issue, though, was not so much their continued loyalty to the military but rather their loyalty to the military's political leader, Nasser. For he, like Primo and Franco in Spain, relied on members of the military as the most trustworthy (and perhaps competent) individuals available to hold posts in civilian organizations. Even in civilian employment the officer corps showed 'a high degree' of loyalty to Nasser and his programme, and 'the army came to represent for Nasser a personnel pool for far-reaching extramilitary tasks'.[31] In fact about a third of the army's 1952 officer corps were eventually used in non-military roles by Nasser's regime.[32] But if Nasser was using the military as an instrument of his personal rule, by the 1960s he was losing control of that instrument. By then he was losing his undisputed leadership of the military and with it much of the degree of personal rule that he had established in the 1950s.

Nasser's Personal Rule

The unique feature of Nasser's regime was his loss and then recovery of a degree of personal rule. After establishing a strong personal position in the later 1950s (as the popular hero of the Suez Crisis, the political leader of the military, a powerful President, and the leader of the regime party), Nasser then lost much of it in the 1960s before eventually restoring his personal rule in the aftermath of Egypt's military disaster of June 1967.[33] The key to this loss and subsequent recovery was Nasser's relationship with the military. For having reversed in the mid-1950s the principal–agent relationship between the military and himself, he then in the 1960s lost his hold over the military – and perhaps even faced the prospect of becoming nothing more than its agent – before in 1967 transforming it again into an instrument of his personal rule.

In the mid-1950s he had established himself as the authoritative political leader of the military, and at first one of the sources of this control over the military was the fact that his close friend and ally, Amer, had been appointed Commander-in-Chief of the armed forces by the RCC junta. However, in time Amer (perhaps inadvertently) became not Nasser's agent but his rival for leadership over the military.[34] As their Commander-in-Chief and spokesman for military interests Field Marshal Amer could expect to attract the professional loyalty and support of the officer corps. But he had also become the 'Father-in-Chief' of the military by showing a paternal solicitude for his officers' individual welfare and by (more prosaically) ensuring that officers personally loyal to him held the key posts.

The apparently close relationship between Nasser and Amer was evident in such measures as Amer's being made Governor of the Syrian half of the merged Egypt–Syria United Arab Republic in 1959 and his being appointed Nasser's First Vice-President in 1964.[35] A few years later, though, there would be revelations about the strained relations between the two men in the early 1960s and about Nasser's having had implicitly to recognize Amer's autonomous control over the military.[36] Nasser's weakened hold over the military had also seriously weakened his personal rule over the regime. 'Given Nasser's towering prestige and his personal ties with Amer, a genuine military coup against him was unlikely', but 'a gentler process of "kicking him upstairs" into some purely honorific position did appear to be a real possibility'.[37]

For the military was discontented about the prominent role that Nasser was assigning to the ASU.[38] The privileged political position of the military was jeopardized by Nasser's emphasis on the new Arab Socialist Union – he even referred to the ASU, rather than the military, as the vanguard of the revolution. The concern within the military about the role of the ASU led to Amer's going so far as to make a public attack on the concept of allowing the ASU a political (party) monopoly. Such attacks not only indicated that the military was out of Nasser's control but also suggested that it was worried about the power the ASU was acquiring.

However, Nasser was unable to use his position as leader of the new regime party as a means of strengthening his personal position within the regime.[39] For he found that his supposed agent for the day-to-day running of the ASU, Secretary-General Ali Sabri, was freeing himself from Nasser's control and creating a personal power base within the ASU in similar fashion to Amer's take-over of the military in earlier years. During 1965–6 an uneasy and wary Nasser publicly criticized the development of 'centres of power' (outside his personal control). And by 1967 the ASU was being criticized for becoming a centre of power that had sought to be above or alongside the government rather than in its proper place of behind the government.

So virtually by elimination Nasser's personal position was based increasingly upon his post of President and his public standing. The Presidency bestowed extensive powers upon him as head of state and government. Even after constitu-

tional changes in the 1960s theoretically increased the power
of the National Assembly ,'all laws appeared in fact, if not
always in name, as presidential decrees'.[40] A more personal
basis of his position was the continuation of the personality cult that had been virtually thrust upon Nasser by his
many Egyptian and other Arab admirers after his Suez triumph. He was viewed by the people as a miracle worker,
and the 'highly personal adulation' of Nasser has been referred to as the 'Nasser cult'.[41] He was also viewed as being Egypt's Rais (*ra'is* or *rayyes*), the country's political and
moral leader – the 'keeper of the nation's conscience'.[42]
This political and moral leadership of the Egyptian people
was epitomized by his role as the main official source of
ideology and was reinforced by the oratorical skills he displayed in frequent speeches on radio and to huge public
rallies.[43]

But the personality cult of the 1960s could not celebrate
the same sort of successes that Nasser had achieved do-
mestically and internationally in the 1950s. The failure of
the union with Syria in 1961 had been followed by the
debilitating and frustrating war in Yemen and by a decline
in economic growth after 1963.[44] His 'regime had reached
the lowest ebb in domestic and external status by the spring
of 1967'.[45] And in June this trend of failure culminated in
the disastrous Six Day War with Israel. Therefore it is all
the more surprising that when Nasser announced that he
accepted total responsibility for the defeat and would resign all his public and political offices, the response was
mass demonstrations (successfully) begging Nasser not to
resign.[46]

Armed with this popular mandate Nasser took over direct, operational command of the demoralized and discredited armed forces – having forced Amer and his close
associate Defence Minister Badran to resign – and instituted
a sweeping purge of the senior and then middle ranks of
the officer corps.[47] Amer reacted by preparing a defensive
coup but this was quashed in September and he committed suicide, leaving Nasser in undisputed personal control
of the military.[48]

Nasser also regained full control over the ASU. In March
1968 he announced a plan to rebuild the ASU by intro-

ducing elections at every level of its structure, which was transformed into an NU-style pyramid of elected councils.[49] Having removed Sabri's hierarchical apparatus of militant officials, Nasser could afford to allow the democratized ASU a theoretically more prominent role in policy making.[50] Sabri himself would continue as its Secretary-General but had already lost much of his power by the time Nasser finally removed him in September 1969.[51]

Thus, paradoxically, the June War débâcle seems to have left Nasser in a stronger personal position than before. It has been argued that his 'position after June 1967 closely resembled that of King Faruq fifteen years earlier' – indeed some Egyptian critics viewed his rule as 'modern pharaohism'.[52] But Nasser's reign would be very short. He died of heart failure in September 1970, leaving behind a grief-stricken and anxious population bereft of its Rais.

2   NE WIN'S BURMA

The territory of the present-day state of Burma (or Myanmar as it was renamed in 1989) was conquered and incorporated into the British Empire in the nineteenth century. The new colonial territory of Burma was established in 1886 and was governed as a province of India until 1937 when it became a separate colony with a degree of self-government. However, ethnic Burmans, who were devoutly Buddhist, comprised only about three-quarters of the territory's population. The ethnic minorities, the Karens, Shan, Kachin and so forth, were to be found largely on the fringes of the territory and tended to be either animist or, later, Christian rather than Buddhist. Problems associated with these ethnic minorities, including secessionist tendencies and rebellions, have plagued the independent state of Burma, which inherited its boundaries and ethnic composition from the British colonial territory.

Burma gained its independence in 1948 and experienced a decade of democratic government, albeit troubled by ethnic and Communist insurgency, before the military took over in 1958. The military take-over had its origins in a split within the dominant party, the Anti-Fascist People's Freedom League, which had easily won the 1951–2 and 1956 elections. (The party had been founded by the leader of the wartime Burma National Army, General Aung San, who would have become independent Burma's first Prime Minister if he had not been assassinated in 1947.) The split in the AFPFL and its division into two separate parties left the Prime Minister, U Nu, without a stable majority in the parliament. The growing political crisis, complete with indications that the army might intervene, led to U Nu's inviting the commander of the army, General Ne Win, to form a caretaker government that would prepare the country for new elections. General Ne Win was elected Prime Minister by the parliament and chose a Cabinet of civil servants and other non-party civilians. Free elections were eventually held in 1960 and U Nu's party won a convincing victory at the polls. He took office as Prime Minister but held power only until March 1962, when the army staged a typical military coup and set up a military regime.

The army's second stint in government would be quite different from the first.[53] Instead of maintaining the constitutional proprieties, the army abrogated the 1947 Constitution, dissolved the parliament, and imprisoned the Prime Minister and many other political leaders. A military junta, the Revolutionary Council, comprising General Ne Win and sixteen other high-ranking officers, took over the legislative and governing powers of the state. (However, a new government of seven military men and one civilian was also set up to take charge of the Ministries and to implement the Revolutionary Council's decisions.[54]) What is more, the military soon established an ideological one-party state, with the Burma Socialist Programme Party as its regime party and Burmese socialism as its ideology.

Burmese Socialist Ideology

Within two months of its seizure of power, the army had published *The Burmese Way to Socialism*, in which the establishment of a socialist economy and society took precedence over all other goals and problems.[55] The new attitude was evident in the tract's declaration that the old form of democracy had failed to produce socialism and would have to be replaced by a socialist democracy based upon democratic centralism. The main theme of *The Burmese Way to Socialism*, though, was the existence of a specifically Burmese form of socialism and way of attaining it. The ultimate goal was to have all the means of production owned by the state, co-operatives, or 'collective unions'. But there was to be a transitional period during which a Burmese capitalist sector would be allowed to operate, under state control, alongside the extensive nationalized sector of the economy. During this transitional period the people would be re-educated for socialism by being taught that a person's dignity is derived from his or her labour and that moral truth is to be found in every religion or culture. Not only during the transitional phase but also in the final socialist society, everyone would be rewarded according to the quality and quantity of his or her contribution to society.

Early in 1963 another ideological work, *The System of Correlation of Man and his Environment: The Philosophy of the Burma Socialist Programme Party*, was published by the regime. As the title suggests, it was a more philosophical document.[56] It covered such topics as the nature of 'man' and society, and whether a person's relations with others and with the means of production were exploitative or co-operative. Capitalism and Communism were said to have erred in basing themselves on materialism and in either encouraging or overly restricting human egotism. In this criticism and in other areas the (unacknowledged) influence of Burmese Buddhist ideas about the inherent spiritual/ material and altruistic/egotistic nature of humanity was very evident.

A radically new, socialist economic policy was legitimated by the programme laid down in *The Burmese Way to Socialism* and by the philosophical pronouncements of *The System*.[57] The state took over much of industry and commerce and prohibited any new private-sector enterprises. There was no attempt at either collectivization or a redistributive land reform – only some rather ineffective laws against the village landlords. But the state took control of marketing rice, and compulsory quotas had to be sold to the state at below market prices.

The regime actively encouraged industrialization with a huge increase in public investment in industry.[58] The emphasis was on import substitution as part of an implicit overall goal of self-sufficiency that led one foreign observer to describe the economy as autarkic. (In keeping with its desire for economic self-sufficiency and independence the regime sought little in the way of foreign aid or loans.) There was also a public commitment to central planning but the new regime was either unwilling or unable to publish an economic plan during the 1960s.

As Burmese socialism was supposed to be a programme or set of ideas that could be altered to fit changes in circumstances, no great ideological crisis accompanied the 1972 decision to shift away from industrializing and xenophobic economic policies.[59] The new Four Year Plan(s) not only gave a higher priority to agriculture but also sought and received much more foreign aid and loan finance from capitalist countries and such multilateral agencies as the World Bank. The next radical change in economic policy did not occur until 1987, when the peasants were freed from the obligation to sell their rice to the state. In the following year a raft of liberalizing economic reforms aimed at encouraging the private sector and foreign private investment was announced. But there was still no official questioning of the socialist basis of the economy and society.

The ideology's legitimation of the regime was complicated by the fact that it legitimated both military *and* party rule through its notion that a transitional period of military rule would precede party rule.[60] *The Burmese Way to Socialism* specified that a temporary phase of military rule would occur, during which the people would be re-educated for socialism, before power would be transferred to the people and 'their' party, the Burma Socialist Programme Party. The Party and its corps of leaders would thereafter 'ensure that the purpose of the state is successfully carried out by moral men and women who are able to provide the remainder of society with proper leadership'.[61] (The regime's ideologists emphasized later that the Party differed from Communist parties in being the vanguard of not just one class but of all the people, except exploiters.) In the meantime, as the Revolutionary Council explained, the Burmese army was the sole legitimate standard bearer of the revolution that had been begun by Aung San many years earlier with the struggle for independence and was now being completed by the army's seizure of power and transformation of Burma into a socialist society.[62]

Some years later, at the BSPP's first Party Congress in 1971, General Ne Win would announce the ideologically foreshadowed and legitimated transfer of power from the military to the Party. But this formal transfer of power would be nullified in reality by the military's continuing dominance of the Party from within. Or as the Party's General Secretary put it: 'The Burma Socialist Programme Party and the *Tatmadaw* [armed forces] must be indivisible like water is indivisible. The *Tatmadaw* exists as the main pillar of the party.'[63] From the early 1970s onwards the military would rule indirectly, by means of or through an apparently all-powerful regime party. The BSPP would be given a strong governing role (in relation to the civilian state apparatus) as well as having its leadership over the state officially recognized in the regime's Constitution and ideology. But the Party would be the internally controlled instrument of the military. This use of a strong-party-state disguise was by no means an innovation – a Communist party-state façade had been adopted by the Cuban military a decade earlier – but the Burmese military would develop a perhaps uniquely comprehensive example of this disguised form of military-party regime.

The Burma Socialist Programme Party (and the Military)

The new regime was just as quick to found a regime party as it was to espouse an ideology. In July 1962 the only 4-month-old military regime announced the formation of its Burma Socialist Programme Party, also known as the 'Lanzin' party.[64] The other parties suffered increasing repression by the military regime until finally in March 1964 all parties except the BSPP were officially banned by the Law to Protect National Solidarity.[65] This legally recognized monopoly would be reaffirmed in the 1974 Constitution, with Article

11 declaring that the BSPP was Burma's sole political party.[66]

The BSPP was intended to be a transitional and elitist party which would begin the country's move towards the goals of Burmese socialism and would identify and train the new corps of leaders needed to take the people through to these goals.[67] What was unusual was the position the military held in the party and the method it used during the 1960s to exert its control over the BSPP.[68] The party was so elitist that for several years the members of the Revolutionary Council were almost the only full members of the party – in 1966 there were only 20 full members and more than 185 000 candidate members. By 1969 there was reported to be still only 100 full members and some 300 000 candidate members. But after the public decision of that year to transform the BSPP into a 'people's party', the number of full members increased rapidly to over 73 000 in 1972 – of whom more than half were military men.

Eventually, in the 1980s, the Party would have more than 2.3 million members (out of a population of nearly 38 million) and would boast some very extensive attached organizations – a youth organization of well over 3 million members, a workers' organization that incorporated more than a third of the workers, and a peasants' organization that incorporated more than four-fifths of the peasantry.[69] An extensive administrative apparatus was also created, as the Party had adopted a typical 'leftist' structure of national, regional and township elected executive committees, layers of Party sections and cells, and an accompanying apparatus of administrative secretaries.[70] The BSPP's Party Congress of 1971 declared that the party would thereafter no longer be run in an uncompromisingly – almost military style – centralist fashion but instead operate according to the principle of democratic centralism.[71] However, in practice the BSPP remained at least as hierarchical and disciplined as the Communist and other parties in the world which adhered to the principle of democratic centralism.

That the Party was to be a multi-role regime party, performing both political and governing roles, was made quite clear in the 1974 Constitution.[72] Article 179 gave the BSPP the responsibility and political role of drawing up the list of candidates for the new People's Assembly and other elected public bodies, notably the new People's Councils that were to be set up at regional, town and local level.[73] The People's Assembly and People's Councils were only rubber-stamping bodies but at least the Party's political role had been enshrined in the Constitution, in rather similar fashion to the 1936 Soviet and 1964 Ghanaian Constitutions.

The governing role of the Party was enshrined in Article 11, which declared that the BSPP was to lead the state, and in Article 205, which gave the Party the right to 'advise' all levels of government on any topic.[74] However, as its standing Executive Committee did not act as a Politburo-like *de facto* government, the Party did not have a policy-making governing role. (Although the Council of Ministers did not make decisions or take action without the approval of Party Chairman Ne Win, this was probably because of his personal power rather than because he was Chairman of the Party's Executive Committee.[75]) But the Party did perform a strong supervisory governing role. There was an informal requirement that every civil servant holding a position of responsibility be a member of the Party or one of its affiliates or in some other fashion have the trust of the Party.[76] And, unlike in some other regimes, such Partyization was accompanied by a strong, Communist-style supervision that converted the civil service into an 'appendage' of the Party, which actually took over administration at the local level.[77]

The obvious weakness in the Party's otherwise strong supervisory role was its relationship to the military. Unlike in Egypt, there were very extensive contacts between the military and the regime party; most of the military belonged to the Party and indeed contributed a large proportion of its membership in the early 1970s. But, as in Egypt, it was the military which controlled the Party, not vice versa. As was pointed out earlier, the military used the Party from the early 1970s onwards as an indirect, disguised means of continuing to play a powerful (but not as prominent) part in an outwardly civilianized regime.

From the outset in the early 1960s the military had played a very prominent part in the regime. In addition to the policy-making governing role performed by the military's

Revolutionary Council junta, the military had a near monopoly in the formal government, totally dominated the new
regime party, and soon had a powerful military presence
in the civil service. Within a few years of the coup 'most
of the secretaries [secretary, deputy secretary, assistant sec-
retary] and a good number of the directors of departments
were men in uniform'.[78] Included among them was the director-general of police, and most of the other top posts in
the police were taken over by military men.[79] So the military was well positioned to supervise the most powerful
sections of the civilian state apparatus.

In the early 1970s the regime carried out an Egyptian-
style 'civilianization' of the regime.[80] In 1972 Prime Minister Ne Win and nineteen other leading 'political' officers
retired from the military. The all-military government was
thus transformed at a stroke into a supposedly civilian government in which only three of the fifteen Ministers bore military titles. The last remnants of military rule were supposedly
put to rest in 1974 when the Revolutionary Council formally transferred all its powers to the new People's Assembly and was officially abolished. However, ex-General Ne
Win was elected by the Assembly to be the country's head
of state, the chairman of the Council of State. What is more,
the Council of Ministers elected by the Assembly was composed predominantly of military men, most of them retired
from active service, and in fact by 1981 retired officers would
comprise the whole government.

These choices by the Assembly were hardly surprising
considering that (a) the Assembly had been selected by the
BSPP in choosing its candidates for the one-candidate elections, and (b) Ne Win and other retired or serving officers
dominated the central organs of the BSPP. The Central
Committee elected by the delegates to the 1971 Party Congress was composed very largely of military men (151 out
of 200 members) and in turn elected military men to all
but one position on the standing Executive Committee and
to the post of General Secretary – not to mention electing
Ne Win as Party Chairman.[81] Therefore, like the 1956
civilianization in Egypt, the changes in outward appearance did not reflect the realities of the situation. The military had lost the policy-making governing role that it had

performed through the Revolutionary Council junta. But it had retained a strong and extensive supervisory role in relation to the Party and, through the Party, in relation to the civilian state apparatus.

For example, the supposed civilianization of the regime in the early 1970s brought to an end a unique way in which the military had dominated the administration of Burma at the regional and local levels – the Security and Administration Committees.[82] In 1962 a hierarchical structure of these committees was established, stretching from a Central SAC, responsible directly to the Revolutionary Council, down through the various levels of administration to a village Security and Administration Committee. The Committees were chaired and dominated by the local military commander and also included representatives from the police and the civil service.[83] On the face of it the Committees were aimed primarily at strengthening security from ethnic-minority or Communist insurgents and any other threats to law and order. But the SACs' main function seems to have been that of strengthening the hold of the centre over the regions and localities.[84] The SACs became the military regime's principal administrative organs in the regions and localities, being given a wide range of duties and being presented as helping to prepare the way for the development of a socialist society.[85] As part of the civilianization of the regime, the SACs were replaced in 1974 by the new, elected People's Councils set up at the regional and local levels.[86] However, as the military indirectly controlled the People's Councils through the BSPP, in reality there was a change only in the form rather than in the extensiveness of military control of state and society in the regions and localities.

The Party continued to be an internally controlled instrument of the military in the later 1970s and the 1980s even though the continuing growth in Party membership diluted the military's numerical presence in the BSPP.[87] The military's hold on the higher Party offices and organs was sufficient to ensure its dominance of the BSPP. By 1981 no less than 125 of the 260 members of the Party's Central Committee were retired officers and, together with the 57 active-service military members, they ensured that the military could elect whomever it wished to the standing Executive Committee, General Secretaryship and Party Chairmanship.[88] In particular, the key office of Chairman of the Party was still held by ex-General Ne Win and would continue to be until the year of the regime's demise. But, somewhat paradoxically, it could be argued that the main weakness in the military's control of Burma was in fact its lack of control over Ne Win, who by the 1980s had established a degree of personal rule.

Ne Win's Personal Rule

There seems little doubt that by the 1980s Ne Win was not just an agent of the military. But just what degree of personal rule he enjoyed was difficult to discern and was a matter of dispute among foreign observers at the time. It was argued that he 'presided more than ruled' and that the regime he presided over was 'not a highly personalized one'.[89] But on occasions observers explicitly or implicitly compared him to a traditional monarch.[90] The 'old man', as he came to be known by the politically sophisticated inhabitants of Burma, was clearly the regime's 'Number One', but his power seemed to rely very heavily on personal ties of loyalty that gave him influence over other powerful figures but not the public image of personal rule.[91]

The most important of these personal ties of loyalty and respect were those that bound the senior ranks of the military to him and enabled him to continue exercising a degree of leadership over the military after he resigned from active service in 1972. The army's senior officers owed their promotions to him, their commander in the 1950s and 1960s, and even after his supposed retirement from politics in 1988 the military's commander and 'other military leaders indicated that they loved and respected him'.[92] It is true that in 1976 a plot to assassinate him was uncovered within the military, but the perpetrators, fourteen middle-ranking officers, belonged to a younger generation than the senior officers with whom he had established his personal ties. Furthermore, the plotters were opposed to the military-party regime and its economic policies, not just to Ne Win personally.[93] There seems little doubt he was the leader of at least the (crucial) higher ranks of the military.

Ne Win also held several powerful or prestigious state posts during the early part of his political career but dispensed with them as he grew older – in itself an indication of the growth of his purely personal authority. He had been the powerful Chairman of the Revolutionary Council until its demise, head of government until 1974 and head of state (chairman of the Council of State) from then until 1981, when he relinquished this largely ceremonial post to a crony. In addition to such state posts, from the 1960s until his political retirement in 1988 he held the Party post of Chairman and thus a formal leadership position over this hierarchical and disciplined regime party. But in the 1977 elections for Party Chairman he received only the third highest number of votes and two more ballots had to be held before he was eventually re-elected to the post.[94] Therefore, there must be some doubts about how strong a personal leadership he exercised over the Party.

Nor was he the object of a personality cult; indeed it was argued that Ne Win's power 'has always seemed strangely disembodied'.[95] The only official personality cult was the cult of the martyred Aung San, the officially recognized founder of modern Burma, whose assassination in 1947 was commemorated by the most sacred of the regime's annual holy days, Martyrs' Day. However, in a manner reminiscent of the Lenin–Stalin cult the regime's propaganda emphasized that Ne Win had been a close associate of Aung San and had received from him the mantle of leadership of the country. What is more, Ne Win was portrayed, like Aung San, as a founding father of the modern state of Burma.

A *post facto* indicator of the degree of personal rule that Ne Win had achieved by the 1980s was provided by his official retirement from political life and his accompanying resignation from all his political and public offices. His supposed retirement was one of a series of political measures taken in 1988 to placate the increasingly extensive and militant public opposition to the regime. The failure of these measures led to the military coup of September 1988 that set up an old-fashioned military regime under a junta called the State Law and Order Restoration Council

(SLORC). The non-revolutionary, almost reactionary title of the military's SLORC political committee was soon accompanied by the military's disengagement from the promotion of Burmese socialism and from the BSPP itself. Instead of being an ideological one-party state the regime had been converted into avowedly a military caretaker regime, preparing the country for a return to multi-party democracy. Its subsequent refusal to accept the result of the 1990 elections and to relinquish power suggests that SLORC may have been envisaging some form of continuing military rule behind the new façade of a multi-party system rather than a one-party state.

Whatever was the case, the key point is that Ne Win, even in retirement, seems to have played a leading, albeit hidden, role in bringing about the change in type of military regime. In the twenty-four hours before the coup of 18 September Ne Win was apparently visited twice at his residence by the military's Commander-in-Chief,[96] which suggests he either instigated the coup or at least had the power to veto any such move. 'Ne Win's ... influence on major initiatives and his capacity to veto were critical to events in 1988 and probably continue to be important.'[97] That he could continue to have such an influence long after retiring from the military and after relinquishing his public and Party offices indicates that in the pre-1988 era he enjoyed a quite strong degree of personal rule. But, in contrast to Nasser, his personal rule was seriously weakened by his lack of public standing. Whereas it was public demonstrations of support that stimulated the revival of Nasser's personal rule after the 1967 June War débâcle, it was public demonstrations of opposition to his regime that forced Ne Win into supposed retirement and into supporting the 'retirement' of his ideological one-party state.

9 Third World 'Multi-Party' Case Studies

1 PERÓN'S ARGENTINA

In the early 1940s Argentina was the most economically developed country in South America but had been plagued by a series of fraudulent presidential elections in which conservative Presidents had hand-picked their successors. The widespread dislike among the military for the prospect of another fraudulent presidential election produced a hastily organized army coup in June 1943 that resulted in General Rawson taking over the Presidency. When General Ramírez succeeded General Rawson as President only days after the coup, he bestowed upon one of his allies, Colonel Juan Perón, the number two post in the War Ministry. And when General Ramírez was himself replaced as President by his War Minister, General Farrell, the vacant post of War Minister was taken over by the lowly ranked Colonel Perón, albeit officially on only an interim basis. Perón now had sole and formal charge of the extensive powers of that office and could further pursue his ambition of establishing a large personal following in the army. 'By manipulating assignments, promotions, and retirements, he was able to isolate his enemies and reward his friends', and he also implemented a series of military reforms that strengthened his reputation as a promoter of the military's interests and welfare.[1]

His wider political ambitions (and his political foresight) were revealed by his appointment to the vacant post of Vice-President in July 1944 and his increasingly obvious moves to prepare the civilian support he would need for an attempt to win the Presidency by electoral rather than military means. Late in 1943 Perón had become Secretary of Labour and Welfare and began using the Secretariat/Ministry's powers and officials to build a personal following among trade unions and the wider working class. Perón's

170

decrees gave workers such new rights as paid holidays and security from arbitrary dismissal and such new welfare programmes as medical insurance and retirement benefits.[2] He also strengthened labour's position in industrial relations, and even had his state officials intervene in collective bargaining between employers and employees, usually in such a way as to win major concessions from the employers.[3] Whether won over by Perón himself or by the support for him among their members, many of the union leaders became allies and sometimes strong supporters of Perón. Those trade unionists who resisted his overtures were neutralized and those who opposed him, such as the Communists, were imprisoned or had to flee the country. As early as mid-1944 the main trade union federation was controlled by allies of Perón and with his support it went on to incorporate most of the unions which were not already within its fold – by the second half of 1945 only a few independent unions remained.[4]

This working-class following of Perón's was to prove absolutely vital when his enemies within the army staged an intra-army coup against him in October 1945. A massive street demonstration in Buenos Aires by his working-class supporters on 17 October led to a compromise with the coup leaders which left Perón free to contest the elections scheduled to be held early in 1946. On voting day, 24 February, the military ensured an honest vote by guarding the polling places and ballot boxes, and so despite being the Farrell government's preferred candidate, Perón won only 52.4 per cent of the vote.[5] However, in the simultaneous congressional elections the three parties supporting Perón (of which the newly formed Labour Party was easily the most important) faced a divided opposition rather than the anti-Perón coalition put together for the presidential election. They won a massive majority of the seats in the Senate and Chamber of Deputies and all but one of the provincial Governorships. In the light of his overall electoral triumph it is surprising that Perón re-emphasized his military background by first having the outgoing government restore him to active-duty status and promote him to Brigadier-General and then wearing his army uniform at his presidential inauguration.[6]

But here Perón was already indicating the direction he would take in the later 1940s when he would convert the newly restored democracy into a military type of ideological (substantive) one-party state. The regime party would have its electoral victories ensured by undemocratic methods, and Perón himself would provide an official ideology – Peronism.

Peronist Ideology

For four years after 1945 Peronism was little more than such slogans as 'social justice', 'economic independence', and 'political sovereignty'.[7] Nevertheless, this provided some ideological legitimation for the first Five Year Plan, announced in 1946, which was an economically radical programme of state-promoted import-substituting industrialization. It was justified by stressing (a) the social as well as economic advantages of industrialization, and (b) the extra economic and political independence that industrialization would give the nation.[8]

The development of a full-fledged ideology to replace or incorporate the Peronists' sloganistic doctrines can be traced to a paper that Perón presented to an international philosophy conference held in Argentina in April 1949.[9] He argued the need for a 'Third Position' between extreme collectivism and extreme individualism and presented the doctrine of 'Justicialismo' as the answer to that need. By 1952 several of the regime's ideologists had written books and articles that gave Justicialismo more substance and a claim to philosophical rigour.[10] The developed ideology held that there are four forces in society – idealism, materialism, collectivism and individualism – that are in constant conflict with one another yet are each indispensable and beneficial. Injustice and tyranny were said to occur when one or more of the four forces is suppressed and not allowed to exercise its proper role in society. (For example, in a Communist dictatorship materialism and collectivism suppress the other two forces, and in a capitalist society materialism and individualism suppress the other forces.) Justicialismo was said to seek the correct, socially optimal equilibrium among the four forces, aiming 'to establish justice, to give each force its rightful place' in accordance with the relative value of each of them.[11] As one American observer pointed out, the right point of equilibrium 'is whatever Perón says it is; *Justicialismo* is whatever he does' and 'Justicialist theory is, basically, a philosophy of opportunism'.[12] Such an easily manipulable ideology could be used to justify virtually any policy Perón deemed to be expedient.

The Peronist ideology also continued to be embodied in such slogans as 'Dignification of Labour', 'Humanization of Capital', and 'Solidarity among Argentines'.[13] Alongside them were the sacred concepts of 'the new Argentina', 'the revolution of 1943', and the *descamisados*.[14] The *descamisados* was a pejorative term (meaning literally the 'shirtless' people or, more freely translated, the uncultured lower classes) which was converted into a positive political symbol emphasizing the regime's support from and commitment to the underprivileged. Another important concept was the ideal of an 'organized' society, community or nation, which became prominent in Perón's public utterances from 1950 onwards.[15] The newly prominent ideal legitimated the regime's attempt in 1953–4 to organize various sectors of society into a set of official organizations.[16] The Union of Secondary School Students and the General Confederation of University Students were aimed at youth, while the General Economic Confederation was aimed at businessmen and the General Confederation of Professionals at professional men and women.[17]

A new ideological basis for legitimating the regime was provided in Perón's 1952 book, *Conducción política*, which described his concept of the Conductor and theory of *conducción*. The latter term 'implies leadership' but the Conductor 'is much more than a mere *Caudillo*, for he is a creator as well as a leader, an artist more than a technician'.[18] The direct contact between the Conductor and his mass of followers was depicted as 'pure' democracy as distinct from a formal democracy that was out of touch with reality and manipulated by economic interests and selfish political parties. To Perón and his supporters the fact that he was supported by the people meant that his regime was democratic.[19]

The text of the second Five Year Plan, published at the end of 1952, began with a heavy dose of Justicialist and *conducción* ideology and presented a vision of an organized and organic state or political community with a government implementing the will of the people.[20] Yet the new Plan was an economically more orthodox document than the first Five Year Plan. By 1952 the country's foreign exchange reserves were exhausted, inflation was running at over 35 per cent, real wages had fallen significantly, and the economy was stagnating.[21] Therefore the regime fell back 'on old-fashioned recourses little envisaged in 1946, such as increased rural production, free enterprise, a reluctant acceptance of more foreign capital, and the discouragement of free and easy public demands'.[22] There was little in Peronist ideology that could have been used to legitimate this retreat to economic orthodoxy; the regime was instead using a heavy dose of irrelevant ideology to obscure the fact that 'Peronist' economic policies had been abandoned. Here ideology was being used more as a smoke screen than as a legitimator of policy.

The Peronist Parties (and the Military)

One of the distinctive features of Perón's regime was that its eventual regime party was surreptitiously transformed from a standard democratic party into an implicit 'official' party as Perón in the later 1940s and early 1950s surreptitiously transformed the regime from a democracy into a military type of substantive one-party state. A Peronist party had been formed in 1946 out of the three parties which had backed Perón in the February elections. The new party was originally titled the Partido Unico de la Revolución Argentina but was soon renamed the Partido Peronista, and would have to be renamed again in 1949 when a female Peronist party, the Partido Peronista Feminino, was established. Although the initial, 1946 name of the Peronist party suggests that Perón had thoughts of a literal one-party state, he did not advocate abandoning the multi-party system.[23] He preferred to give his party only a monopoly in effectiveness rather than one in law or in fact. He had found weapons less blunt than explicit or implicit prohibition to prevent the electoral dominance of the Peronists being threatened by its Radical and Socialist competitors.[24]

During the election campaigns of the late 1940s and early 1950s the non-Peronist parties were denied police protection against physical attacks by Peronists, could obtain hardly any time on radio or permits for political rallies, and were restricted by press censorship. A law of October 1949 prohibited parties from forming electoral coalitions like the one the anti-Perón parties put together in the 1946 presidential elections. The severe gerrymandering of the congressional districts meant that Peronist candidates in the congressional elections of 1951 won ten times the number of seats won by the Radicals with only twice the number of votes. A variety of often devious means was used to close down the opposition press, and by the time of the 1951 elections the only newspapers still being published were either pro-Perón or were 'neutral'.

More drastically, many of the opposition leaders were either jailed or exiled.[25] The regime's ability to use such measures was enhanced by the decreeing in 1951 of a state of 'internal warfare' that allowed the executive 'to suspend constitutional guarantees and to detain individuals without trial'.[26] An extensive political–police apparatus was developed and often used coercion and torture in dealing with opponents or suspected opponents of the regime.[27]

The result of these various undemocratic measures was to produce clearly disproportionate election victories for the Peronists without the need for any vote-rigging. Perón had established a sophisticated example of semi-competitive substantive one-party state, in which the regime party enjoyed a monopoly in effectiveness behind a multi-party, democratic façade that was made all the more convincing by the obvious degree of autonomy retained by the party's competitors.

The (main) regime party, the renamed Partido Peronista Masculino, did not make its membership figures public but one estimate puts the figure at the beginning of the 1950s at 250 000 to 300 000 – around 4 per cent of the male population.[28] The Party also deployed so many full- or part-time officials to administer its extensive structure (extending from the Basic Units to district and then regional units and finally the national organs) that the degree of bureaucratization has been blamed as one of the reasons for the Party's inability to expand its membership rapidly.[29] The Party certainly developed a quasi-bureaucratic degree of hierarchy and discipline. Although there were Conventions or Congresses of elected delegates held at district, regional and national level, the Party was subject to centralized rule by its unelected Supreme Chief of the Movement.[30] (The Party's rules even specified that if a Party member became President of the country, he automatically became the Party's Supreme Chief.) His decisions were reinforced by a Tribunal of Party Discipline whose function was to inform members of the Party line and ensure that it was adhered to, with any deviant usually being expelled from the Party. Perón had made clear in a 1948 pamphlet on Party organization that he wanted a virtually paramilitary degree of hierarchy and discipline, and the formal organization of the Party seems closer to that ideal than would be expected of a political party which denied any similarity with such rightist parties as the PNF in Italy or the FET in Spain.

The Women's Peronist Party was founded in 1949 – just after women acquired the vote – by Perón's wife, Eva. It was structured like its male counterpart but by 1952 was more extensive, with a membership of some 500 000.[31] Although it has been described as only the 'women's auxiliary' of the male Peronist Party, it elected its own members to public office and was more than just the Peronist equivalent of the Italian Fasci Femminili.[32] Instead the establishment of the female Peronist Party was a unique innovation that produced a dual, partnered combination of regime parties that was no more incongruous for a one-party state than was the continued existence of competing, non-Peronist parties. After his wife's death in 1952 Perón took over her position as head of the Women's Peronist Party rather than allow anyone else to succeed to such an important post.[33]

The primary role of both parties was political – to select Peronist candidates for public office and to ensure the voters elected them in what was a much more competitive political environment than most other regime parties have ever faced.[34] In the March 1948 congressional elections the Peronists increased their share of the vote from 54 per cent to 60 per cent, and then pushed it even higher to nearly 63 per cent in 1954.[35] But the high point in the parties' performance of their political role was the vital set of elections in November 1951. Perón won the Presidency with over 62 per cent of the vote, the Peronists won all the seats in the Senate, no fewer than 135 of the 149 seats in the Chamber of Deputies, and all the provincial Governorships.

As for the Peronist parties' social role, changing public attitudes to conform to the regime's ideology 'was the particular responsibility of the Party, which was to create these new attitudes by an indoctrination (*adoctrinamiento*)'.[36] However, it is unlikely that the two Peronist parties were very successful in instilling Peronist ideology in the hearts and minds of the people (especially in explaining the finer points of Justicialismo) and even the urban working-class heartland of the Peronist movement showed little commitment to Peronism when it faced its final crisis in 1955.

The two parties never acquired any policy-making governing role or any significant supervisory role. The 'overwhelming majority' of civil servants and municipal officials became members of the (male) Party.[37] (Many joined only in order to protect their careers, and indeed in parts of Argentina public employees could be dismissed for failing to secure Party membership.[38]) But the Peronist parties were not allowed by Perón to supervise state employees in any fashion at all – leaving frustrated Peronist militants to bemoan the continuing existence of a politically neutral civil service.[39]

The Peronist parties did not even have any connections with, let alone supervise, the military arm of the state.[40] Perón was too shrewd and wary ever to contemplate an attempt at Party-izing an officer corps which was very attached to its professional, non-party tradition. Active-duty officers were permitted to stand for public office and those holding federal public office were permitted to participate fully in the affairs of political parties. But a Brigadier-General was relieved of his command for joining his local unit of the Peronist Party. This does not mean there was no attempt to politicize the military. After the 1951 election's apparent ratification of Peronism as the *doctrina nacional*, the study of this national doctrine was incorporated into all levels of the army's instructional programme. There were also compulsory lectures and classes praising Perón's achievements and denigrating the civilian political leaders of the past. By 1953 the Army Ministry had even prepared and issued a Manual of National Doctrine and Organization. However, as in the rather similar case of Nazi Germany, such indoctrination was carried out by the army itself and did not involve any contacts with the regime party.

Although Perón used the hackneyed 'backbone' analogy when referring to the military's role in the 'organized community' he was creating in Argentina,[41] military men did not play a prominent role in his military-party regime. It was calculated in 1952 that, on average, half of Perón's appointees to ministerial office were military men and that since 1943 close to half of the provincial Governors or their equivalents had been army officers.[42] But somewhat paradoxically, during the military-party period of Perón's rule, from the late 1940s onwards, the Cabinet was predominantly civilian, with only one of the civilian (as distinct from the four armed-service) Ministries or Secretariats being given to a military man.[43] Furthermore, the military was not given a number of posts in the civilian state apparatus or the regime party, as it had in Spain under Primo de Rivera and then Franco. Yet despite the lack of any obvious role for the military in the regime, the extent and degree of military support was a key factor in determining how long Perón could maintain the personal rule he had attained at the head of his military-party regime.

Perón's Personal Rule

Perón obviously had always been more than just an agent of the military but he was never the leader of more than a part of the military. He was himself a General and had already won the leadership of a substantial section of the army before becoming President. And as President he was titular Commander-in-Chief, with appointment powers over the most senior military positions. On the other hand, he had also aroused the opposition of a substantial section of the military and he lacked the military prestige and rank of a Franco or a Ne Win.

In 1948–50, as he moved away from democracy, Perón attempted to strengthen his personal hold on the military. He ensured that the highest command positions of the army were in the hands of his supporters, and he boosted his military rank to more impressive heights.[44] In May 1950 Congress approved his being promoted to Major-General, despite his lack of the necessary years of service, and then in September approved his further promotion to the (in the Argentinian army) rare and exalted rank of Lieutenant-General. Perón also catered generously to the military's corporate interests by providing promotions for the senior officers, generous inflation-compensating pay increases for all, new equipment, military-influenced industrialization, and even improved accommodation.[45] Even the attempted politicization of the military in the 1950s may be seen as largely an attempt to strengthen Perón's personal hold on the military. For the process of politicization 'involved efforts to promote a sense of personal identification and ideological affinity with the President and his movement; it also involved measures that would strengthen the military men's sense of appreciation, personal and professional, for favorable treatment accorded them and their institutions.'[46] In fact by 1954 senior commanders were encouraging what was virtually a Perón personality cult within the military, including naming military units and installations after him.[47]

However, these various measures and efforts were not entirely successful – and, as will be seen later, some of them were counter-productive. Perón's failure to become the leader of all the military was apparent not only in the navy's hostility towards him and the uneasiness within part of the army about his shift from democracy to dictatorship, but also in a small-scale attempted coup in 1951 and a plot uncovered in 1952.[48] To secure his personal position Perón had to maintain his non-military bases of personal rule.

The very important constitutional/state basis of Perón's personal position was his office of President, which made him head of state and government and gave him 'vast powers of patronage'.[49] The legislative powers conferred on the

Congress were also under Perón's control thanks to his authoritative leadership over the party which dominated both
houses of Congress. The very name of the party expressed
the fact that it was the personal instrument of President
Perón. As the Supreme Chief of the Movement he had the
formal right to veto or change any Party decisions, including the selection of the Party's candidates for public office
and of candidates for office within the Party itself.[50]

Perón had won a deal of popularity among wide sections
of the population in 1943–6 and this strong public standing was supported by a personality cult propagated by
Peronists and the tame mass media. The high priestess of
this cult was Eva Perón, and at times her public praise
and adoration of her husband did actually verge on the
religious.[51] However, Eva Perón herself became the object
of a personality cult and eventually established a personal
relationship with the masses that seemed to overshadow the
one Perón had established in the mid-1940s. She became
not only the head of the increasingly important female wing
of the Peronist movement but also the informal head of
the trade union wing which Perón had worked so hard to
establish in 1943–5, and which had saved his political career in October 1945. Almost as important was her position
as the head of the Eva Perón Welfare Foundation.[52] By the
end of the 1940s this (heavily) publicly as well as privately
funded welfare organization was running more than 1000
schools and a dozen hospitals, as well as children's homes
and other welfare and medical facilities. It also provided
her with ample funds for her well-publicized personal dis-
bursements of aid to individual needy cases. The result was
the at least partly spontaneous and genuine cult of 'Evita'
that saw her crowned with such titles as 'The Workers'
Plenipotentiary', 'The Mother of the Innocents', and 'The
Lady of Hope'.[53] Her name (like Perón's) was to be found
'throughout the country, on railway stations, parks, aque-
ducts, schools, plazas, ports, avenues, ships, in city districts,
and much else'.[54] When Eva died in July 1952, the outpouring of grief and the emotional extravagance of her
funeral were evidence of the genuineness and depth of the
cult of Evita and of the Peronist regime's reliance upon her.[55]

What made her loss all the more serious politically was

that the regime's popularity was being put under strain by the end of the post-war economic boom and thus the end of the regime's ability to deliver material benefits to the workers. But it was the military's disenchantment with Perón that was the direct cause of his downfall. The decline in the intensity of popular backing for the regime would contribute only indirectly, by leaving Perón without the possibility of another 17 October 1945 to overturn or indeed deter a move by his military opponents.

By 1954 there was significant opposition within the army's officer corps to the politicization of the army, the Perón personality cult indulged in by the army's senior commanders, the simplicities and artificiality of the national doctrine in which the officer corps were being indoctrinated, and the tendency towards identifying the army with a particular person rather than a system, order, or institution that was independent of any individual.[56] However, when a large-scale military rebellion began on 16 September, most of the army stayed neutral or loyal to Perón and although many army officers in apparently loyal units were no longer prepared to put up a serious fight in defence of Perón's regime, the rebels were soon contained and in some places defeated.[57] The decisive blow came from the navy, which was entirely under rebel control and on 18 September blockaded the country's coast and threatened to bombard the main oil refinery and storage facilities.[58] Faced with a split in the military and the possibility of civil war, the army's senior Generals were prepared to abandon Perón and re-establish an old-fashioned military regime like that of 1943.[59] With the masses not rallying to Perón as they had in October 1945, he himself recognized the hopelessness of his situation and escaped to Paraguay and to an international exile that would last nearly twenty years.[60] In June 1973 he would return in triumph to Argentina and in September be elected President once again, only to die from natural causes in July 1974.

2   SUHARTO'S INDONESIA

The very large and populous (now over 180 million people) Indonesian archipelago was once a Dutch colony, known as the Dutch East Indies. However, in 1942 the Japanese defeated the Dutch and occupied the colony, allowing the local anti-colonial nationalists the freedom to develop a major political movement. When the Japanese surrendered to the Allies in August 1945, the nationalists responded by declaring the independence of the new state of 'Indonesia'. A constitution was promulgated, known later as the 1945 Constitution, and the most prominent nationalist leader, Sukarno, was chosen to be the new country's first President.

However, the Dutch government did not accept this bid for independence and used military force to reinstitute colonial rule. The result was a prolonged guerrilla war against the Dutch that did not end until 1949, when they finally agreed to Indonesia's independence. In 1950 a constitution was promulgated that differed from the 1945 Constitution in making the Cabinet responsible to parliament rather than to the President and in other ways reducing the powers of the Presidency. The parliamentary elections of 1955, however, produced a splintering of the vote among many parties. President Sukarno's party, the PNI, won the largest share of the vote with only 23 per cent, closely followed by two Muslim parties and the Communist party.

In the later 1950s army commanders on some of the outer islands rebelled against the central government, leading it to impose martial law on the whole country. Although the rebellion was militarily defeated in 1958, this did not bring an end to the state of martial law. Instead, President Sukarno declared in 1959 that the military role in administering the country would continue and that the presidential 1945 Constitution would replace the existing parliamentary Constitution. Indonesia had entered an era of what Sukarno termed 'Guided Democracy', which eventually saw him declared President for life.

His dictatorial rule over Indonesia was based upon the support of the military and of two major political parties – his own PNI party and the Indonesian Communist Party (PKI). The military was given a major role in running the country, not only through the administration of martial law and holding a number of provincial Governorships, but also in the form of several Cabinet posts and substantial representation in the new, appointed parliament. However, the army became increasingly hostile towards another of Sukarno's allies – the outwardly moderate but large and rapidly expanding Communist movement.

In October 1965 the army smashed the Communist movement in reaction to a PKI-supported coup attempt against the military high command by officers claiming to be protecting Sukarno from an army plot. In March 1966 he was pressured into signing over his presidential powers to the army's supreme commander, General Suharto, and Sukarno was placed under a form of 'palace arrest' until his death in 1970.[61]

General Suharto moved patiently and cautiously to consolidate the new, military regime.[62] In 1967 his use of the presidential powers was regularized by his being named acting President, and in March 1968 he was appointed President for a five-year term by the Provisional People's Consultative Assembly (MPRS). He had promised the MPRS that parliamentary elections would soon be held and they eventually were in 1971. The by no means free and fair elections produced a large majority, nearly 63 per cent of the vote, for the new regime's electoral standard bearer, Sekber-Golkar. Along with this regime party, the military had established an official ideology and created a very distinctive example of the military type of ideological (substantive) one-party state.

The Dwifungsi and Pancasila Ideology

The military had already developed principles or concepts to justify its playing a prominent and permanent part in the political and social life of the country.[63] During the era of Sukarno's Guided Democracy, the army had espoused the concept of 'the Middle Way' (that is, between the two 'extremes' of the military's being either apolitical or taking over the government) to justify its claim to permanent representation in the country's administration, Cabinet and parliament. Then in April 1965 a new term, *dwifungsi* (dual function), was formally adopted by the army to describe its dual function as both a 'military force' and a 'social-political force', with the latter covering 'the ideological, political, social, economic, cultural and religious fields'.[64] In August 1966, following the military's take-over of power from Sukarno, the army explained that it had been forced to adopt this dual function because the people's hopes were centred on the military.[65] By early 1980s the *dwifungsi* doctrine maintained that although the army's dual function was permanent, the social-political component of its dual function could shrink if there was no longer as great a need for the military's social-political involvement. But the doctrine itself had not declined in importance, being enshrined in the 1982 law on the Basic Provisions for the Defence and Security of the Republic.

The military had no comprehensive ideological doctrines, though, about the nature of society and politics. The new regime used the slogan of establishing a 'New Order' which would be 'a "correction" of what were considered to be deviations from the 1945 Constitution perpetrated by Sukarno's Old Order'.[66] Yet apart from fervent anti-Communism and a more positive attitude to capitalism and foreign aid/investment the New Order did not appear to have much ideological content. Its key slogans or concerns were order (especially stability) and national development (especially economic growth).[67] What has been termed the New Order's 'development ideology' legitimated a series of Five Year Development Plans.[68] Instituted in 1969 the first of these Plans contained little in the way of actual planning apart from emphasizing some priority areas, notably rice production, in which the state would supplement market forces.

Despite its relatively positive attitude to capitalism, the New Order could not have legitimated much in the way of economic deregulation and movement towards a more market economy.[69] For the New Order was ideologically bound by its commitment to the 1945 Constitution's favouring of state control of the economy. Article 33 of the Constitution has been paraphrased as containing three stipulations:

> (1) the economy is organized as a joint venture (*usaha bersama*) based on the family principle (*asas kekeluargaan*); (2) the sections of production [that are] important for the state and that encompass the basic needs of the people are controlled by the state; and (3) natural resources are controlled by the state for the benefit of the people.[70]

The new regime did free up trade and investment but this was aimed only at attracting foreign investment and strengthening the export sector. The general thrust of economic policy was along the statist and interventionist lines legitimated by the often-cited Article 33. In the 1970s state-owned enterprises grew to be a major part of the economy, and even the development of a significant corporate private sector was facilitated by state subsidies and protection. When the country's substantial oil revenues (which had financed the expansion of the state sector) were hit by the collapse of oil prices in the 1980s, the regime introduced deregulatory policies in an attempt to broaden the export base of the economy. But by the 1990s there was pressure 'to revert to the ideological purity demanded of the New Order by its strict adherence to the 1945 Constitution'.[71]

The regime's most important decision in the field of ideology was its support for Indonesia's already existing official creed of Pancasila, the Five Pillars or Five Principles, which became the ideological foundation of the New Order regime and policies.[72] Although the Pancasila had originally been formulated (in July 1942) by the now deposed Sukarno, it had been included in the military's sacred 1945 Constitution and had become since independence the ideology of the Indonesian state rather than that of any particular regime. Therefore it is not so surprising that the new military regime decided to maintain ideological continuity – and also acquire a ready-made wide political-social ideology – by committing itself to Pancasila. And the degree of commitment to Pancasila seemed to increase with time, as by the 1980s the Political Parties Amendment Bill and the Mass Organizations Bill were demanding that all political and social 'mass' organizations acknowledge that Pancasila was their sole ideology.[73]

The first of the five Pancasila principles was nationalism, including the creation of an Indonesian national solidarity overriding the various ethnic divisions to be found in the archipelago. The second principle was internationalism or humanitarianism, which balanced the potentially harmful international effects of nationalism by encouraging nations to live in peace with one another. The third principle was usually translated as 'democracy' but it was democracy of a consultative and consensual Indonesian type, not of the supposedly conflictive and divisive Western type. (Thus the military regime branded as 'alien' the Western concept of voting in which '50 plus 1' constitutes a majority and a democratic decision.[74]) The fourth principle was social justice, on an international scale as well as in Indonesia itself. Finally, the fifth principle was belief in the one, supreme God – a principle which had been liberally interpreted by Sukarno as meaning religious tolerance and freedom.

Golkar (and the Military)

One of the unique features of the Indonesian military-party regime was the nature of its regime party, Sekber-Golkar.[75] The name Sekber-Golkar was an abbreviation of Sekretariat Bersama Golongan Karya, the Joint Secretariat of Functional Groups, which had been originally set up by the army in 1964 to co-ordinate the activities of those functional or occupational groups which were opposed to the Communists. Hundreds of organizations and groups, ranging from trade unions and professional associations to religious and youth groups, had attached themselves to Sekber-Golkar by 1968. After being reorganized into a more effective political instrument – under tight military control at the top – this conglomeration of affiliated functional groups was deployed as the military regime's standard-bearer in the 1971 parliamentary elections. The post-election revamping of Sekber-Golkar involved only minor changes in name, to Golongan Karya Pusat (Functional Groups Centre), and in structure, with the Joint Secretariat being replaced by a national council. During the rest of the 1970s Golkar continued to expand and to win overwhelming election victories through its affiliated-functional-group structure, and not until 1983 were steps taken to convert Golkar into something that would look more like a political party. The organization's Third National Congress voted to abandon the affiliated-functional-group structure and shift to a standard form of party structure based on individual members, who were to be led and organized by an extensive corps of well-trained cadres. By 1987 Golkar was claiming some 28 million individual members or about 15 per cent of the population.[76]

The unique functional-group structure of Sekber-Golkar was overlaid and administered by a territorial structure of indirectly elected executive committees at national, provincial and district levels. In practice Golkar was so centralized that critics accused it of having adopted the 'Command System' and of having a bureaucratic structure very like that of a ministerial department.[77] But in the 1980s this quasi-bureaucratic discipline was disturbed by moves towards encouraging lower-level democratization, by a factional struggle to control delegates to the National Congress, and by discernible internal divisions over policy.[78] Golkar had certainly not been as disciplined as might be expected of the regime party of a military type of one-party state.

Golkar's monopoly in effectiveness has been ensured by means that, as in the case of Perón's Argentina, preserve the appearance of a competitive multi-party system. But the Indonesian example of a semi-competitive substantive one-party state has actually come quite close to the approach of the puppet-party *non*-competitive system of Communist people's democracies in developing its unique system. For in Indonesia the competing parties not only have been restricted and denied the state aid accorded the regime party but also have been deprived of much of their autonomy. In the 1971 elections the regime intervened in the parties' internal affairs and disqualified hundreds of their candidates as well as banning any criticism of the new regime's policies.[79] After the elections the interventionist strategy became more sophisticated. All political parties apart from Golkar were made to merge into two new parties, one Muslim (PPP) and the other nationalist (PDI). On the face of it this forced merger strengthened Golkar's electoral competitors, who had been splintered into nine different parties in the previous election. But their merger into just two parties made them easier for the regime to control, and they have been plagued by continual factional problems and internal disunity that have in turn facilitated the regime's interference and control.[80]

The interventionist strategy was formalized in the Political Parties Bill of 1975, which allowed only the three officially recognized parties – Golkar, the PDI and PPP – to contest parliamentary elections. The government argued that 'the three sanctioned and strictly controlled parties provided sufficient "facilities for the channelling of opinions and ideas of members of society"', and the parties were told to be 'complimentary' rather than antagonistic to one another.[81] To ensure that elections would not become too heated or produce inappropriate members of parliament the government's Election Institute vetted each party's list of candidates, striking off the names of those deemed to be irresponsible or too strongly anti-government.[82] It is hardly surprising that the PDI and PPP have 'tended to act as little more than minority wings of Golkar'.[83]

As well as neutering the competing parties, the regime strengthened Golkar's vote-winning capacities in various ways. From the 1971 elections onwards the civil service has been mobilized to support Golkar by using officials' influence over village and urban society to win votes for the party. The Department of Internal Affairs, in particular, was used 'to create a patronage machine that would win over supporters from other parties'.[84] After the 1977 elections it also became formally obligatory for all civil servants to campaign on behalf of Golkar and to promise that they and their families would vote for it.[85] In the lead-up to the 1982 elections all village headmen were classified as civil servants, which at a stroke provided Golkar with a layer of influential grassroots activists and increased the pool of guaranteed Golkar votes from civil service families to around 20 million – a sixth of the total electorate.[86] Another form of state aid for Golkar was the use of intimidation, especially in the 1971 elections, by the network of locally deployed military units, which constituted an effective electoral machine in its own right.[87]

The state resources in personnel, patronage and intimidation that were deployed on Golkar's behalf enabled it to win a succession of overwhelming election victories without the need for widespread vote-rigging, for police repression of electoral opponents, or even for close and comprehensive control of the media. Golkar won nearly 63 per cent of the vote in 1971, just over 62 per cent in 1977, over 64 per cent in 1982, and 73 per cent in 1987. In fact Golkar's main purpose or role has been the winning of elections, and during the 1970s it virtually went into hibernation between elections.[88]

Therefore Golkar clearly was not a multi-role party. Like the Peronist regime parties, it concentrated its efforts upon performing the political role of selecting candidates for public office and mobilizing voting support for them from the electorate. The key public offices in the Indonesian case were the 400 contested seats in Indonesia's parliament, the DPR, which was by no means only a rubber-stamping body. (The government's legislation was sometimes subjected to heated debate and prolonged deliberation, with amendments and even an occasional withdrawal being wrung from the government as the price for maintaining the image of consensual Pancasila democracy.[89]) In the 1980s a restructured Golkar did envisage also performing something of a social role in the sense of propagating Pancasila among at least its own members.[90] But Golkar has never looked like taking on a policy-making or supervisory role of any kind; only the military has performed any sort of governing role in the Indonesian military-party regime.

The prominent part played by the military in the Indonesian military-party regime was very much in line with the official *dwifungsi* doctrine of the armed forces' right and duty to perform civilian roles. It is true that there has not been a junta or martial law, and even the military presence in Cabinet has been erratic and sometimes quite small.[91] But the Indonesian military has developed some innovative and still unique means of maintaining a pervasive and powerful presence in the regime.[92] For example, a block of seventy-five, later a hundred, seats in parliament was officially reserved for military appointees, retired or active-service officers. And the army's deployment of its soldiers in rural areas included stationing a soldier in every village, no matter how small, as the military's local representative. The most important innovations, though, were the new systems developed for supervising the regime party and the civilian state apparatus.

The military has always been the most powerful component of Golkar – the most important of its affiliated functional groups – and military men, especially retired Generals, have almost monopolized the key executive posts, notably general chairman, chairman, deputy chairman, and secretary-general.[93] But the military also inserted a unique supervisory apparatus into Golkar's administrative structure. Golkar's central, provincial and district executive committees were each supervised by an accompanying council of advisers that was in turn dominated by military men.[94] These advisory or supervisory councils, not the executive committees that they supervised, were the most powerful organs in Golkar and therefore ensured tight military control from central to district level.[95] In 1978 an apparent civilianization occurred when it was decided that regional and district army commanders would no longer automatically head their local council of supervisors and that officers on active service would no longer be allowed to hold executive posts in Golkar.[96] But the key central supervisory and executive posts continued to be held by retired officers, usually by retired Generals.

In performing a supervisory governing role over the civilian state apparatus the military again developed a new and unique system – the *karyawan* or Civic Mission system.[97] The *karyawan* (functionary) officers were active-service military men on detachment to civilian posts in state and society (no fewer than 16 000 of them in the early 1980s) who maintained regular contact with a Karyawan Management Board in the Non-Military Affairs unit of the military's General Staff. The Karyawan Management Board received quarterly reports from the *karyawan* officers and sent official policy decisions and other information to them. There were also many more thousands of retired rather than active-service officers holding important posts in state and society. They held such non-state posts as local chief of the official trade union movement and, together with active-service officers, occupied about half of the higher-ranking posts in the central civil service.[98] In the later 1960s military men held over a third of the Ministries' key posts of secretary or director-general as well as seventeen of the twenty-four provincial Governorships, and more than half of the mayoralties and rural district Governorships.[99] By the late 1970s some four-fifths of the ministerial secretaries and directors-general were military men and so were more than two-thirds of the provincial Governors and more than half of their district equivalents.[100] But by then it was also clear that the military man who held the most important of all civilian posts, that of President, was not simply an agent of the military – Suharto had attained a degree of personal rule.

Suharto's Personal Rule

Although the prominent and extensive military presence in the regime has not been converted into just an instrument of Suharto's personal rule, neither can he be seen as being in any way an agent of the military. He has clearly escaped, though not reversed, any principal-agent relationship between himself and the military.

When Suharto took over the Presidency in the late 1960s, he was the army's commander but by no means its leader.[101] He had no widespread following or great reputation and had acquired command of the army almost literally by elimination, after the previous commander and several other senior Generals had been killed by the rebels in October 1965. However, during the 1970s Suharto established a degree of control, if perhaps still not leadership, over the armed forces. He used his powers of appointment to fill the key posts in the armed forces with his supporters or with non-political officers who would obey him as their formal superior. (In 1973 he retired from his military post of Commander of the Armed Forces and his government post of Minister of Defence but his appointment powers as President and titular Supreme Commander allowed him to continue this personnel policy.) Over time Suharto was also able to win the respect of the military for his personal virtues and its gratitude for his ensuring that the military enjoyed the prominence in state and society that had been envisaged by the military's own *dwifungsi* doctrine – and that provided many opportunities for material benefits and career development. Finally, there was no credible alternative figure to Suharto, and an increasingly professional military establishment abhorred the prospect of such potentially divisive political interventions as attempting a coup against him. Therefore by the later 1970s Suharto appeared 'to be directly in control of the military' and to have 'succeeded in confining it to policy-implementation'.[102]

However, Suharto's control over the military was still based more on his position as President than on any personal leadership over the military; in implementing his policies it was not acting as simply his personal instrument. Although his overall relationship with the military was markedly better than was Perón's with the Argentinian military, the security of his personal rule was perhaps almost as dependent as Perón's upon such other bases for personal rule as his leadership of the regime party and his hold on the extensive powers of the Presidency.[103]

He has been careful never to assume formal leadership of Golkar, preferring to maintain the image of a President who is in a sense 'above parties'. However, the powerful supervisory apparatus which the military built into Golkar's structure provided him with the opportunity to hold a discreet but powerful post.[104] In 1973 he became the Supreme Adviser of Golkar's central supervisory council and in 1978 assumed the chairmanship of this council of supervisors or advisers. Through the eventually very extensive powers of his supervisory position he acquired a formal control over Golkar. And by the time of his 1988 re-election as chief supervisor by the party's Fourth National Congress it was clear that he was Golkar's '*de facto* leader'.[105]

His control and leadership over Golkar did not provide Suharto with a very powerful basis for his personal rule but it did secure his hold on the very powerful constitutional office of President. According to the 1945 Constitution the President is elected every five years by the People's Consultative Assembly (MPR), which comprises the members of parliament and an equal number of appointees/representatives from the regions and various political and social organizations. Control of Golkar, together with the block of his carefully chosen military appointees in the MPR, has guaranteed him a majority in this electoral college for the Presidency. (In practice Suharto has always been re-elected unopposed in a manner that maintains the image of consensual Pancasila democracy.) Under the 1945 Constitution the President is head of government as well as head of state and possesses not only decree powers but also appointment powers over the civil service and the armed forces – of which he is titular Supreme Commander.[106]

Suharto has emphasized his constitutional legitimacy as the choice of the MPR and has also presented himself as having acquired a form of popular mandate from the people themselves by being the unanimous choice of the People's Consultative Assembly.[107] He has also sought to portray himself as a man of the people, as being a product of Indonesian culture and recent history, and as having the humility and simplicity of life-style that are traditional Javanese virtues.[108] But although he acquired the informal title of 'father of development', until recently there was no attempt to develop any sort of Suharto personality cult.[109]

In the early 1980s the President held practically all decision-making power both inside and outside the military, including deciding upon appointments to all key executive posts with little or no consultation.[110] But in the later 1980s a threat to his position arose from his advancing years (though he was only in his late sixties) and from the inevitable conjectures about when he would retire, who would succeed him as President, and whether the succession would be smooth. In fact by the end of the decade 'senior military figures, both active and retired, had begun working quietly to seek his removal'.[111] However, as these military opponents would not contemplate the use of force against him, Suharto was in a virtually unassailable position. The only apparent victory his opponents won was the removal in 1988 of a Suharto henchman, Vice-President retired-General Sudharmono, from the general chairmanship of Golkar.[112] Suharto himself went on to be re-elected President unopposed in 1993.

Part III
Transformations from One Type to Another

10 From Party-State to Military-Party Regime

1 KUOMINTANG CHINA

As the last dynasty of Emperors in China were Manchus in ethnic origin, the overthrow of the Imperial regime in 1911 was a nationalist as well as republican uprising. However, the nationalism evident in the 1911 revolution did not carry over into post-revolutionary national unity, not at least in the political and administrative sense. The new Republic's central government in Peking was very weak, and in reality the eighteen provinces were ruled by the *tuchüns* (military Governors) of the provinces – the famous or notorious 'warlords'.[1] These warlords accepted the right of the Peking government to be the national government and to represent China to the outside world. But after the death in 1916 of the second President of China, the military strongman Yüan Shih-k'ai, the warlords would not allow the central government in Peking to interfere in their running of the provinces. Thus after 1916 China was almost a confederation of provincial military regimes with a weak central government in Peking handling foreign relations on behalf of the confederation.

The standard bearer of the struggle for a united China was the Kuomintang movement based in the southern city of Canton. The Kuomintang (National People's Party) was formed in 1912 and espoused the political doctrines of China's leading nationalist figure and most well-known politician, Sun Yat-sen. The fundamental concern of the Kuomintang, or the 'Nationalists' as they were often called by Westerners, was the unification of China and the establishment of a strong central government that would end foreign domination and exploitation of China. In pursuit of this goal Sun was prepared to ally his Kuomintang movement with the Communist regime that by the early 1920s was firmly in charge of the former Russian Empire and was

197

looking outwards to the south-east as well as to the west. In 1923 the Communist regime began sending advisers to Sun's base in Canton to help him train a Kuomintang army and to reorganize the Kuomintang itself. (As part of the new alliance the small Chinese Communist Party would also join the Kuomintang in a 'united front'.) The Kuomintang was to be restructured to fit the Leninist model of a revolutionary party, which had proved its capability in Russia by not just staging a revolution but also winning the post-revolutionary civil war and establishing a strong central government. So began what was virtually a second founding of the Kuomintang, referred to as the 'Reorganization of 1924', that established a Leninist party structure based upon a centrist interpretation of democratic centralism.

With Sun's death in March 1925 the Kuomintang entered a period of collective leadership somewhat similar to that being experienced by the Soviet Communist Party in the mid-1920s after the death of Lenin. There was the same sort of factional squabbling in the central Party organs and the steady elimination of potential successors to the founder-figure's leadership of the Party. One of the three most likely successors to Sun's leadership position was assassinated, another (Hu Han-min) found it necessary to retire temporarily from politics, and the third (Wang Ching-wei) was prevented from consolidating his position as the apparent successor by military intervention in March 1926 by the leader of the military wing of the movement, General Chiang Kai-shek, the commander of the Kuomintang's National Revolutionary Army.[2]

In 1926–8 the Kuomintang carried out its long-awaited military campaign, known as the Northern Expedition, aimed at freeing China from the warlords and uniting it into a modern nation-state. During the campaign Chiang, in April 1927, turned on the Kuomintang's Chinese Communist allies, instituting a savage wave of anti-Communist repression. But despite such 'distractions', through a combination of military victories and alliances with warlords sympathetic to the Kuomintang, by June 1928 the Chiang-led armies had reached Peking. The Kuomintang government in its new capital city of Nanking could make an apparently credible claim to rule over a unified China. The Kuomintang was also establishing what would be the first Asian example of an ideological one-party state – and would later be one of the few examples anywhere to be transformed from a party-state to military-party regime.

Kuomintang Ideology

The new party-state regime was well endowed with ideology. The deceased founding leader of the Party, Sun Yat-sen, had left his devoted followers a body of sacred script to guide them and their regime through the difficult years ahead. In one of the most extreme examples in history of bestowing official status upon an ideology, the Kuomintang regime declared in 1928 that Sun's writings would be viewed as having the force of law.[3]

The essence of Sun's political thought was his Three People's Principles, which were first formulated in the early 1900s. They are often translated as (1) nationalism, (2) democracy, and (3) socialism. However, the Chinese terms are not exact equivalents of these English words; the second principle would be more accurately translated as 'the people's rights or power' and the third principle actually means 'the people's livelihood', with a connotation of material well-being.[4] The nationalism of the first principle had developed an anti-imperialist emphasis in the 1920s, denouncing the control of Chinese affairs by the Western powers and Japan, and looked to an international anti-imperialist revolution by oppressed nations which would eventually produce a global commonwealth of all mankind.[5] But even when dealing with the problem of foreign imperialism, Sun's nationalism displayed a concern for national solidarity which makes 'nationhood' perhaps a better translation of the first principle than 'nationalism'. For he viewed 'the lack of cohesive spirit among the Chinese people ... to be a major source of China's internal weakness in the face of external threats. As a remedy for Chinese national fragmentation, he proposed a revived national consciousness on the basis of language, livelihood, tradition and common blood of lineage.'[6] Sun even talked of basing the new national solidarity on the traditional loyalties of clan and family and advocated a revival of the ancient Confucianist morality.[7]

As for the Principle of People's Power (or Rights), Sun initially believed in simply copying Western representative democracy, which he viewed as the political 'wave of the future'.[8] But he became disillusioned with Western democratic institutions and practices and developed a strong attachment to ideals of participatory democracy (as at the local-government level) and absolute popular sovereignty (as with the use of referendums and recall in addition to ordinary elections). From his earliest formulations of this second People's Principle until his death Sun also maintained that there would need to be a transitional period of *tutelage* during which his party would hold a monopoly of political power and prepare the people for constitutional democracy.[9]

The third People's Principle, the People's Livelihood, was the vaguest of the three. Sun was, though, 'a staunch proponent of state capitalism' in industry and of the need for the state to lead and regulate the private sector.[10] And his unrealistic prescriptions for solving the problems of rural China reflected his urban and industrial bias – he was looking to a Western-style industrial revolution to lift the people's livelihood onto a new plane.[11]

In the first few years of the Kuomintang regime the concept of Political Tutelage was perhaps the most important component of its Sunist ideology.[12] It provided the ideological justification or legitimation for the Kuomintang's dictatorial regime, in which the government was chosen solely by and was responsible solely to the Party.[13] Although the Party's Central Executive Committee promised in June 1929 to complete this tutelage within six years,[14] obviously there was every opportunity for the period to be extended on the grounds that the educative goal had not yet been attained. As the Kuomintang regime never made any serious attempt to provide the masses with training in democratic, constitutional self-government, it gave itself good reason to claim that the period of tutelage would have to be longer than first envisaged.[15] The end result was as open-ended a justification for transitional party rule as that which Lenin had provided for his Communist regime in the Soviet Union with his doctrine of rule by the proletariat's party during the transitional dictatorship of the proletariat.

However, the Kuomintang ideologists were keen to distinguish their form of party dictatorship from that in the Soviet Union by emphasizing that their Party represented the interests of not just the proletariat but all national classes.[16] Certainly the Kuomintang regime did not wage any class wars against the urban and rural capitalists, large or small, in carrying out its economic and social policies. For example, its belated attempts after 1932 at reconstructing the rural economy were hampered by the regime's rejection of any form of land redistribution and its persistent upholding of landlord rights.[17] As for Sun's vision of state-led industrialization, little was accomplished apart from the establishment in 1932 of what became the National Resources Commission. The NRC aimed 'to create state-run basic industries for steel, electricity, machinery, and military arsenals' but 'was directly under Chiang and the military'.[18] In fact the regime's industrial interests and policies in the 1930s were probably affected – and legitimated – more by its perceived military needs than by the economic component of Sunist ideology.[19]

The Kuomintang

The proclamation of a period of political tutelage by the Kuomintang in 1928 meant that it was explicitly claiming to be the regime's official party.[20] In practice the Kuomintang also sought a complete political monopoly. The ruthlessness shown in suppressing the Communists in 1927 was scarcely less evident in the Kuomintang's determination to eliminate the few and small non-Communist parties. The repression was supported in law by the January 1931 Law for the Speedy Punishment of Crimes Endangering the Republic – an equivalent of the Law for the Defence of the State that had been used against political parties in Fascist Italy. After the Japanese take-over of Manchuria in 1931 the Kuomintang's repression of non-Communist parties was relaxed, but they were still prohibited from any open political activity.

The Kuomintang was one of the least extensive regime parties in history, in part because of the Leninist-style elitist procedures for ensuring that new members were dedicated revolutionaries.[21] In 1930 there were only about 300 000 civilian Party members in China, and although by 1935 membership had increased to nearly 500 000, this was still a very small percentage, much less than 1 per cent, of a population numbering in the hundreds of millions.[22] What is more, the membership was heavily concentrated in cities and towns and in central and south-east China.[23] In 1933 less than half of China's provinces could boast a proper provincial Party committee, and less than a fifth of China's counties contained any Party branches.

Like its fellow Leninist party in the Soviet Union, the Kuomintang had an extensive and hierarchical apparatus of Party administrators that supported a centralist and 'disciplined' interpretation of democratic centralism. Although the secretaries found at each level of the Party's administrative apparatus usually lacked the power of their Communist counterparts, the Party's central administrative departments seem to have been at least as powerful as their Communist equivalents. The most important department was the Organization Department, which supervised the administration of the Party down to local level and made and unmade lower Party committees.[24]

The Kuomintang's failings as a multi-role regime party were quite unusual in the sense that the Party combined a strong governing role with a very weakly performed social role and the lack of any political role. As the Kuomintang regime did not stage any elections or referendums during the period of tutelage, the Party did not perform a political role. Neither did it really perform anything in the way of a social role. For the Party was simply too small and urban to be an effective instrument for indoctrinating the people in the Kuomintang's national solidarity-building ideology. In any case, the Party lacked programmes – and any enthusiasm – for indoctrinating its own members, let alone for training them to instil the ideology in the hearts and minds of the public.[25] When the regime felt the need in 1934 for a major effort at indoctrinating the public, the task was handed to a wholly new organization, the New Life

Movement, which was kept separate from the Party.[26]

As for its governing role, in theory what the Kuomintang regime established in 1928 was a full-fledged party dictatorship, with a strong policy-making and supervisory governing role for the Party.[27] Like the Russian Communists from whom it had borrowed so many political ideas, the Kuomintang not only filled government posts with Party members but also transformed a political committee of the Party into the *de facto* government of the country.[28] An extra complication in the Chinese case was the existence of two separate political committees. The increasing membership of the Central Executive Committee, from only 24 full members in 1924 to 222 full members in 1945, meant that a smaller body was soon needed to take over the week-to-week running of the Party. But this authoritative smaller body was called not the Political Bureau but the Standing Committee of the CEC. For in 1924 the Kuomintang had already established an equivalent of the Communist Politburo – the Political Council subcommittee of the CEC. The Political Council was responsible for governmental and political as well as Party affairs and in practice there seems to have been a Party/government division of labour between these two Politburo-like political subcommittees, with the Standing Committee leading the Party and the Political Council going on to become the governmental policy-making body. The Political Council also became the key organ of Party rule over the government, legislature, and other central state organs. It soon showed a strong tendency to expand far beyond the size of a Politburo and eventually divided itself into a set of functionally specialized committees, enabling it to exercise 'a general control over legislation, appointments, and administrative matters' within the state institutions and apparatus.[29] It appears to have been performing in part a supervisory as well as policy-making governing role.

The Party's Organization Department and other administrative departments also exercised strong supervisory powers over the civilian state apparatus. The civil service was rapidly and extensively Party-ized and was brought under Party control at the central level by the Organization Department's taking control of the personnel units in the Ministries.[30]

The Party's central and provincial administrative departments often intervened in state officials' administrative activities or exercised a direct, quasi-state power over society, especially at provincial and county levels.[31]

The Party's relationship with the military was not very similar to Communist practice, despite the Kuomintang's 1924 decision to follow the Leninist model of a Party-ized army.[32] The Kuomintang actually went one step further than the Communists by conferring Party membership automatically on all officers and enlisted men of its National Revolutionary Army – a practice which was continued into the 1930s. More importantly, the Kuomintang also adopted the Communist system of political commissars, who in China were given the right to intervene or take command if the military commander was incapacitated or treacherous. However, the commissars were abolished in 1927 and therefore the new Kuomintang regime set up in the following year did not inherit a system of relatively strong Party supervision of the military,[33] and throughout the regime's life the Party would not perform a strong governing role in relation to the military arm of the state apparatus. All that remained of the Kuomintang's original vision of a Party-ized army was the disproportionately large number of military men holding Party membership. In 1932 the military membership was 670 000 and in 1935 it was over 1 million – that is, double the civilian membership.[34]

The Kuomintang party-state regime did not have a personal ruler or even an individual regime leader. Despite the obvious importance of General Chiang Kai-shek, he ruled in alliance with one or other of the two leading civilian figures in the Party. When Chiang became President of the National Government, his ally Hu Han-min became head of the legislature and the two men ran the Party and government in partnership until 1931.[35] Then Hu formed an alliance with the other leading civilian figure in the Kuomintang, the leftist Wang Ching-wei, and together they demanded that Chiang quit his public offices as the price for their maintaining Party unity – which had become all the more important in the face of the Japanese take-over of Manchuria in September 1931.[36] In December Chiang agreed to resign from both the Presidency of the National Government and his recently acquired post of head of government. But the new government could not operate without Chiang's support (for example, the regime's central armies would not back the new government) and it collapsed before the end of January.[37] Forming an alliance now with Wang, a vindicated Chiang returned to political centre stage. He did not take up his former offices of head of state and head of government – the latter being acquired by his new ally, Wang. But Chiang's new military post, Chairman of the Military Council, would soon prove more powerful than any civilian office as the Kuomintang regime was transformed from a party to a military type of ideological one-party state.

From Party-State to Military-Party Regime

From the outset the Kuomintang one-party state was in a sense partly a military-party regime. For most of the territory nominally under its control was in reality ruled by warlords who had allied themselves with the Kuomintang during the Northern Expedition, on the understanding that they would retain their existing autonomy in their new roles as the Kuomintang equivalent of provincial Governors.[38] It has been estimated that in 1929 the Kuomintang central government 'controlled only 8 percent of the nation's area and 20 percent of the population'.[39] Outside this Kuomintang heartland, centred upon Shanghai and Nanking, China remained more like a confederation of military regimes.

The shift to a thoroughly military-party regime occurred in the mid-1930s when the Kuomintang's central military command acquired the right to rule over the provinces which were under the Kuomintang's control. The transfer of authority to the military arose from the Kuomintang's desire to eliminate the threat posed by its former ally, the Chinese Communist Party.[40] The local military campaigns of 1930 and early 1931 against the Communist strongholds to the south-west of the Kuomintang heartland were military failures, much to the consternation of the authorities in Nanking. These failures led to the Kuomintang army's high command being given power over civilian authorities as well as military forces within the Communist-affected provinces, which were classified as 'Bandit Suppression Zones'. Eventually even the regime's two most firmly controlled provinces, Kiangsu and Chekiang, joined eight neighbouring provinces in being classified as Bandit Suppression Zones. What is more, the Party's CEC and Political Council passed resolutions in 1931 that gave the military high command clear authority over Party as well as state affairs in these Bandit Suppression Provinces.[41]

This ruling authority was handed over to the National Military Council (or Commission), an administrative organ which had recently been set up by the regime to direct and co-ordinate the military and political–administrative activities of the central Kuomintang military forces. By handing over such authority to this military administrative organ the Party authorities were in a sense – and doubtless inadvertently – transforming it into a *de facto* government. It was acquiring a policy-making governing role without the need for a coup or any other form of military intervention in politics. What is more, the Military Council soon developed an 'extensive administrative apparatus of its own', whose administrative activities often overlapped with those of the government Ministries and of the Party's central headquarters.[42] The Secretary-General and Secretariat of the Military Council headed an administrative apparatus that extended down through the provinces, the administrative inspectorate districts, and the counties, to the towns and villages.[43] This extensive apparatus of military administrators exercised the authority over Party and state bestowed on the Military Council and used that authority to implement a form of military control over the administration of the Bandit Suppression Provinces. In other words, this military administrative apparatus was acquiring a strong supervisory governing role in relation to the Party and state components of the regime.

On the face of it such apparently only 'administrative' changes bore fruit for the Kuomintang regime. There was not only a more effective implementation of military strategy, culminating in the successful 1933–4 campaign which forced the Communists into their famous Long March to the north, but also an extension of the regime's central authority into the eight, at least partially warlord-control-led, provinces included among the Bandit Suppression Provinces.[44] However, this was an extension of not the Kuomintang's authority but that of the Military Council's administrators, who 'exercised political control in the Bandit Suppression Provinces'.[45] The Military Council itself had clearly become in practice the *de facto* government of the provinces under the regime's central control. During the anti-Communist military campaigns of 1932–3 'the actual center of the Kuomintang regime shifted from Nanking to Nanchang', the location of the Military Council Chairman's field headquarters and of the Secretary-General and Secretariat of the Council.[46] Later the centre of the regime would shift with the Chairman's field headquarters to Wuchang and then in 1935 to Chunking. 'It was in these temporary headquarters that major military, party and administrative policies were actually discussed and determined; then they were submitted to Nanking for formal ratification' by the appropriate Party and state organs.[47]

In theory the regime remained under party, not military, rule. The CEC or the Political Council was supposed to set the policy guidelines for the Military Council and had the right of final decision over even military matters.[48] But such safeguards were nullified by the fact that the Chairman of the Military Council was also the pre-eminent figure in the Party – Chiang Kai-shek. And he was able to win such control over the Party's CEC, the Central Executive Committee which wielded ultimate executive authority over the Party, that it authorized whatever policies he wanted.[49]

Chiang could count on the strong support of a very powerful Party faction known as the CC Clique or Organization (Department) Group.[50] The members of this faction viewed Chiang as the leader of China and were loyal to him personally, irrespective of whatever formal positions he held in the Party or regime. The CC or Organization faction was made up largely of conservative middle- and lower-level Party officials and an increasingly large proportion of the Central Executive Committee was linked to this faction in the early 1930s. When combined with the less organized support that Chiang could count on from other members of the Party as a bastion against the Communists and as leader of the (central) Kuomintang's military wing, this enabled him to win control of the Party CEC by the end of 1932.

To maintain and extend his support within the military membership Chiang had been able to deploy another personally loyal Party faction – a unique secret movement or 'party within the party' that was commonly referred to as the Blue Shirts. The most credible explanation of the origin of the name Blue Shirts is that it was 'used first by the Japanese to slander the movement by equating it to Mussolini's Black Shirts'.[51] Thereafter it was commonly used by members themselves, as well as the general public, to refer to this secret-society-like political movement. So secret was the Blue Shirt movement that historians still differ over what its real name actually was, but the organization in its widest sense and most public face was probably known as the (Chinese) Restoration (or Revival) Society.[52] Chiang had initiated the founding of the Blue Shirts in 1932 and was from the outset their permanent leader.[53] They demanded absolute obedience to Chiang from not only fellow Blue Shirts but also the Party and all Chinese, on the basis that he was the supreme leader of China. However, Chiang never actually publicly acknowledged the Blue Shirts' existence, and the public knew of them only by rumour. The movement seems to have had a membership of over 10 000, was structured very much like a Leninist party and was dominated by the many army officers among its membership. In fact Chiang appears to have viewed the Blue Shirts as primarily an instrument for controlling and extending his support within the military. The Blue Shirts 'almost completely dominated political training and the party organization within the military' and held a similar position in the military's officer-training schools or academies.[54] More importantly, the Blue Shirts had a dominant presence in the Military Council's administrative apparatus and thus ensured that the administration of military rule was in the hands of officers personally loyal to Chiang as the leader of their secret movement.[55]

By the end of 1935 Chiang Kai-shek was clearly the individual leader and probably the personal ruler of the Kuomintang regime. He had reacquired from Wang the post of head of government and was 'acting chairman' of both the Standing Committee and the Political Council of the Party.[56] Chiang now no longer needed to ally himself with any other Party figure – he had no need of even a junior or token political partner.

Chiang and the military acquired yet more power with the outbreak of war with Japan in 1937. The Military Council became China's publicly acknowledged *de facto* government, with even the Party's administrative departments placed under its control.[57] In the provinces the newly created military War Zone commanders were not only given authority over provincial governments but also made the top-ranking Party officials in their zones – a unique example of military 'supervision' of the regime party.[58] In January 1938 an Organic Law of the Military Council regularized the Military Council's position by bestowing on its Chairman the formal powers of Commander-in-Chief, and, more importantly, empowering him 'to direct the people of the whole nation for the purpose of national defense'.[59] The ultimate confirmation of military rule – or rather personal rule by a military leader – was the Party's 1938 decision to provide Chiang Kai-shek with a dictatorial and formal leadership position over the Party – the post of Tsung-ts'ai of the Party.

However, as early as 1935 the regime had clearly shifted from a party to a military type of one-party state. The shift in type brought more changes to the Party's roles than to the content of the ideology. The Party had given up its governing role to the military, and the military regime leader and then personal ruler had no inclination to restore that role to the Party. Chiang's long-standing position on the question of Party-state relations was that Party control over the state 'only meant that party ideology should be used to guide the state'.[60] As for that ideology itself, the inauguration of the Chiang-backed New Life Movement in the mid-1930s added a vulgarized Confucianism to the corpus of officially recognized sacred principles and virtues. The New Life Movement's creed or dogma was *li-i-lieu-ch'ih* – a combination of four moral and social virtues which can be loosely translated as 'propriety-justice-honesty-sense of self-respect'.[61] This has been described as 'a Confucianism for the masses', 'a sloganized Confucianism' that had been reduced to its 'ethical essentials' for mass consumption.[62] The doctrine of the New Life Movement had been heavily influenced by Chiang's strongly Confucianist views and orientation, which had become more obvious after his ending of the Communist alliance in 1927.[63] When he finally came to write a full-scale ideological text of his own in the early 1940s, *China's Destiny*, the Confucianist orientation was apparent in his advocating of a psychological reconstruction of the nation 'through educational programmes that would generate the restoration of China's ancient values and virtues'.[64] Chiang also asserted in *China's Destiny* that the country's future rested entirely with the Kuomintang.[65] The ideological commitment to the one-party state had continued long after the shift to military rule and it would be continued by the regime's otherwise very different successor, the Communist party-state regime of 1949 onwards.

2   COMMUNIST POLAND

The Polish shift from the party-state to military-party type of one-party state differed greatly from the Kuomintang example. The Polish Communist party-state regime ruled by the Polish United Workers' Party was a Soviet satellite state, in which the governing role performed by the Party in typical Communist fashion was affected by the latent threat of Soviet intervention. The political threat which provoked the shift from party to military type of one-party state was very different from the situation which produced the shift in regime type in Kuomintang China. And the transition from party-state to military-party regime in Poland occurred quite literally overnight and without prior authorization from the Party's Politburo and Central Committee. In fact the military wing of the Communist Party and regime took power on 13 December 1981 in a manner that resembled a typical military coup – declaring martial law and establishing a military junta. The period of military rule was also apparently more short-lived (less than two years) than in Kuomintang China. Martial law was suspended in December 1982 and formally ended in July 1983, the junta was

dissolved, and power was seemingly handed back to the Party.
However, the differences between the Chinese and Polish
cases are not as great as they at first appear. In reality the
military take-over in Poland was not as abrupt as the 'coup'
of 13 December might suggest; the military had become
increasingly involved in politics in the period leading up to
the declaration of martial law. And, as in the Chinese case,
a military leader continued to rule – and thus a military-
party regime continued to exist – until the one-party state's
demise. Although not as powerful as Chiang Kai-shek became, General Jaruzelski would still come as near to being
a personal ruler as seems possible in a Soviet satellite state.

The threat facing the Polish Communist one-party state in
the lead-up to becoming a military-party regime was very
different from the rebellious warlords and insurrectionary
Communists plaguing the Kuomintang party-state regime
in the early 1930s. Economic decline and the unpopularity
of an incompetent and corrupt party élite had forced the
Communist leadership in 1980 not only to remove First
Secretary Gierek as head of the Party and regime but also
to allow the development of an independent trade union
movement, Solidarity, which soon was powerful enough to
force other changes in Party policy. Moreover, the explosive growth of Solidarity to an eventual membership of some
10 million had in turn stimulated a liberalizing, democra-
tizing attitude among the ordinary membership of the Party.[66]
Many disillusioned members left the Party and even more –
about a third of its membership – remained but also joined
Solidarity.[67] The Party's beleaguered and fragmented Politburo responded to the pressure from below by allowing
decentralization and democratization at the lower levels of
the Party, and only a fraction of the discredited Central
Committee and Politburo were re-elected at the Party Congress in July 1981.[68] Therefore the Party was facing a threat
to its disciplined cohesion as a Communist party at the
same time as it was facing a threat to its monopoly of power
from Solidarity's increasingly confident claims to have a say
in policy making. In other words, there was a threat to the
traditional Marxist–Leninist view of both the nature and
leading role of the Party. Such a view was still held by

Party conservatives and of course by the same Soviet leadership which had ordered the invasion of Czechoslovakia in 1968 to maintain Communist orthodoxy in that Soviet satellite.

Therefore the ideologically conservative military wing of the Party took charge of a drastic attempt at crushing Solidarity and dealing with Poland's economic crisis. The key figure was the long-time (since 1968) Defence Minister and virtually *de facto* leader of the military, General Jaruzelski, who was not only a long-standing (since 1971) member of the Politburo but also was well trusted by the Soviets – during the 1970s he had dealt with them directly on military matters.[69] In 1980 he secretly fended off the prospect of a Polish replay of the Soviet invasion of Czechoslovakia by promising the Soviet leaders that the Polish military would itself eliminate the threat posed by Solidarity.[70] Planning for a possible use of martial law began as early as August 1980 and – under Soviet pressure – had reached a mature stage by March 1981. The plans were further developed with the use of political intelligence gathered by military detachments deployed in October–November ostensibly to help with food distribution. Jaruzelski himself had become Prime Minister in February (thereby becoming formal head of the National Defence Committee that was coordinating planning for martial law), a close military associate became Minister of the Interior in August, and another close associate, the army's Chief of Staff, became an alternate member of the Politburo in October. The continuing refusal of the politically weak head of the Party, First Secretary Kania, to authorize the use of force against Solidarity ensured his replacement by Jaruzelski in October. Thus there had been months of creeping militarization, both open and hidden, of politics and rule in Poland before Jaruzelski announced to the nation on 13 December that, in accordance with Article 33 of the Constitution, a State of War – of martial law – had been declared. From then on Poland was very clearly a military type of one-party state.

The structure of this new military-party regime resembled a typical military regime more than the Kuomintang regime had done. Unlike in China, there was a military junta, the Military Council of National Salvation (WRON), comprising twenty senior commanders and claiming that it had a mandate from the Polish military to carry out its tasks.[71] The degree to which this political committee of the military was actually a *de facto* governing body – in the sense of making the week-to-week policy decisions – is still disputed, but there is no disagreement about its having held the ultimate formal authority within the regime.[72] The new regime's key administrative bodies, the military–civilian National Defence Committee and provincial Defence Committees, were somewhat similar to the Security and Administration Committees set up by the Burmese military-party regime. The Polish committees differed from the Burmese in being the legally prescribed governmental bodies in a State of War and being officially headed by, respectively, the Prime Minister and the provincial Governors.[73] But of course Jaruzelski was now Prime Minister and eventually nearly half (ten) of the provincial Governorships were held by military men.[74] Furthermore, the provincial Committees of Defence had very influential military deputy-chairmen and were officially supervised by military commissars to ensure compliance with the decisions of the Military Council and National Defence Committee.[75] A conglomeration of such military plenipotentiaries, commissars, Inspection Teams and Operational Groups acted as the representatives of the Military Council and National Defence Committee and performed a supervisory, governing role that went far beyond that of Primo de Rivera's military *delegados* – extending from the central Ministries down to the villages and even to many factories.[76] The regime's militarization of the factories also went far beyond Franco's policy of having strikers tried by military courts. In Poland employees of major factories were placed under military discipline and could be tried by military courts if they disobeyed any work-related instructions.

The central Party organs that had formerly been the fount of political authority now had little more than an advisory role in policy making. Like their Kuomintang counterparts, they simply rubber-stamped key policy decisions made by the military leader and his close associates or assistants.[77] In the regions the Party's organs and officials were not explicitly subordinated to the military as their Kuomintang counterparts were in China, but they were now, in the words of a Central Committee member, 'nowhere to be seen'.[78]

However, one of the new regime's (and the Soviet leaders') main concerns was that the Party be rebuilt into an orthodox Communist regime party that would carry out and defend its leading role in standard Communist fashion. The rebuilding of the Party involved (a) a recentralizing and redisciplining of the Party's structure and processes and (b) an extensive purge of its membership, including its administrators.[79] The centralizing and disciplining returned the Party to something much closer to the norm for a Communist party, controlled from the top down by its hierarchical administrative apparatus. The purge was aimed not just at liberals and those moderates deemed to be unreliable but also at any corrupt Party bosses and administrators of the 1970s who still remained in power – altogether more than half the Party's full-time officials were removed. (The purge of ordinary Party members was carried out by the Party's own control commissions but the purge of its administrative apparatus was carried out or supervised by military men.) But when the rebuilt Party took up its leading role again, it would be as an instrument of the military leader who had become its First Secretary and had used the purge to further consolidate his hold on the Party.

Although the obviously military aspect of the regime ended in 1983 with the end of martial law and the junta, Poland remained a military-party regime – albeit now a quite civilianized example – because General Jaruzelski did not relinquish the personal power he had acquired in 1981–2. In fact he would come as close to being a personal ruler as could be expected in a Soviet satellite state. Even before becoming First Secretary and thus informal head of the Party, he was already Prime Minister, head of the National Defence Committee, and Minister of Defence. During the period of martial law he was also head of the Military Council junta, and in 1985 he became head of state, the Chairman of the Council of State. (Changes to the structure of the National Defence Committee allowed him to remain its chairman and the military's *de facto* Commander-in-Chief despite relinquishing in 1985 his post of Prime Minister to a civilian technocrat, who thus took over the responsibility and blame for the continuing economic crisis.[80]) It is true that he lacked a personality cult like that enjoyed by Ceauşescu in Romania, but Jaruzelski's leadership of the military provided him with a source of power that was not available to any of the other rulers of Communist Eastern Europe except Tito in Yugoslavia. Moreover, Jaruzelski had quickly secured his personal hold on the Party and after the ending of martial law he ruled largely through his Party posts as informal head of the Politburo and formal head of the Secretariat.[81] He had introduced several of his cronies and assistants into the Politburo in the months before and after martial law was declared and he had come to dominate it as well as the Secretariat.[82] As First Secretary he had quickly adapted the Secretariat and its departments to his own purposes, using the Secretaries as his 'agents' for controlling the Party, and had 'brought to the fore apparatchiks personally loyal to him'.[83]

Like other military rulers, though, Jaruzelski used military men as trusted instruments of his rule, even after the end of the martial law period.[84] For example, Generals close to Jaruzelski held the posts of Minister of the Interior (including the police), Minister of Local Administration, chief of the Prime Minister's personal cabinet, and head of the Secretariat's Cadres (Personnel) Department. He also allowed a degree of military supervision, if only at a monitoring level, to continue on after 1983. There were periodic inspections at regional and local levels by military officers who reported back through military channels to Jaruzelski's National Defence Committee.

The 10th Party Congress in 1986 officially marked the end of the rebuilding of the Party into an orthodox and 'trustworthy' Communist regime party.[85] But the Congress also 'demonstrated that Jaruzelski had achieved a degree of personal power unprecedented in postwar Polish politics'.[86] For example, the election of a new Politburo saw the dropping of the last independent voices among its membership and the introduction of yet more of Jaruzelski's cronies and associates. Three more Generals and two of his most trusted Party administrators became full or alternate members. What is more, the presence of the new Soviet leader, General Secretary Gorbachev, at the Congress clearly signalled the Soviet Union's continuing approval of Jaruzelski's actions – his Soviet principal clearly approved of his achieving a degree of personal rule within the Polish regime.

The military-party regime added little of note to the ideology of the Polish one-party state. At first there was an attempt to legitimate the regime by emphasizing nationalism, patriotism, and national solidarity, with the military justifying its rule by claiming that 'the Polish soldier-patriot had been compelled to act to save the nation from fratricidal conflict'.[87] But Jaruzelski's half-hearted espousal of nationalism was soon replaced by a renewed emphasis on the inherited body of Marxist–Leninist ideology and its belief in proletarian internationalism rather than 'bourgeois nationalism'.[88] The only new ideological elements were the regime's legalism and emphasis on work discipline – indeed the Military Council junta's slogan was 'Law, Order, and Work'.[89] The legalism was displayed in the regime's preference for promulgating policies in the form of laws passed by parliament rather than in the form of decrees issued by the junta itself.[90] The emphasis on work discipline was not only displayed in but also legitimated the regime's two most prominent policies. The first of them, of course, was the elimination of the Solidarity movement, and the second was the attempt to increase productivity by militarizing the factories – the regime's only new economic policy.[91] The continuing failure to develop any effective new economic policies eventually destroyed the regime's credibility and self-confidence, leaving it ready to relinquish power peacefully at the end of the 1980s as part of the general collapse of Communism throughout Eastern Europe.

11 From Military-Party to Party-State Regime

1 POST-REVOLUTION MEXICO

The Mexican example of ideological one-party state is easily the oldest surviving example and is also one of the few to have been transformed from a military-party to party-state type. The origins of the Mexican one-party state lie in the Mexican Revolution that began in 1910 in opposition to the constitutionally clothed dictatorship of General Porfirio Díaz, who had been President almost continually since 1876. The revolutionary uprising, demanding political and land reforms, finally dislodged him from power in 1911. But Mexico was soon left in a virtually anarchic condition as the revolutionary leaders and forces fought among themselves for control of the country. The continual civil wars and general disorder cost as many as a million lives and also spawned a host of political–military leaders, the *caudillos.* Hundreds of these self-taught military commanders, who had been middle-class civilians before 1910, acquired their title of 'General' in command of personal armies that had been recruited from the populace of the commander's region or locality. Zapata and 'Pancho' Villa became the most widely known of Mexico's revolutionary leaders, the former as a classic example of the leader of a peasant revolt and the latter as a classic example of a *caudillo* with bandit-like tendencies. But it was Vanustiano Carranza who eventually emerged as the victor in the struggle for power and became the first President of Mexico to take office under the terms of the new federal Constitution promulgated by a constitutional conference in 1917.

As a civilian politician and social conservative Carranza had difficulty in maintaining the support of the socially radical military wing of his loosely knit following. The military wing comprised the victorious revolutionary Generals and their armies of poorly trained ex-peasants, ex-workers,

217

and ex-bandits, which since May 1917 had collectively borne the title of the National Army. But its commanders were *caudillos*, exercising independent political as well as military power in their regions and localities. (Many of them were allied to or supporters of political parties, which were usually regionally based or had been formed by trade union or peasant leaders to represent their organization's interests.) Therefore an obvious comparison can be made with the Chinese warlords of the same era, though the stronger central government in Mexico meant that it was less a confederation of regional military regimes and more like the federal system that its Constitution claimed Mexico to be. Another, more important, difference was the ideological influence of the Revolution, which ensured that the country was outwardly a working multi-party democracy.

The Revolution's ideology and the Constitution prohibited a President from being re-elected, and when Carranza began to prepare an obscure civilian to be his successor, he ran into furious opposition from the already disgruntled military wing of his following. In April 1920 the powerful north-western section of the military revolted against Carranza, claiming that he was preparing to impose the next President upon the country. The rebels' preferred candidate for the Presidency was General Obregón, the Revolution's most famous and brilliant military commander. Support for Carranza soon collapsed as Generals from other regions joined the revolt, and he was murdered by one of his few remaining followers. With General Obregón's election as President the regime became fully military in nature despite the outward respect it showed for the constitutional and democratic principles contained in the Revolution's ideology. For the presidential elections of 1920 and thereafter were so subject to rigging and influence by the federal government – and by the 'official' candidate's regional backers – that they certainly cannot be described as democratic.

President Obregón could dominate civilian politics at the national level, where the success of political parties in Congress and elections depended upon his support. But as the manner of his acquisition of the Presidency had shown, the military dimension to the country's politics was more important than the civilian. Obregón made some attempt to civilianize the regime by including only three military men in his Cabinet and encouraging officers to concentrate on their military duties and stay out of politics.[1] Yet he also chose another military man as his successor.

Obregón was able to have his Minister of Government (the Interior) and former revolutionary comrade-in-arms, General Calles, succeed him as President in 1924 – though not before facing a major military revolt by Generals opposed to his choice. Calles continued Obregón's policy of professionalizing the military. Many of the *caudillo* officers were sidelined and substantial progress was made towards transforming the rest of the National Army into a professional army.[2] But a more immediately significant development was the amending of the Constitution to allow a President one, non-consecutive re-election – a move which cleared the way for Obregón to return to the Presidency. After he and Calles defeated a military revolt led by his presidential rivals, Obregón duly won the 1928 presidential elections. However, months before his inauguration President-elect Obregón was assassinated by a religious fanatic, leaving a dangerous political vacuum.

As part of his response to this political crisis Calles broached the idea of establishing a new, official party that would incorporate the whole coalition of forces that had carried out the Revolution – the peasantry and the working class as well as the party bosses and the military. In his words, he sought to shift from 'personalist' to 'institutionalist' politics.[3] He officially founded the new party on 1 December 1928, the day that his term as President ended, and called it the Partido Nacional Revolucionario. Although not all the Revolutionary parties would join the PNR, the new party would become the regime's official party in all but name and law. In establishing a regime party Calles was also transforming an already ideological military regime into a military-*party* regime and an ideological one-party state. The ideological component had emerged from the Revolution more than a decade earlier, being expressed programmatically in the sacred 1917 Constitution.

The Revolutionary Ideology

The 1917 Constitution encapsulated in one sacred document the varied goals of the many different groups that
had taken part in the overthrow of Díaz and the fratricidal civil war among the revolutionaries themselves. The
new Constitution would be depicted as the banner of the
Revolution, the bearer of the Revolution's programme, and
the repository of solutions to Mexicans' common problems.[4]
In total it provided a set of ideological goals or principles
that could legitimate a regime and a wide range of quite
radical policies – extensive land reform, workers' rights,
nationalism, anticlericalism, and a liberal democracy centred upon a strong Presidency with a one-term tenure.

The Mexican Constitution was the first in the world to
include an extensive set of 'social' provisions.[5] It declared
that the nation had the right to impose limits on the size
of land holdings and to redistribute land. Limits were to
be set on the size of the big landowners' holdings and the
excess used to restore the communal land lost by the villages and to ensure that each village was relatively self-
sufficient. The Constitution also contained measures
improving the lot of the working class, such as making the
eight-hour day obligatory, and measures designed to increase
workers' power, such as provisions which facilitated strikes
but hampered lockouts.

A nationalist attitude was evident in the Constitution's
ban on foreign individuals and companies owning land without government approval. Other provisions reserving the
ultimate ownership of all subsoil wealth to the government
were also nationalistic, as the exploitation of Mexico's min-
eral wealth was very largely in foreign hands. Anticlericalism
was evident in the provisions banning religious organizations from holding land and from having anything to do
with the promised free and compulsory elementary school
education. The Church was also prohibited from taking
any part in political activities – the clergy were even denied the vote – and political parties were prohibited from
including any religious reference in their name, such as
calling themselves Catholic or Christian.

As for the Constitution's specifically political content, the revolutionaries' opposition to Díaz's continual re-election as President was reflected in the provision prohibiting a President from serving more than one term. Apart from this ban on re-election the political content of the Constitution followed the lines of many other liberal-democratic constitutions in the American hemisphere. In addition to federalism there was an extensive list of civil liberties and personal rights, checks and balances between separate executive, legislative and judicial branches, and a bicameral Congress comprising a Senate and a Chamber of Deputies. However, the President was given stronger powers than his United States equivalent, such as the power to issue decree legislation over a wide range of matters.[6]

Although there was therefore ideological legitimation available for a sweeping set of reforming policies to be implemented by a powerful Presidency, this opportunity was not properly exploited by the military regime of the 1920s. Obregón's and Calles's governments did make some effort towards implementing the Constitution's promises to workers and peasants but there was still a long way to go to meet the goals set by the constitutional provisions on land reform. And while it is true that Calles actually went well beyond the Constitution's anticlericalism in launching a full-scale attack against the Church, this had the effect of producing a serious rural revolt, known as the Cristero rebellion or the Cristiada, that lasted for several years and cost many lives.

The creation of a one-party state seems eventually to have had an effect on policy. For in the early 1930s a new and radical social programme emerged within the Party in the form of a Six Year Plan to be implemented during the 1934–40 presidential term. (In fact some of the Plan's goals went beyond and outside the Revolutionary goals described in the Constitution.[7]) After his inauguration President Cárdenas quickly set about implementing the Plan and during his term more land was distributed to the peasantry than had been in the whole 1917–34 period, with the result that by the time he left office nearly half of Mexico's arable land had been redistributed since the Revolution began.[8] Cárdenas even met some of the Revolutionary nationalist aspirations by having the railroad and oil industries taken over from foreign ownership or control. During the presidential term of his successor, though, there was a moderating or 'consolidation' of Cárdenas's policies. President Ávila Camacho was ideologically a moderate and was a professed Christian, not a committed anticlerical like Cárdenas. With the shift in 1946 to a civilian, party-state regime under President Aleman, the country also began to experience the alternating shifts towards and away from capitalism that would become characteristic of the policy direction of the Mexican one-party state.

As for the Constitution's legitimating the regime itself, the military and then military-party regimes were legitimated by the Constitution only because they disguised their military nature behind a façade of liberal democracy. The liberal and democratic principles expressed in the Constitution had to appear to be adhered to if the regimes were to maintain their ideological legitimacy. So there was never any real possibility that the regime party established in 1929 would be given a complete political monopoly – that Mexico would become a literal one-party state. Other political parties and supposedly competitive elections had to be allowed to exist to provide a credible disguise for the undemocratic nature of the regime party's hold on the Presidency and the many other public offices.

The PNR and PRM (and the Military)

Throughout its long history and under three different names (PNR, PRM, and PRI) the Mexican regime party has enjoyed a monopoly in effectiveness that has been based upon not only the use of state patronage but also a more direct form of state aid – vote-rigging. The Ministry of Government was responsible for supervising, or rather controlling,[9] the country's domestic politics and had the informal responsibility of ensuring that the 'correct' election results were achieved. To that end the Ministry of Government officials administering the electoral system were quite prepared to rig the vote. One reason for the several military revolts of the 1920s was the realization that the President's control of the election machinery through the Ministry of Government made it impossible for his opponents to defeat him and his 'official' candidate with ballots rather than bullets. From 1929 onwards the Ministry supported the regime's official party and helped to create a classic example of the semi-competitive form of substantive one-party state.

But Mexico by no means provided a classic example of a disciplined regime party; on the contrary, the official party at first was an extreme example of a loosely knit political party.[10] The delegates to the founding conference of the PNR in 1929 were meant to represent equally the military, the peasants and the workers, but the two civilian sectors were split into a multitude of various parties and groups. In addition to the peasant and labour unions and other interest groups, there were the many regional political parties, often led or dominated by *caudillos*. The delegates decided that each party and interest group would retain its identity and independent structure within the new party. Only the Generals were given individual membership of the PNR; everyone else had to be content with an indirect, affiliated form of membership through belonging to one of the parties or groups incorporated into the PNR. The new regime party was therefore more like a political confederation than a political party and is still a unique example of how far the confederal approach can be taken in constructing a party.

However, the state assistance – the patronage and vote-rigging – which guaranteed the Party's dominance over its competitors also had the effect of strengthening the position of the central Party organs and officials that controlled the distribution of these 'resources' within the Party.[11] The centralizing tendency was institutionalized in 1932 when another PNR national convention replaced its confederal structure with a more normal party structure based upon individual membership. The confederated regional parties were dissolved and the interest groups were excluded from actual membership of the Party.

In 1938 the PNR was renamed and radically restructured.[12] It was renamed the Partido de la Revolución Mexicana and was reorganized into four different functional/occupational sectors – an innovation in party structure that would remain unique until the arrival of the Golkar regime party in Indonesia. The agricultural or peasant sector of the PRM incorporated the various peasant unions and associations, while the labour sector incorporated most of the trade unions. The 'popular' sector was a residual, catch-all grouping which incorporated a wide range of groups: skilled-workers' trade unions, small-business associations, youth organizations, the medical and legal professions, and the federation of state-employee unions. Finally, there was the military sector. The PRM's explicit inclusion of the military as an official component of the Party was in itself an innovatory move and provoked a heated public debate. But, as Cárdenas himself pointed out, the military would be confined by the Party's rules to having only a minority influence within the PRM. For the Party operated according to the principle of giving equal weight to each sector's views, despite the disparity in size between the sectors – the peasant sector, for example, contributed more than half of the Party's official membership of almost 4 million.[13]

The new party's administrative apparatus appeared to be quite weak, being 'little more than a skeletal framework of committees following a vertical-horizontal arrangement corresponding to the national, state, and local levels of government'.[14] But the vertical restructuring of the regime party into functional/occupational sectors strengthened the centralizing tendency that had been evident ever since the regime party's founding. In fact this restructuring 'had the effect of sounding a death-knell for the political machines of the once all-powerful local *caudillos*'.[15]

Although it was in some degree a multi-role party, the Mexican regime party was primarily concerned with its political role of selecting and electing candidates to the many federal, state and local public offices, especially to the powerful executive offices. The PNR/PRM and the interest groups incorporated within the regime party did perform something of a social role in keeping the Revolution alive in the hearts and minds of the people. But the regime party performed little in the way of a governing role.[16] It is true that the Party quite often seemed to initiate official policies and activities. And at each level of government, from federal to local, the chief of the relevant executive committee of the Party was regarded as an unofficial but important part of the governing circle. The Party and state became so intertwined in even their own officials' minds that the Party laid claim to the petty privileges enjoyed by a state organ. However, the Party organs and officials did not act as a *de facto* government or perform anything more than a monitoring supervisory role. The chief of a Party executive committee was unofficially a subordinate and (often) an appointee of his state equivalent – be it the federal President, the state Governor, or the municipal president. The unofficial relationship between the regime party and the state in Mexico actually seems similar to Party-state relations in Fascist Italy and Primo de Rivera's Spain, despite the Mexican regime's very different ideology and policies. It was the military, rather than the regime party, that for a time performed a significant governing role in Mexico.

Initially the military continued to play as prominent a part in the new military-party regime as it had in the 1920–8 era military regime. Although there was still no junta, military men 'were so dominant during the *Sexenio* [1929–34], that they did not even feel obliged to seek civilian support'.[17] They held the Presidency, a number of Cabinet posts, and half of the state Governorships. As for their hold on the regime party, not only was Calles the undisputed leader of the PNR but also he and other Generals dominated the Party's executive committee – one of them, General Cárdenas, also became President of the Party. Furthermore, the political influence wielded by regional and local *caudillos* meant that military men were in a position to exercise strong supervision over the grassroots of the regime party as well as over its summit.[18]

Through their control of federal, state and local government, military men also had the means to exercise strong supervision over the civilian state apparatus.[19] Public employees in Mexico did not in practice enjoy the protected status of a career civil servant and were subject to the vagaries of an unofficial 'spoils' system. They were all to some extent the political followers of members or controllers (mostly military men) of federal, state, or local governments. If the Mexican military had been a more disciplined or even just a more united organization, it could have performed a strong and extensive, rather than only a significant,

supervisory role. Certainly military men played a very prominent part in the early years of the Mexican military-party
regime.

However, the part played by the military in the Mexican
one-party state began to decline or shrink after 1934. In
part this was owing to changes in the nature of the National Army which had the effect of depoliticizing most of
the military. By 1934 the Army was no longer a collection
of personal armies and was becoming much more of a hierarchical, corporate organization. Generals Cedillo and
Almazán were the last remaining examples of regional
caudillos commanding powerful forces who were loyal to them
personally rather than to the Army hierarchy.[20] The other
caudillos had been eliminated during the several military
revolts of the 1920s or had allowed their armies to be properly assimilated into the increasingly professional National
Army.[21] During his term as the country's President in 1934–
40 General Cárdenas implemented a programme of further
professionalizing the Army, which had the effect of encouraging the middle and junior ranks of the officer corps to
stay out of politics.[22] Thus the better trained, younger officers
viewed the Army's Revolution-era Generals as less qualified
to command than they were themselves because these Generals, the old *caudillos*, 'were politicians rather than soldiers'.[23] Although military men still held more than half
of the chief executive and Cabinet posts at federal and state
levels,[24] the junior and middle-ranking bulk of the officer
corps was becoming quite uninterested in assuming any
responsibility for running the country.

The depoliticization of the officer corps was evident in
the part the military sector played within the PRM. The
'election' of military delegates to the national Party conventions was supervised by the War Ministry on behalf of
the President, the constitutional Commander-in-Chief, who
gave the delegates instructions and had them explicitly agree
that they would participate in the Party as ordinary citizens rather than as representatives of the military.[25] Therefore, in practice the military sector's delegates were really
no more than a source of loyal support for President
Cárdenas within the Party. His successor as President, General Ávila Camacho, actually eliminated the Party's mili-

tary sector in December 1940. Any officers wishing to remain in the Party – and significantly most did not – became members of the popular sector.[26] By the 1940s the momentum of civilization was so great that even the Presidency itself would be relinquished to a civilian at the next presidential election. However, the smooth transition to civilian rule and a party-state regime was greatly assisted by the fact that Cárdenas was one of the two examples of personal rule that were produced by the military-party regime.

Personal Rule

The first example of personal rule was provided by Calles in the years following the end of his term as President in 1928. Although these years saw the military play its most prominent part in the regime, General Calles was clearly more than just an agent of the military. As the PNR's *jefe máximo* (supreme chief) and the unofficially titled Supreme Chief of the Revolution he 'controlled the nation's affairs from behind the throne of three successive presidents: Emilio Portes Gil (1928–1930), Pascual Ortiz Rubio (1930–1932), and Abelardo Rodríguez (1932–1934)'.[27] This was the era of what some Mexicans labelled *callismo*.[28] However, Calles now lacked the constitutionally powerful and historically prestigious office of President. Nor was he the sole and undisputed leader of the military; it was jointly led by a quinumvirate of five senior Generals of whom Calles was only 'first among equals'.[29] As Cárdenas was one of these five leading Generals (as well as being a popular War Minister and a leading figure in the PNR), it is hardly surprising that when he was elected President in 1934, he was not prepared to be another of Calles's tame or puppet Presidents. A trial of strength between the two Generals was not long in coming and resulted in Calles's being forced into retirement and then exile.

Cárdenas emerged from the struggle against Calles in a stronger personal position than his rival had ever achieved. Unlike Calles, he held both the powerful Presidency and control over the regime party. (Although Cárdenas would not seek the title of *jefe máximo* of the Party, in reality from now on every federal President would automatically become the *ex officio*, if informal, leader of the regime party.) What is more, Cárdenas attained the highest public standing of any Mexican President thanks to his speedy implementation of the Six Year Plan's social programme and then later his take-over of the foreign-owned or foreign-controlled oil and railroad industries – a move which brought him public acclaim from all sectors of society.[30]

But the key question was his relationship with the military. As has already been mentioned, Cárdenas was one of Mexico's most prestigious Generals and in further professionalizing the National Army would undermine the position of other Revolution-era Generals. The professionalization programme also brought about central control over the Army's thirty-three regional, military-zone commanders, ensuring that the holders of these key posts were obedient subordinates of the President and his War Ministry.[31] And thanks to the many benefits Cárdenas conferred on them during his time as War Minister and now as President, he would win the personal support of the junior officers and the enlisted men.[32] In fact he probably could have converted the Army into an instrument of his personal rule if he had not instead been intent on 'constitutionalizing' as well as professionalizing the Mexican military.

Yet despite the strength of his personal position, when Cárdenas had his War Minister, General Ávila Camacho, adopted by the PRM as the Party's presidential candidate, the Revolution-era Generals led an attempt to prevent Cárdenas from imposing his choice of successor upon the country.[33] No fewer than thirty-four of the Revolution-era Generals took leave from the Army to campaign for one of their number, General Almazán, and against Ávila Camacho, who had been only a junior officer during the Revolution and had made his reputation as a military administrator rather than a battlefield commander. On the other hand, the rest of the Army showed no opposition to Cárdenas's choice of the politically moderate War Minister. So when the government announced that Almazán had won only 128 574 votes as compared to Ávila Camacho's 2 265 199 in the presidential election of 1940, the losers' justifiable claim of election fraud did not lead to a military rebellion

– the Revolution-era Generals returned quietly to active duty.[34]

From Military-Party to Party-State Regime

The large degree of personal rule achieved by Cárdenas would be crucial in securing his successor's position, strengthening the Presidency, and later assisting his successor to bring about in turn a smooth transfer of power to a civilian President. To many Mexicans' surprise Cárdenas made no attempt to become another Calles by turning Ávila Camacho into another puppet President.[35] On the contrary, although 'the millions of agrarian and trade unionists and the hard core of the Mexican army looked first to Cárdenas', the former President used his influence to secure his successor's position.[36] He became Ávila Camacho's Defence Minister and brought all his personal power to the service of the new President and government.[37]

The President and Cárdenas together hand-picked a civilian successor to Ávila Camacho and ensured a smooth transfer of power to the first civilian to be elected President since Carranza.[38] The new President, Miguel Alemán, was a 43-year-old lawyer and former Minister of Government. He was the son of a leading General killed rebelling against Calles and was an experienced politician, having been Governor of Veracruz and then Ávila Camacho's campaign manager before becoming his Minister of Government.

His election as President marked the beginning of the party-state era in the long history of the Mexican one-party state – since then all Mexican Presidents have been civilian members of the Party. (The shift was marked by another renaming of the regime party, for the Party conference which nominated Alemán for President also renamed the PRM as the Partido Revolucionario Institucional.[39]) It is true that many vestiges of military rule remained under the civilian Presidencies of Alemán and his first few successors. The post of President of the Party would be bestowed upon a succession of Generals, and dozens of military men would acquire state Governorships.[40] But Cárdenas and Ávila Camacho had transformed the Presidency into a unique, institutionalized regime-leader position that had some of the characteristics of personal rule, including a (mild) form of personality cult.

Cárdenas had set the pattern for this by his extensive election campaign of 1934. From then on the Party's candidates for President would use 'cars and planes, motion pictures and radio to bring their faces and their voices to more people more often than even the local *políticos* had ever succeeded in doing'.[41] Just as Cárdenas had campaigned upon the basis of the programme contained in the Six Year Plan, so future Presidents would ensure their government's programme was identified with them personally. The benefits bestowed upon the people by the government were to be seen as 'the product of *cardenismo, avilacamachismo,* or *alemanismo,* not the normal functioning of an abstract and lifeless government'.[42] Even the Party apparatus devoted its energies to furthering a personality cult which depicted the President, not the Party, as the standardbearer and spokesman of the Revolutionary movement.[43]

In fact the shift from military to party type of one-party state had not brought the regime party a much more prominent part in the regime. The Party still lacked not only a significant governing role but also a principal–agent relationship with the holder of the office of President. That even a civilian President was not simply an agent of the Party is hardly surprising considering that in reality he owed his office not to the Party but to his predecessor. For in practice each President informally chose the Party's official candidate for the next presidential election.

In reality the Party was still as much an instrument or agent of the President as it had been under Cárdenas. For example, the Party was used as an instrument for implementing presidential control over not only the legislative and other activities of Congress but also the executive offices at the state and local level.[44] With the help of the Party a new President exercised an informal power to select most of the supposedly independent and elected state Governors. (Moreover, disobedient or embarrassingly unpopular Governors could be removed by using the Constitution and the Party's control of the federal and states' legislatures.) As the Governors in turn informally selected and controlled the key local public officials, this meant that the whole state apparatus, from federal to local level, was in effect the personal administrative machine of the President.

Such a concentration of power in the hands of the regime leader may seem reminiscent of the absolutist personal rule enjoyed by Hitler in Nazi Germany or Franco in Spain. But in Mexico (a) power was derived from holding the office of President and was not in any way personal, (b) there were some informal restraints within the regime on just how dictatorial or arbitrary a President could be in using his power, and (c) there was that crucial limitation on how long anyone could hold the office of President. Just as the original ancient Roman office of dictator was limited to a period of only six months, so the Mexican equivalent was limited to his six-year term of office.[45] That truly republican distaste for informal as well as formal monarchy which was evident in the Revolution and the 1917 Constitution has lived on in the refusal to countenance the re-election of a President. The Mexican one-party state has produced a truly original and still unique form of party-state regime, in which the holder of the office of President is an institutionalized regime-leader figure who is more than just an agent of the regime party but enjoys only a relatively short tenure of the office that provides his power.

2   CASTRO'S CUBA

Like the Mexican Revolution, the Cuban Revolution brought forth a military type of one-party state but the Cuban example did not follow the Mexican path of post-revolutionary development. In particular the shift from military to civilian rule has yet to occur in Cuba and by the end of the 1980s was already several years 'overdue' when compared with how long it had taken in Mexico to shift to a civilian type of one-party state. This tardiness can be explained in part by two of the other differences from the Mexican case. First, the military man who has been Cuba's personal ruler since the Revolution, Fidel Castro, has shown the typical monarchical desire of a regime-founding personal ruler to continue ruling 'his' regime until his death.

Secondly, the Cuban military-party regime disguised itself behind a Communist party-state façade, not the liberal-democratic façade used in Mexico. (The disguise would have been more convincing, though, if Castro had been prepared to resign from his military post of Commander-in-Chief.) The use of a party-state disguise has reduced the pressure to shift from a military to a party type of one-party state, as the regime has gradually been civilianized and has acquired an increasingly strong resemblance to a genuine party-state regime. In fact by the end of the 1980s all that was required for the transition to be completed was for Castro to be replaced by a civilian Party leader or collective leadership.

The Cuban Revolution, like the Mexican, was begun by civilians taking up arms to overthrow a military dictator, in this case President Batista. In January 1959 the small revolutionary army of guerrilla fighters entered the capital, Havana, as victors over Batista's army and regime. (The revolutionary army would soon be transformed into the new military arm of the state under the new name of the Revolutionary Armed Forces.) The *caudillo* of the revolutionary army, Fidel Castro, became the country's Commander-in-Chief and Prime Minister.

However, the Cuban Revolution soon showed a major difference from the Mexican Revolution in refusing to establish even a façade of liberal democracy. The revolutionary army saw itself as the 'vanguard of the revolution' and sought to oversee the implementation of what was becoming an increasingly radical programme of land reform and state intervention in the economy. Moreover, the revolutionaries' nationalist opposition to American political and economic dominance of Cuba led to such a sharp deterioration in relations with the United States that the new regime was forced to look for a military as well as economic alliance with the Communist superpower. The Soviet Union, though, would take on the commitment of a full-fledged military alliance only with a Communist party-state regime, not with a revolutionary military regime. Under the impetus of an attempted invasion by American-backed Cuban exiles in April 1961, Castro moved further towards the Soviets by setting up an incipient Communist regime party in July. Finally, in December he publicly announced that he was a Marxist–Leninist. Thus by the end of 1961 the regime had clearly opted to become an ideological one-party state and in theory a Communist party-state regime.

An obvious ideological difference from the Mexican case was that the Cuban regime had adopted a foreign or international ideology, Marxism–Leninism, instead of espousing a new ideology developed during the Revolution. But within a few years the Cuban regime had produced some ideological innovations that together constituted a new 'interpretation' – known as Castroism or *fidelismo* – of Marxism–Leninism.[46] The most important ideological innovation was the doctrine of the parallel rather than consecutive development of socialism and communism.[47] Instead of following the orthodox Marxist–Leninist view that a society must go through a socialist stage before being able to attain full communism, Castro argued that Cuba could and should undertake the parallel construction of both socialism and communism at one and the same time. Not only Cubans' social life but also their economic activities were now to be based on the morality and social consciousness appropriate for a communist society. The Cuban people's acquiring of this communist *conciencia* (a process which was also depicted as the creating of a communist 'New Man') was expected to contribute as much as the socialist development of technology and industry towards the construction of the material basis for a communist society.

The doctrine of the parallel development of socialism and communism legitimated (a) the policy of relying very much on moral incentives, rather than (scarce) material incentives, to motivate the work-force, and (b) the wider economic policy of adopting an extreme version of the Communist economic model.[48] The approach to economic policy became more moderate in the 1970s but this shift towards material incentives, (limited) decentralization, and a more pragmatic attitude was not accompanied by any major changes in ideology that might have legitimated such a change in approach to policy making. The 1980s did see a new ideological development with the launching of the Rectification of Errors and Negative Trends campaign in 1986.

However, the Rectification campaign sought to shift the balance back towards the 1960s approach, with a renewed emphasis on central control, moral incentives, and communist *conciencia*.[49]

In addition to the doctrine of parallel development an innovative theory of revolution was incorporated into the official ideology in the 1960s. In light of the Cuban experience Castroism argued that in Latin America a revolution could be carried out by intellectuals taking up the 'vanguard role of the guerrillas' and leading rurally based guerrilla bands in an armed struggle against the capitalist state. What is more, Castroism implied that after the revolution the guerrilla army would continue to provide elitist 'leadership' over the masses – a notion which served to legitimate the prominent part played by the Cuban military in a regime avowedly committed to the Leninist doctrine of party rule.

The first regime party, the Integrated Revolutionary Organizations (ORI), was meant to be a transitional movement that would lead on to the creation of a United Party of the Socialist Revolution (PURS), but the ORI's failings led to its actual dissolution in 1962 and a fresh start to the development of PURS.[50] This party was in turn reconstituted in 1965 as the Communist Party of Cuba (PCC), complete with Politburo, Secretariat and Central Committee. However, the Communist Party was a very small regime party, which in 1969 still had only 55 000 full and candidate members (0.6 per cent of the population) and a comparably small administrative apparatus.[51] The Party's small size, weak administrative apparatus, and other deficiencies made it incapable of effectively performing the supervisory governing role that was assigned to it by Castro in standard Communist fashion. Although the Party apparatus 'dominated, even in some instances supplanted', the civilian state apparatus, 'it was simply unable to keep track of what the state apparatus was doing'.[52] Nor did the Party perform a policy-making governing role, as the Party's central organs met only rarely and even more rarely issued policy directives.[53]

One of the predictable weaknesses in the Party's performance was its weak supervision of the military.[54] The Revolutionary Armed Forces had already ensured in 1962 that their newly acquired 'revolutionary instructors' in political–ideological matters did not develop into commissars. And when the Revolutionary Armed Forces were Party-ized in standard Communist fashion, they ensured that the structure of Party units within the military followed the contemporary Soviet pattern of having an auxiliary rather than a supervisory role. That the Party was relegated to such a weak position within the Revolutionary Armed Forces was quite predictable considering that military men completely controlled the Party's central organs and played almost as dominant a part in this avowedly Communist regime as the military had played in the Mexican military-party regime in 1929–34.

However, the prominent part played by the Cuban military in the 1960s was only as the instrument or agent of a personal ruler. The Cuban Revolution's sole *caudillo*, Castro, had become the personal ruler of the country as well as undisputed leader of the military. The Commander-in-Chief's leadership over the military was assured when his personally loyal guerrilla army became the basis of the new military state apparatus, the Revolutionary Armed Forces. Former guerrillas monopolized the high command and the key posts in the Ministry of Defence – of which Castro's brother Rául has been Minister since its inception.[55] Castro was also head of the all-powerful revolutionary government (with its legislative as well as executive powers), was First Secretary and leader of the regime party, and enjoyed great prestige and popularity. The personality cult of the *líder máximo* reflected this great public standing and his very visible, direct, impatient, and sometimes impromptu style of personal leadership.[56] His very direct form of personal but also populist and popular rule was one reason why the regime was still operating in a quite provisional or *ad hoc* fashion a decade after the seizure of power.[57]

Castro used his trusted military followers from his original guerrilla band as the main instruments or agents of his personal rule. They completely dominated the central organs of the regime party and held many key posts in government and the civilian state apparatus.[58] Military men comprised an overwhelming majority, almost three-quarters, of the Party's Central Committee – the active-service officers alone constituted more than half of the Committee's members. Seven of the eight members of the Politburo were also military men, six of them having the rank of General. The military also held a number of important Ministerships (such as Interior, Industry, Transportation and Education) and held many posts in the Ministries, particularly in the powerful Ministry of the Interior. When Castro invested his personal prestige in the massive propaganda campaign surrounding the attempt to reach a record sugar harvest in 1970, he had the military supervise the harvesting operation, deploy troops to help with the cane-cutting, and even take over the management of the most important sugar factories.[59]

The failure to reach the 10-million-ton harvest target was a severe political blow to Castro personally and resulted not only in the shift to a more moderate economic approach but also in an 'officially declared shift from individual to collective leadership'.[60] Castro abandoned his very direct form of personal rule and allowed the institutionalization of the regime.[61] The 1970s saw the promulgation of a Constitution and the creation or strengthening of political and administrative institutions, such as the creation of a pyramid of elected Organs of People's Power and the strengthening of the Party. The First Party Congress in 1975 'marked a major advance in elevating the supremacy of the PCC', which 'took on the trappings and functions of a genuine Leninist party'.[62] It had also by then taken on something of the size required of a genuine regime party. Membership had grown to over 200 000 (more than 2 per cent of the population) and some 6000 cadres were being trained in Party schools.[63]

One of the less obvious examples of institutionalization was the professionalization of the military.[64] For example, non-serving officers in civilian posts were banned from using their military titles and discouraged from wearing their uniforms.[65] As had occurred in Mexico, the professionalization of the former revolutionary army brought a measure of depoliticization and a reduction in the army's hold over the regime party.[66] In 1975 the new and enlarged Central Committee included a markedly lower proportion of mili-

tary men, with the active-service officers in particular now
comprising less than 30 per cent instead of 57 per cent of
the Committee.[67] Military men were actually a minority of
the Central Committee elected by the Second Party Congress in 1980 and indeed the active-service officers now
comprised less than 15 per cent of the Committee – approaching the norm for a Communist regime and distinctly
less than in the Burmese military-party regime.[68] 'Civilian
party leadership was clearly asserted' at the 1985 Third
Party Congress.[69] Military representation in the Central Committee fell yet again, and apart from the Castro brothers
there was now only one active-service officer among the fourteen full members of the Politburo.[70]

Yet in reality the process of relinquishing military control of the regime party had not progressed beyond the
stage reached in Mexico when General Cárdenas had incorporated the military into the PRM as only one of its
four sectors. And it seemed very unlikely that Castro would
continue moving down the Mexican path to full civilianization
and a genuine party-state regime. It is true that he (a)
had presided over the post-1970 professionalization and
depoliticization of the military, (b) had taken on the newly
powerful post of President in 1976, and (c) wished to be
succeeded by his Defence Minister. But at the end of the
1980s Castro seemed most unlikely to follow Cárdenas's lead
and go on to relinquish power to his chosen successor(s).
Castro hardly seemed ready to retire from the leadership
of 'his' regime, which he had presided over since 'his'
Revolution. The highly personal nature of his rule was il-
lustrated by the fact that his preferred successor, Defence
Minister Raúl Castro, was his younger brother.[71] In fact
Raúl Castro had long been the number-two man in the regime; in addition to being Defence Minister and General of
the Army he was Second Secretary of the Party and First
Vice-President of both the Council of State and Council of
Ministers.

Nevertheless, some variation of the Mexican pattern (of
the succession passing from a personalist military leader
to a professionalized military officer and finally to a hand-
picked civilian) seemed a much more likely prospect than
a repeat of the Burmese or Polish patterns. The Burmese

and Polish examples of quite personalist military rule disguised as a party-state regime were replaced in the late
1980s by, respectively, an old-fashioned form of military
regime and a democracy. Neither of these fates seemed as
likely a prospect for Cuba as the shift to civilian rule and
a genuine party-state regime. Revolutionary origins and a
period of popular personal rule have been shown by the
Mexican case to provide a secure basis for a long-standing
party-state regime – albeit one disguised by the façade of
a multi-party democracy.

12 From Party-State to Military-Party to Democratic Regime: Turkey since 1908

As with the Communist regime in Russia, the origins of the Turkish ideological one-party state lay in the massive military defeats suffered in the First World War. But Turkey fought alongside rather than against Germany, and Turkey as a separate country had not existed during the war – it had been the heartland of the much larger Ottoman Empire established by the Ottoman Turks several centuries earlier. When the Ottoman Empire entered the war in September 1914, it still contained within its borders a very large part of the Middle East, including Anatolia, Syria, Palestine, Iraq and Arabia.

During the Tanzimat (Reorganization) era of 1839–76 the Empire's hereditary and supposedly absolutist monarch, Sultan Abdulmecid, had introduced a series of Westernizing reforms aimed at arresting the centuries-old decline of the empire – reforms which culminated in the granting of a Constitution and an elected parliament.[1] But the successor to this reforming Sultan was a reactionary who dissolved the parliament in 1877 and established a despotic rule that re-emphasized the Islamic aspects of his dynasty and the Empire. The most important symbol of this Sultan Abdulhamid's policy was his attempt to claim the title and religious authority of Caliph, the office of leader of Islam which had been established after the death of Mohammed and had many centuries ago fallen into disrepute and disuse. Abdulhamid re-emphasized an old Ottoman claim that in the sixteenth century the last hereditary claimant to the by then virtually meaningless title of Caliph had transferred his claim to the Caliphate to the Ottoman Sultan of that time and thus, by hereditary succession, to all later Sultans.[2]

However, during the reign of the now Sultan-Caliph Abdulhamid a new form of Western 'infection', ethnic nationalism, was becoming established among the Turkish intelligentsia, including its Western-trained army officers.[3] The emphasis on the Turkish language, culture, history, and even 'race' (in the wider 'Turanian' sense) was a very different approach to building solidarity from that of the dynastic and statist approach of the Tanzimat era. For although Turkish was the official language of the Empire, it was not widely spoken outside the Turkish ethnic homeland of Anatolia. Moreover, many ethnic Turks lived outside the borders of the Empire, in the Central Asian territories of Russia and China.

By the early 1900s a new nationalist movement known as the Young Turks was winning substantial support among the lower-ranking military officers and civil servants and within the professions.[4] The most important group of Young Turks, the secret society known as the Committee of Union and Progress, would go on to establish a new regime that appears to be the first party-state regime – and indeed one-party state – of the twentieth century.

1   THE PARTY-STATE REGIME OF THE COMMITTEE OF UNION AND PROGRESS

The 1908 Young Turk Revolution, as it is often called, was sparked off by military members of the Committee of Union and Progress in the movement's heartland of Macedonia.[5] After the Sultan capitulated to the rebels by sacking his government and restoring the 1876 Constitution, the CUP did not itself attempt to take power and indeed did not acquire control of the government until five years later.

After its take-over of power in 1913 the CUP unleashed a wave of repression against its enemies and, as a result, was the only organized party that took part in the 1913–14 elections.[6] But the unwillingness of the CUP to dissolve or outlaw all other parties 'enabled the Committee to maintain the fiction of a multi-party system and representative government in the years to follow'.[7] It was therefore the first regime party to opt for a monopoly in effectiveness behind a multi-party democratic disguise. In 1913 the CUP also reorganized itself into a structure more like that of a normal – and democratic – political party and less like that of a secret society.[8] (Although a CUP parliamentary party known as the Parliamentary Party of Union and Progress had existed since 1909, a small Central Committee at the CUP headquarters in Salonika had guided the activities of the CUP to an undefined and secret extent.) Yet despite these internally democratic reforms, during the 1914–18 war the Central Committee regained its dominant position in the movement, confirming the party's tendency towards centralization and discipline rather than democracy. On the other hand, the CUP regime never developed into a form of personal rule. A triumvirate of three leaders, not any one person, seemed to rule the CUP and its regime in the 1914–18 period – and it may even be 'an over-simplification to talk of the rule of the triumvirs (Enver, Talât, and Cemal) after 1914'.[9]

The CUP performed an important political role as winner of parliamentary elections and it may even have performed a governing role. For the power of the CUP Central Committee and the CUP's hold on provincial government might be viewed as early examples of a policy-making and supervisory governing role. But the party could never have performed a social role for the simple reason that it lacked any ideology to instil in the hearts and minds of the people. More importantly, this lack of ideology also means that despite the 1913–18 CUP regime's clearly having a party-state structure, it cannot be included as an early pre-First World War example of the party-state subtype of ideological one-party state.

The members and leaders of the CUP do not seem to have had any clear idea of what the truths and goals of the regime were, apart from the hardly novel ones of saving the Empire and establishing a modern state.[10] The CUP 'did not concern themselves very much with political ideas' and they 'had no guiding principle for future action save an opaque notion of constitutionalism'.[11] The regime's pragmatism and lack of ideology was revealed even in the one area, nationalism, where an ideological commitment could most be expected from a Young Turk party and regime.[12]

Turkish nationalism was not officially viewed as being a sacred truth, principle, or goal. Instead, first the secular Ottomanism of the Tanzimat era and then the Islamist Ottomanism of old were used to try to hold the Empire together. However, the Young Turks had certainly been affected by Turkish nationalism, indeed by Pan-Turkism (Pan-Turanism). The apparently non-nationalist policies of 1913–14 represented not so much a lack of Turkish nationalism as a continuing reluctance to have it interfere with the CUP's ultimate, almost sole goal of preserving the Empire. The outbreak of war with Russia, France and Britain stimulated and brought out into the open the CUP leaders' expansionist Pan-Turanism version of Turkish nationalism, which supplemented the traditional, Pan-Islamic element in the regime's wartime rhetoric. However, a political and more narrowly defined 'Turkish nationalism, centered around the Turks in Anatolia, was in the process of development in 1914. It was to emerge out of the defeats of World War I, only after Pan-Turanism and Pan-Islam had proved to be mere dreams.'[13]

The CUP regime would not live to see the triumph of the new Turkish nationalism. Defeated in war, the regime and the CUP itself committed suicide before the Empire's capitulation to the Allies – the CUP dissolved itself at its last Congress in October 1918.[14] There would be a hiatus of several years of nationalist political and military struggle before a new regime would emerge to replace it. The continuity between old and new regimes would be clear – many of the key figures in the new regime would be former dissident or second-ranking CUP leaders and its initial, nationalist political organization would have been founded in many places by former CUP members.[15] But the new regime would be an *ideological* one-party state and would be of the military rather than party type.

## 2	THE SHIFT TO A MILITARY-PARTY REGIME

The period from the armistice of 30 October 1918 between the Ottoman Empire and the Allies to the signing on 24 July 1923 of the Lausanne peace treaty between the state of Turkey and the Allies was a complex and confused historical interlude. It spanned (a) the end of the Ottoman Empire and its CUP party-state regime, and (b) the creation of the state of Turkey and the beginning of a military-party regime under the leadership of Mustafa Kemal. The years in between can perhaps best be described as a period of political and military struggle led by Turkish nationalists to prevent the victorious Allies from carving up among themselves any more than just the Arab part of the pre-war Ottoman Empire.

The success of this struggle to defend the inviolability and sovereignty of the Anatolian Turkish fatherland resulted in the setting up of the new state of 'Turkey', which became the Republic of Turkey in October 1923. The Sultanate had been abolished in November of the previous year, having lost credibility with many nationalists after the Sultan-Caliph's 'collaboration' with the Allies during the postwar nationalist struggle. (In 1924 the accompanying position of Caliph would also be abolished.) The nationalist struggle had instead been led by the Turks' greatest military hero of the 1914–18 war, General Mustafa Kemal, who had won yet greater glory by commanding the army that in 1921 decisively defeated the invading Greek army of occupation and so ensured that the nationalist cause would eventually triumph. It was hardly surprising that this saviour of the nation was elected as the first President of Turkey by the National Assembly in 1923 – and would remain so until his death in 1938. Kemal would also establish a military-party type of ideological one-party state through his RPP regime party and by providing the regime with a full-fledged ideology.

Kemalist Ideology

Although the ideology of the Turkish military-party regime is and was often referred to as 'Kemalism', most of its components can be traced back to the ideas of Young Turk intellectuals and in some cases even back to the ideas of the Tanzimat reformers.[16] These seminal ideas in turn were often derived from imported Western ideas that had been adapted to the Turkish situation. Nevertheless, it was Kemal who brought the various components together into an officially recognized package that legitimated the policies and very nature of the regime he headed. Unlike his contemporary Communist and rightist leaders, he did not provide sacred interpretative texts but instead allowed the RPP – and only the RPP – to present and interpret the official ideology.[17]

From the outset Kemal's regime had an at least incipient form of ideology. 'Westernization and modernization were constantly heralded as its aim', and four of its basic principles, 'republicanism, nationalism, populism and secularism, were developed in the 1920s'.[18] However, the six sacred principles which formed the basis of the definitive Kemalist ideology were first presented as a group in a manifesto published by Kemal in 1931 and were immediately adopted by the RPP as its official principles, being symbolized by the Six Arrows insignia that became the RPP's emblem.[19] In 1937 the six principles were incorporated into Article 2 of the Constitution as a formal recognition that they were the ideology of the state as well as of the regime party.[20]

Secularism was the most prominent of Kemalism's principles.[21] Although primarily concerned with the separation of Church and state, it also sought to separate religion from the social activities deemed to belong to the secular world, such as education. Secularism legitimated the 1924 abolition of not only the Caliphate but also the religious courts enforcing Islamic law (the *Şeriat*). And it legitimated the series of supplementary secularizing measures implemented in the later half of the 1920s. Religious titles and the religious brotherhoods or orders (but not the official religious functionaries, the *ülema*) were abolished, the wearing of religious garb was restricted, and the Islamic calendar was officially replaced by the Western, Gregorian calendar. Islamic law was replaced by new civil, penal and commercial law codes based on European examples, and the article in the Constitution that declared Islam to be the state religion was removed. Later, in 1935, the weekly day of rest was shifted from the Islamic Friday to the Western Sunday and religious instruction in the public schools was discontinued.[22]

The importance of the principle of republicanism was two-fold.[23] First, it legitimated the abolition of the Sultanate and, secondly, it indicated the goal to which the regime was supposedly heading – a democracy like the Western democratic republics of France and America. Kemal himself argued in 1933 that a republican regime inevitably was committed to democracy. However, democracy had a lower priority in his reform programme than those other Westernizing reforms that he valued more highly and that could be implemented only in an undemocratic, authoritarian fashion. The regime would continue on as a legalistic and only mildly repressive example of one-party state, with the formal norms of the apparently democratic parliamentary Constitution being carefully observed and a large degree of dissent or criticism magnanimously tolerated. But independent political activity was prohibited, and the newspapers were controlled, to prevent the tolerated criticism of the regime and government from ever being mobilized and publicized.

The principle of nationalism was used to legitimate the creation and strengthening of a Turkish nation-state.[24] This official nationalism was based upon an ideal of Turkish linguistic and cultural, not religious or racial, similarity and solidarity. Thus it could incorporate Christian minorities and such ethnic minorities as the Kurds. The official nationalist ideal was also territorially confined to the boundaries of the state of Turkey – Kemal was just as opposed to Pan-Turkist as to Pan-Islamist ideology. For his cautious state-preserving foreign policy would have been endangered rather than legitimated by an expansionist Pan-Turkist ideal. Nor did official Turkish nationalism contain any chauvinist claims to Turkish superiority to the encroaching Western civilization. Kemalists actually considered Western civilization to be inherently superior to Near Eastern civilization. This allowed and in a sense legitimated the copying of Western practices, of which the most well-known example was the 1928 change from the Arabic to the Latin script for writing the Turkish language.

The principle of populism was a particularly convoluted and ambiguous one.[25] Although it contained both the democratic principle of popular sovereignty and a concern for the welfare of the people, in the Turkish context 'populism' also had a more unusual meaning – the social solidarity of the occupational groups, not classes, that comprised Turkish society. The populist espousal of solidarity between the society's occupational groups ideologically countered the Marxist idea of class conflict and provided the nearest thing to a justification of the regime party's political monopoly. For with such a high degree of social solidarity there was supposedly no need for competing parties to defend conflicting social interests and the RPP could represent the interests of all occupations.

Revolutionism is another difficult concept to convey because, again, of its specific Turkish meaning. The Turkish word actually 'implies radical change executed with order and method'.[26] In practical terms, though, the principle of revolutionism expressed and legitimated the RPP's determination to replace any traditional institution deemed to be inimical to the Party's Westernizing or modernizing programme.[27]

'Étatism' (statism) referred to all forms of state intervention in society but primarily served as the ideology's economic principle – the state's leading and indeed directive role in the development of the economy.[28] The measures taken by the state to combat the effects of the Depression were presented as a new policy which was soon transformed into one of the sacred principles of Kemalist ideology. It legitimated the adoption of a statist approach to the industrialization drive of the 1930s. The national economic plans, especially the first Five Year Plan, and the state's industrial projects were influenced by the Soviet example but there was no collectivization of agriculture and no state monopoly of industry and commerce. In fact there was never any significant redistributive land reform and not even a façade of reformist labour legislation until the 1936 labour code. Even then the code continued the regime's 'even-handed' approach (of prohibiting strikes as well as lock-outs) and its 'populist' policy of not allowing class-based trade unions to be formed.

The Republican People's Party (and the Military)

Kemal had been at least as much a political leader as a military commander during the post-war nationalist struggle of 1919–23. In particular he had been the leader of the political organization, the Society (or Association) for the Defence of the Rights of Anatolia and Rumelia, that had organized support for the nationalist cause. But by 1923 he had seen the need for a more disciplined and reliable political organization than the Defence of Rights association, and it was transformed into the (Republican) People's Party in September 1923, with Kemal duly elected President-General of the new party.[29]

Except for two brief periods the RPP would enjoy a complete monopoly, enforced through legal and other means by Kemal's regime.[30] The first period of multi-partyism began in 1924 with the establishment of the Progressive Republican Party and ended in June 1925 with that same party being abolished by Cabinet decree. The second period of multi-partyism occurred in 1930 when Kemal encouraged the creation of a 'loyal opposition', the Free Party. But he soon became disillusioned with his experiment, and the new party's leaders dissolved it before the year was out.

The RPP has been described as an elitist party dominated by 'the official elite and local notables' and as using its difficult entrance procedures to restrict membership to such groups.[31] (In contrast, although civil servants were required in theory and in law to be 'non-political', this was very loosely interpreted and in reality nearly all of them became Party members.[32]) Nevertheless, the Party has also been estimated to have had, by 1935, as many as 1 million members – more than 6 per cent of the population.[33] Not only the national level of the Party but also the various provincial, county and township subdivisions and the local branches were equipped with elected executive committees and one or more members of the extensive apparatus of secretaries. However, the chairman of the executive committee, not the secretary, was the most important Party official at each level except the national, where the President-General was supreme.[34]

The RPP was an openly centralized and disciplined party.[35] The permanent President-General of the Party, Mustafa Kemal, was the formally recognized head of the Party who appointed both the Vice-President-General and the Secretary-General and together with them constituted the Council of the Presidency-General – the political committee of the Party. The Council's authority over the Party was backed up by a strong emphasis on Party discipline. Party regulations specified that the decisions of the Council were to obeyed by Party members 'without reserve or condition'.[36] Moreover, although the Party was formally democratic at its regional and local levels, the officials and committees elected from below had to be approved by higher-level Party organs. On the other hand 'the party did not impose upon its members a strict adherence to its program. Different tendencies and affiliations were allowed to develop within manageable limits.'[37] Freedom of discussion was evident within the National Assembly and especially in the deliberations of the RPP's parliamentary caucus.

The RPP was clearly a multi-role party, even if one of its roles was performed ineffectively and another was dramatically downgraded in 1936. The Party had a significant political role to perform in selecting its parliamentary and local-government candidates and organizing their election to the National Assembly and its various local-government equivalents. An added complication was the use of indirect elections to the National Assembly through elected constituency electoral colleges which chose the parliamentary deputies.[38] And the degree of respect and autonomy accorded to the National Assembly gave an added significance to the Party's selection of its parliamentary candidates.

The Party's performance of its social role, though, was quite ineffective. Although Party regulations specified that its members were to propagate the Party's principles, the RPP was not well equipped to propagate Kemalism.[39] As late as 1938 only about half of this predominantly rural society's villages had any sort of Party branch established in them. It is true that in addition to its own, overt propaganda activities, the RPP also supervised the regime's famous People's Houses, with their various educational and recreational programmes. Yet the People's Houses, too, lacked the extensive presence and also the properly targeted message and activities that were needed to establish a link with the grassroots of Turkey's still largely peasant society.

The Party never acquired a policy-making governing role. But for a time it did perform quite a strong supervisory governing role, including wielding some personnel powers, over the civilian state apparatus in the regions – where the provincial Party chairmen in particular became powerful figures.[40] However, in June 1936 Kemal took the innovative step of having state officials take over the posts and duties of their Party equivalents. The Secretary-General of the Party was dismissed and his office taken on by the Minister of the Interior.[41] In the regions the provincial Governors took over the posts and duties of the provincial Party chairmen.[42] Sub-provincial Governors, too, became heads of their territory's Party unit, taking on the post of chairman of their county's executive committee of the RPP.[43] The Party, though supposedly 'merged' with the state, was in reality now more subordinated to the state than the Fascist Party was in Italy or the UP had been in Primo's Spain. It is not surprising that after Kemal's death the Party quickly moved to restore the pre-1936 *status quo*.[44] But Kemal's innovative move has remained to this day the most clear-cut subordination of party to state to be found in any one-party state.

The military did not play a prominent part in the regime – there was no junta, military Cabinets, supervisory role, or martial law. This is somewhat surprising, for not only had the military won great prestige as the force whose victories had led to the creation of the state of Turkey but also the military had occupied an important political role during the nationalist struggle.[45] However, Kemal had long been known for his strong belief in separating the military from politics, the military career from the political career.[46] Once the military struggle had clearly ended, officer 'politicians' were pressured to choose between their two careers, and in December 1923 the National Assembly decided that in future officers would have to resign from active service before they stood as candidates for election to the Assembly – in fact active-service military men were not even allowed to vote.

Yet the part played by the military in Kemal's regime should not be underestimated. It continued to enjoy a privileged and influential position in the country's government and administration.[47] Moreover, through retired and resigned officers the military until the 1940s contributed on average close to a fifth of the members of the National Assembly and more than a quarter of the country's Cabinet Ministers.[48] In particular, the country's Prime Minister throughout much of the period from the founding of the new state until Kemal's death had been one of the leading military commanders of the nationalist struggle, Ismet Inönü, who retired from the army only in 1927.[49] Finally, the civilianization of the regime in the mid-1920s had deliberately adopted a narrow interpretation of what was meant by removing the military from politics. For Kemal's 'main concern with the army was not to keep it out of politics, but to make sure that it remained completely loyal to him and to the Republic, a court of last resort when needed to support his efforts to build the new Turkey'.[50] The army was in this sense an instrument – if only a weapon kept in reserve – of Kemal's personal rule.

3   FROM PERSONAL RULE TO DEMOCRACY

Kemal's secure position of personal rule was based primarily upon his personal leadership of the military. He had won great personal prestige in the army through his military exploits in the 1914–18 war and as Commander-in-Chief in the nationalist military campaign of 1921. After his decisive victory over the Greeks in September 1921 the National Assembly voted him the title of Gazi or 'Victor' and promoted him to the uniquely high rank of Marshal.[51] As Kemal actually did not retire from active service until 1927 (despite his practice for several years previously of wearing only civilian garb), he was until then the highest ranking officer in the armed forces.[52] Finally, Kemal could count on the 'unquestioned' personal loyalty of the military's commander, the Chief of the General Staff, throughout Fevzi Çakmak's very long (1924–44) tenure of that post.[53] This combination of prestige, uniquely high rank, and personal ties gave Kemal a secure grip on the loyalty of the military throughout the course of his apparently civilianized rule.

The constitutional/state basis of Kemal's personal position was the office of President, to which he was re-elected unopposed by the National Assembly every four years from 1923 until his death in 1938. Yet in itself the Presidency was constitutionally a weak and comparatively powerless office.[54] The President was chosen by the National Assembly, rather than being given a direct democratic mandate by the electorate, and did not enjoy many powers in comparison to the Assembly's. The Constitution of 1924 gave the President the role of being – along with the Cabinet – the 'intermediary' through which the National Assembly exercised executive power. He had the power to choose the Prime Minister but the Prime Minister's choice of Cabinet Ministers had to be approved by the National Assembly, and the Assembly could 'at any time withdraw power' from the Cabinet. All presidential decrees had to be countersigned by the Prime Minister and relevant Minister, and even the President's veto power over the Assembly's legislation could be overridden by a simple majority vote in the Assembly. The President was not given powers of appointment over the civil service or the military, and 'supreme command' over the armed forces was vested in the President only as the representative of the National Assembly – ordinary command in peacetime was vested in the Chief of the General Staff.

However, Kemal's leadership of the RPP regime party ensured his control of the National Assembly and thus not only guaranteed his continual re-election to the Presidency but also enabled him to exercise in practice many more powers than the Constitution gave to him as President. His leadership position over this centralized and disciplined party was formal, authoritative and permanent. The Party Regulations stated that Kemal was both the founder and the *permanent* President-General of the Party.[55]

Kemal also enjoyed a great public standing as a wartime and nationalist military hero, a successful statesman, and the founder of the modern state of Turkey. By the 1930s a largely spontaneous Kemal personality cult was flourishing.

A contemporary Western observer noted that Kemal's 'picture is everywhere; his deeds are recited daily and his praises without end'.[56] By then, too, the informal title of Büyük Önder (Great Leader or Chief) was being applied to him.[57] A more formal 'title' was the surname Atatürk (Father-Turk or father of the Turks) which was bestowed upon him by the National Assembly when a law of 1934 demanded that all Turks adopt the Western practice of having a surname.[58] The widespread and genuine grief shown at his death in November 1938 was an indication of the very high esteem in which he was held by the Turkish people.[59]

Atatürk was succeeded as President by his long-time friend and frequent Prime Minister, Ismet Inönü, who also succeeded to the position of permanent President-General of the RPP in December 1938.[60] Although at the end of 1938 Inönü had taken the title of National Leader and 'soon acquired the status of an institution', he did not succeed to Atatürk's powerful leadership position and did not attempt to do so.[61] In November 1945 he called for (a) the replacement of indirect elections to the National Assembly by direct elections with a secret ballot, and (b) an end to the laws which restricted the liberties supposedly guaranteed by the Constitution, especially those laws which restricted the press and associations and gave extensive powers to the police. He even declared that 'in keeping with the needs of the country and in the proper functioning of the atmosphere of freedom and democracy, it would be possible to form another political party'.[62]

In January 1946 this duly occurred when dissident former members of the RPP formed the Democratic Party.[63] A few months later Inönü discarded his title of National Leader and his right to be the permanent leader of the RPP. The multi-party election of 1946 was marred by its repressive atmosphere – though the Democrats nevertheless won 65 of the 465 seats in the National Assembly. Inönü then led the RPP into accepting the need for truly fair and free competition with the Democrats, with the result that the Democrats won a landslide victory in the 1950 elections and took over power from the RPP. (On the other hand, both parties backed the continuing repression of the left through such measures as the laws prohibiting 'Communist propaganda'.) The 1950 handover of power to the Democrats was the ultimate proof that Turkey had shifted from being a one-party state to some form of democracy.

However, democracy was to have a troubled history in Turkey and there would be military interventions (albeit short-lived) in 1960, 1971 and 1980.[64] The new and fragile democracy instituted under Inönü did not last for more than a decade before being first threatened by an increasingly repressive Democratic government and then ended by a military coup carried out by middle-ranking and junior officers in 1960. Their junta, the National Unity Committee, established a new Constitution in 1961 that was actually more democratic and liberal than its predecessor,[65] and the military handed over the basis for a revived democratic system to the political parties later in the year. Again democracy did not last for more than a decade before military intervention occurred, in 1971, though this time it was intervention by the military high command aimed at repressing the leftist groups that had sprung up since 1961. The military ruled through a non-party civilian government, without a junta, and pushed through a raft of changes to the Constitution that had the effect of returning it to a pre-1961 degree of democracy and liberalism. Power was handed back to political parties in 1973 but yet again democracy did not last a decade. In 1980 the military high command took power once more and ruled through a junta, the National Security Council. It oversaw the introduction in 1982 of a quite authoritarian presidential form of democratic Constitution that was aimed ostensibly at rectifying the political instability and violence of the late 1970s. Democracy was returned to Turkey in 1983 and although severely flawed, by 1993 it had at least survived for more than a decade and did not seem in any danger of suffering another military intervention.

Conclusion

The case studies presented in the preceding chapters have shown the great variety and innovativeness of the ideologies and political structures of the modernized, twentieth-century dictatorships – the ideological one-party states.

The official ideologies contain a huge range of ideas, principles and goals. Liberalism seems to be the only significant ideological or philosophical doctrine not included in any of the ideologies examined or any others that come to mind. If an attempt to analyze or categorize them were to be made, one possibility would be to categorize them into groups according to the ideology's degree of 'particularity' or uniqueness. First there is the group of ideologies which are addressed to a particular nation or race and therefore inevitably have some unique features – such as in Fascism's glorification of the Italian nation or Nazism's of the German Aryan race. Then there is a group which espouses some form of socialism but a form adapted to national or regional requirements, such as Burmese socialism, Arab socialism, and African socialism. A third group, the Communist, comprises those ideologies with a commitment to an apparently standard or universal form of socialism, namely Marxism–Leninism, that is addressed to one or two particular classes – the workers and/or the peasantry. Several of the Communist regimes have developed their own interpretations of the core ideology but such variations as Stalinism, Maoism, Titoism and Castroism are still classed as examples of Marxism–Leninism. A fourth group consists of universally applicable principles that have been combined into particular and unique 'packages' that are relevant to their country of origin but could also be applied to many others. Kemalism, for instance, comprised the six principles of secularism, nationalism, republicanism, populism, revolutionism/reformism and statism. Another example is the Pancasila ideology of Indonesia, which comprises the five principles of nationalism, internationalism/humanitarianism, democracy, social justice and religious tolerance.

There have also been great variations in several different aspects of the political structure of the ideological one-party states. The parties vary in such matters as their type of membership and their structure. The Communists' elitist approach to party membership contrasts with the Guinean PDG's innovation of bestowing membership upon the whole adult population, while the Egyptian ASU was actually meant to have three different types of membership – inactive, active and secret vanguard. There have been such innovations in party structure as the Peronist movement's being organized into separate male and female Peronist parties and the Mexican PRM's opting for an affiliate structure divided into separate sectors for peasants, labour, 'popular' groups, and the military. There have been several examples, each unique in one aspect or another, of the combining of equivalent party and state posts or powers at the regional/local level – in Nkrumah's Ghana, Touré's Guinea, Franco's Spain, and Kemal's Turkey.

As for the state apparatus itself, there have been such innovations as Primo de Rivera's military *delegados* to local government, the Burmese regime's establishment of a pyramid of Security and Administration Committees, and the Indonesian army's creation of the *karyawan* system of supervised officers on detachment to civilian posts. There have even been cases of separate, autonomous instruments of rule being created within the party or the state. The secret Blue Shirt organization was set up within the Kuomintang, and the presidential military/security/bodyguard unit, the National Security Service, was formed within the Ghanaian state apparatus. Finally, the most unique and notorious of all these structural innovations has been the expansion of Hitler's SS into a personal bodyguard/police/military force that also became his instrument for genocide.

It is this innovatory capacity, this political creativity, of the twentieth-century dictatorships which suggests that it is far too early to view dictatorship as an endangered species. The dashed hopes of 1918 for a world 'safe for democracy' should remind democrats not only that such optimism may be premature but also that any new threat to democracy may take the form of regimes that are not yet conceived of or that are not yet recognizable as a new type of regime – as with Communism when still in its Bolshevik infancy or Fascism after the March on Rome. Thus the next century could well see a wholly new, twenty-first-century form of dictatorship.

However, what is more likely is the re-emergence of the innovative twentieth-century form in a new guise, hiding behind a façade of multi-party democracy. A few twentieth-century dictatorships have already shown how the outward forms of multi-party democracy, including supposedly competitive elections, can conceal dictatorship. Two of these regimes were examined earlier as case studies of 'multi-party' dictatorships and suggest two main strategies for such a form of regime – an Indonesian-style multi-party system with one or more official, neutered (not puppet) opposition parties, and a Peronist-style use of material and other benefits to buy an electoral support base sufficiently broad not to need too obvious use of anti-democratic methods against opponents. A further development of these two variants of semi-competitive one-party state would be a regime whose ideology incorporated an explicit commitment to Western-style democracy and whose regime party had only the more subtle methods of state intervention (notably state patronage) used on its behalf in the regime's semi-competitive multi-party elections.

Adopting such a sophisticated façade of democracy would force the twentieth-century form of dictatorship to shed the multi-role aspect of its ideology and party. For in order to maintain the credibility of its democratic façade it would have to use its ideology and party in the same way as a democracy, confining them to the political roles of legitimating the regime and helping with the electoral process. Therefore it would have to relinquish the apparent edge or advantage in modernity that a multi-role ideology and party had given the twentieth-century dictatorships when they were openly challenging democracy in ideological and political combat. But camouflage, rather than combat, will probably be the best survival and revival strategy for the twentieth-century form of dictatorship in the next century. And its resort to camouflage will produce a new and perplexing challenge for the democracies – how to prevent the twenty-first century from being the century of pseudo-democracy.

Notes and References

3 The Fascist Examples

1. For a brief account of the rise of the Fascist movement see P. Brooker, *The Faces of Fraternalism: Nazi Germany, Fascist Italy, and Imperial Japan* (Oxford, 1991), chapter 2.
2. On the other hand, the Socialists and the Catholic Populists had won major victories against the large landowners and leaseholders in *rural* areas of north and central Italy, and it was actually in these areas that the *fasci* movement and its squad violence experienced an explosive growth in 1921.
3. A. J. De Grand, *The Italian Nationalist Association and the Rise of Fascism* (Lincoln and London, 1978), p. 121.
4. H. Finer, *Mussolini's Italy* (London, 1935), p. 215.
5. B. Mussolini, 'The Doctrine of Fascism' (first published 1932), in A. Lyttelton (ed.), *Italian Fascisms from Pareto to Gentile* (London, 1973), p. 47.
6. Brooker, *Fraternalism*, pp. 292, 293.
7. Lyttelton, *Italian Fascisms*, p. 53.
8. Brooker, *Fraternalism*, p. 148.
9. See ibid., pp. 150, 194–5 on implementation of the Corporative State.
10. Brooker, *Fraternalism*, pp. 173–4.
11. R. A. Webster, *The Cross and the Fasces* (Stanford, 1960), p. 110.
12. The adding of Nazi-style racism and anti-Semitism to Fascist ideology in the late 1930s was entirely Mussolini's decision and seems to have been provoked by his new policy of allying Italy with Nazi Germany (Brooker, *Fraternalism*, p. 149). Many committed Fascists opposed this apparent aping of a foreign doctrine, but Nazi-style racial doctrine became part of the regime's official ideology and was in turn used to legitimate such measures as the discriminatory, anti-Semitic laws of 1938 (ibid.).
13. Lyttelton, *Italian Fascisms*, p. 50.
14. A. Lyttelton, *The Seizure of Power: Fascism in Italy, 1919–1929* (London, 1973), p. 267.
15. On the growth, exclusiveness, and statist nature of the Party's membership see D. Germino, *The Italian Fascist Party in Power: A Study in Totalitarian Rule* (Minneapolis, 1959), pp. 53, 52 table 3, 54–6; E. R. Tannenbaum, *Fascism in Italy: Society and Culture, 1922–1945* (London, 1973), p. 78; H. A. Steiner, *Government in Fascist Italy* (New York and London, 1938), pp. 45–6, 55 n. 10.
16. Steiner, *Government*, pp. 45–6; Germino, *Fascist Party*, p. 55.
17. Germino, *Fascist Party*, p. 52 table 3.
18. On the organizations attached to and removed from the Party see

257

Brooker, *Fraternalism*, pp. 154–5, 198–9, 186–9; Steiner, *Government*, pp. 53, 54, table on membership; Germino, *Fascist Party*, p. 43 table 1.

19. See Brooker, *Fraternalism*, pp. 155–6. In urban areas there were also *fiduciarii* heading ward subdivisions of the city *fascio*, and beneath them were layers of *capi* heading sectors, nuclei, and sections of Party members.

20. Ibid., p. 155.

21. Quoted by Lyttelton, *Seizure of Power*, p. 76.

22. Ibid.

23. Ibid., pp. 294–5.

24. Brooker, *Fraternalism*, p. 157. On the Party hierarchy and its discipline see ibid. pp. 156–7; Lyttelton, *Seizure of Power*, pp. 294–5; Germino, *Fascist Party*, pp. 38, 51–2.

25. The opposition parties were able to win more than 50 per cent of the vote in all the large cities except Rome, and it was only the use of nefarious means in the regional strongholds of the Fascists and their allies that ensured the opposition parties won only 33 per cent of the total vote (Lyttelton, *Seizure of Power*, p. 146).

26. Brooker, *Fraternalism*, pp. 307–8.

27. Quoted by R. C. Fried, *The Italian Prefect* (New Haven, 1963), p. 181.

28. G. Gentile, 'The Problem of the Party in Italian Fascism', *Journal of Contemporary History*, 19 (1984), p. 263.

29. Quoted by Tannenbaum, *Fascism*, p. 70.

30. Lyttelton, *Seizure of Power*, pp. 104, 294.

31. Quoted by Finer, *Mussolini's Italy*, p. 277.

32. Brooker, *Fraternalism*, p. 164.

33. Quoted by Fried, *Italian Prefect*, p. 181. See also ibid. pp. 182, 185.

34. Germino, *Fascist Party*, p. 113.

35. Ibid., pp. 54, 113.

36. Ibid., p. 114.

37. Ibid., p. 107. On the development and activities of the Militia see ibid., pp. 107–10, 115.

38. Ibid., pp. 109–10.

39. M. Knox, *Mussolini Unleashed, 1939–1941* (Cambridge, 1982), p. 13. A historian has argued that one of the reasons 'why the Fascists failed to react to the *coup d'état* that toppled Mussolini on July 25, 1943' was 'the dependent and secondary role [in relation to the army] assigned to the Fascist Militia' (R. Sarti, in R. Sarti (ed.), *The Ax Within: Italian Fascism in Action* (New York, 1974), p. 45).

40. Lyttelton, *Seizure of Power*, p. 294.

41. See Brooker, *Fraternalism*, pp. 160, 161.

42. Finer, *Mussolini's Italy*, pp. 260–2.

43. Brooker, *Fraternalism*, p. 161.

44. Gentile, 'The Problem', p. 264. See also P. Melograni, 'The Cult of the Duce in Mussolini's Italy', in G. L. Mosse (ed.), *International Fascism* (London, 1979).

45. D. M. Smith, *Mussolini* (London, 1981), p. 167.
46. Tannenbaum, *Fascism*, p. 74; Smith, *Mussolini*, p. 167.
47. Brooker, *Fraternalism*, pp. 176, 294.
48. Knox, *Mussolini Unleashed*, p. 105.
49. Finer, *Mussolini's Italy*, pp. 315, 333.
50. Brooker, *Fraternalism*, p. 160.
51. Smith, *Mussolini*, p. 164. Although the Grand Council met forty-seven times from 1932 to July 1943, the great majority of these meetings occurred in 1932–3 (A. J. Gregor, *The Ideology of Fascism* (New York, 1969), p. 238).
52. Smith, *Mussolini*, p. 294.
53. Ibid., p. 298.
54. L. Schapiro, *Totalitarianism* (London, 1972), p. 27.
55. See Brooker, *Fraternalism*, pp. 88–91, 148–52, on the sacred elements of National Socialism and Fascism.
56. I. Kershaw, *The 'Hitler Myth': Image and Reality in the Third Reich* (Oxford, 1987), p. 122.
57. A. Hitler, *Mein Kampf*, tr. D. C. Watt (London, 1974), p. 543.
58. Brooker, *Fraternalism*, p. 138.
59. Hitler, *Mein Kampf*, pp. 408, 410.
60. See Introduction to *Mein Kampf* by D. C. Watt, p. xxxix.
61. Brooker, *Fraternalism*, pp. 94, 345 n. 5.
62. Ibid., p. 94.
63. For a more comprehensive listing of these organizations see ibid., pp. 93–4; D. Orlow, *The History of the Nazi Party, 1933–1945* (Pittsburgh, 1973), p. 6; A. L. Unger, *The Totalitarian Party: Party and People in Nazi Germany and Soviet Russia* (London, 1974), pp. 72–5.
64. Orlow, *Nazi Party*, p. 92 table 2.
65. Ibid., p. 95.
66. There was also an administrative headquarters of the Politische Organisation, with a *Reichsorganisationleiter* (national organization leader) of the Party, Robert Ley. He styled himself 'Reich leader' or 'chief of staff' of the PO, but Hess soon squashed Ley's pretensions and left him with only politically unimportant organizational duties, PO training, and statistics-keeping (Brooker, *Fraternalism*, p. 97).
67. Orlow, *Nazi Party*, pp. 93, 172, 197, 222–3, 245, 251, 364; Unger, *Totalitarian Party*, p. 31; M. Kater, *The Nazi Party: A Social Profile of Members and Leaders, 1919–1945* (Oxford, 1983), pp. 204, 236.
68. E. N. Peterson, *The Limits of Hitler's Power* (Princeton, 1969), pp. 165, 25.
69. K. D. Bracher, *The German Dictatorship: The Origins, Structure and Consequences of National Socialism* (Harmondsworth, 1973), pp. 307–9.
70. Brooker, *Fraternalism*, pp. 304–5.
71. Ibid., p. 106.
72. For this paragraph see ibid.
73. Ibid., p. 107. Prussia, by far the largest of the regions, had no Reich Governor but Gauleiter were appointed to several of the

powerful Prussian provincial governorships (ibid). In other large regions, such as Bavaria, Gauleiter might become Minister-President of a county or province (Peterson, *The Limits*, p. 253).

74. Peterson, *The Limits*, pp. 87, 96; R. Koehl, 'Feudal Aspects of National Socialism', *American Political Science Review*, 54, 4 (December, 1960), p. 927.
75. Peterson, *The Limits*, p. 184.
76. The power of Gauleiter varied substantially from individual to individual and often according to such purely personal factors as their political energy and skill and the strength of their personal relationship with Hitler. For an example of a truly powerful Gauleiter see the case of Gauleiter/Governor Wagner of Baden. (See J. H. Grill, *The Nazi Movement in Baden, 1920–1945* (Chapel Hill, 1983).)
77. Peterson, *The Limits*, pp. 341, 351.
78. Ibid., pp. 339–40, 352, 434.
79. Ibid., p. 97.
80. J. Noakes, 'The Nazi Party and the Third Reich: The Myth and Reality of the One-Party State', in J. Noakes (ed.), *Government, Party and People in Nazi Germany* (Exeter, 1980), pp. 16, 23; Peterson, *The Limits*, p. 96. See Brooker, *Fraternalism*, pp. 108–9, on the powers of the Kreisleiter.
81. Brooker, *Fraternalism*, pp. 105–6, 108, 109.
82. R. J. O'Neill, *The German Army and the Nazi Party, 1933–1939* (London, 1966), pp. 69, 70–1, 72.
83. K. Demeter, *The German Officer-Corps in Society and State, 1650–1945*, tr. A. Malcolm (London, 1965), p. 212.
84. O'Neill, *German Army*, pp. 103–4.
85. Bracher, *German Dictatorship*, p. 437; H. Buchheim, 'The SS – Instrument of Domination', in H. Krausnick, H. Buchheim *et al.*, *Anatomy of the SS State* (London, 1968), p. 142.
86. Bracher, *German Dictatorship*, pp. 442, 442–3; Buchheim, 'The SS', p. 172.
87. D. Schönbaum, *Hitler's Social Revolution: Class and Status in Nazi Germany, 1933–1939* (New York, 1967), pp. 227–8 n. 138.
88. See Bracher, *German Dictatorship*, pp. 437, 440.
89. Ibid., p. 439.
90. B. Wegner, 'The "Aristocracy of National Socialism": The Role of the *SS* in National Socialist Germany', in H. W. Koch (ed.), *Aspects of the Third Reich* (Basingstoke, 1985), pp. 445–6.
91. Ibid., p. 446.
92. It is even doubtful whether the SS should be viewed as a single organization rather than a conglomeration or collection of separate organizations that was held together only by a common personal relationship of subordination and loyalty to Himmler (J. Hiden and J. Farquharson, *Explaining Hitler's Germany: Historians and the Third Reich* (London, 1989), p. 76.
93. On the four-year-term Enabling Law's renewal in 1937 see M. Broszat, *The Hitler State* (London, 1981), p. 84.

94. Brooker, *Fraternalism*, p. 105.
95. Bracher, *German Dictatorship*, p. 428.
96. Broszat, *Hitler State*.
97. O'Neill, *German Army*, p. 55.
98. Broszat, *Hitler State*, p. 295.
99. Bracher, *German Dictatorship*, p. 427.
100. For a detailed description and analysis see Kershaw, '*Hitler Myth*'.
101. Kershaw, '*Hitler Myth*', chapters 2–8.

4 The Communist Regime in the Soviet Union from 1917 to 1945

1. N. Tumarkin, *Lenin Lives! The Lenin Cult in Soviet Russia* (Cambridge, Mass., and London, 1983), p. 67.
2. J. Plamenatz, *German Marxism and Russian Communism* (London, 1954), p. 249.
3. D. McLellan, *Marxism after Marx: An Introduction* (London, 1980), p. 89.
4. L. Schapiro, *The Communist Party of the Soviet Union* (London, 1970), pp. 214–15.
5. See J. F. Hough and M. Fainsod, *How the Soviet Union Is Governed* (Cambridge, Mass., and London, 1979), p. 101, for quotations from the resolution laying down the anti-factionalism rule.
6. Schapiro, *Party*, p. 210. See also McLellan, *Marxism*, p. 100.
7. Schapiro, *Party*, p. 215.
8. Ibid., p. 211. On War Communism see R. Pipes, *The Russian Revolution* (New York, 1990), chapter 15.
9. Schapiro, *Party*, pp. 212–13; Hough and Fainsod, *Soviet Union*, p. 103.
10. Schapiro, *Party*, p. 210; Plamenatz, *German Marxism*, p. 272.
11. Tumarkin, *Lenin*, pp. 120–2.
12. For in addition to his narrowly political writings Lenin had covered a wide range of other topics, and his famous economic theory of imperialism was sometimes used to legitimate this and other Communist regimes' foreign policy.
13. While maintaining that he was only a presenter of Lenin's ideas, Stalin soon added a new doctrine, 'Socialism in One Country', to the regime's ideology (McLellan, *Marxism*, p. 122; Plamenatz, *German Marxism*, pp. 267 footnote 1, 268).
14. Stalin's doctrine of Socialism in One Country had already legitimated a shift in approach to economic policy making. See McLellan, *Marxism*, pp. 121–5, on the background to and backing for the new doctrine.
15. Ibid., pp. 132–3. See Pipes, *Revolution*, pp. 729–30, on the problem of defining a kulak.
16. R. C. Tucker, *Stalin in Power: The Revolution from Above 1928–1941* (New York and London, 1990), p. 187.
17. Ibid., pp. 88–9. Here again he was able to find some support for this idea in Lenin's voluminous writings.

18. Quoted ibid., p. XIII.
19. Ibid., p. 331.
20. McLellan, *Marxism*, p. 137.
21. Pipes, *Revolution*, p. 542 table.
22. Ibid., pp. 563, 544–5.
23. Ibid., p. 563. Though 'as a reward for their support against the White armies, the[se] two socialist parties were later reinstated and allowed to rejoin the soviets in limited numbers' (ibid.).
24. See L. Schapiro, *The Origin of the Communist Autocracy* (London, 1955), pp. 205, 127–8, for the final attack on the Mensheviks, the SRs, and the Left Socialist Revolutionaries.
25. Schapiro, *Party*, p. 333.
26. For figures on Party and population size see ibid., pp. 172–3, 235, 313, 317; Hough and Fainsod, *Soviet Union*, p. 52; Tucker, *Stalin*, p. 588.
27. For this paragraph see Schapiro, *Party*, p. 313; M. Fainsod, *How Russia is Ruled* (Cambridge, Mass., 1967), pp. 287, 291.
28. Fainsod, *How Russia is Ruled*, p. 190.
29. W. H. Chamberlin, *Revolution 1917–1921*, ii (New York, 1954), p. 368.
30. Hough and Fainsod, *Soviet Union*, pp. 129–30.
31. Schapiro, *Party*, pp. 313, 324.
32. J. A. Getty, *Origins of the Great Purges: The Soviet Communist Party Reconsidered, 1933–1938* (Cambridge, 1985), pp. 40–1, 46 table 2.1. But the political police were not used against Party members. OGPU at most only provided information on Party members to the Party's internal disciplinary organ, the Central Control Commission and its subordinate local control commissions (Schapiro, *Party*, pp. 323–4). The Party 'jealously safeguarded itself from any encroachments by the OGPU, and retained the privilege of purging itself' (ibid. p. 323).
33. Ibid., p. 243.
34. R. Service, *The Bolshevik Party in Revolution* (London, 1979), pp. 121, 147–8.
35. Fainsod, *Russia*, pp. 353–4.
36. It also mentioned in Article 141 the right of the Party and other 'organizations and societies of working people' to nominate candidates for election (S. E. Finer (ed.), *Five Constitutions: Contrasts and Comparisons* (Harmondsworth, 1979), p. 141).
37. A. L. Unger, *The Totalitarian Party: Party and People in Nazi Germany and Soviet Russia* (London, 1974), pp. 51–2.
38. Pipes, *Revolution*, p. 510. The Communist Party was described as the 'vanguard of the working people' and 'the leading core of all organizations of the working people, both governmental and nongovernmental' (Finer, *Five Constitutions*, p. 139).
39. Quoted by Pipes, *Revolution*, p. 510.
40. See ibid., pp. 512, 531–2; Tumarkin, *Lenin*, p. 57.
41. Schapiro, *Party*, pp. 243–5.
42. Ibid. for figures on meetings.

43. Tucker, *Stalin*, p. 122.
44. On the establishment of Party supervision over the military see Fainsod, *Russia*, pp. 466–8, 474, 481.
45. Ibid., p. 469.
46. Ibid., p. 470.
47. Schapiro, *Origin*, pp. 242–3.
48. Fainsod, *Russia*, p. 471.
49. Ibid., p. 475.
50. T. J. Colton, *Commissars, Commanders, and Civilian Authority: The Structure of Soviet Military Politics* (Cambridge, Mass., 1979), pp. 39, 43.
51. Schapiro, *Party*, pp. 246, 248.
52. Ibid., p. 247.
53. Ibid.
54. Pipes, *Revolution*, pp. 526–9, 555.
55. Ibid., pp. 508–9, 529.
56. Chamberlin, *Revolution*, p. 362.
57. Schapiro, *Party*, p. 248.
58. Ibid., p. 448 footnote 2.
59. Ibid., p. 248.
60. Schapiro, *Origin*, p. 219.
61. Ibid.
62. Schapiro, *Party*, p. 327.
63. Tumarkin, *Lenin*, p. 74.
64. Pipes, *Revolution*, p. 511.
65. Ibid., p. 512; Tumarkin, *Lenin*, p. 57.
66. Pipes, *Revolution*, p. 521. See also ibid., pp. 531–2, 512; Tumarkin, *Lenin*, pp. 57–8.
67. Ibid., p. 60.
68. Ibid., p. 79.
69. Ibid., p. 80. Pipes agrees that the assassination attempt 'inaugurated a deliberate policy of deifying Lenin' (Pipes, *Revolution*, p. 812).
70. Tumarkin, *Lenin*, p. 107.
71. Pipes, *Revolution*, p. 814.
72. Ibid., p. 812. See also Tumarkin, *Lenin*, pp. 60, 103, on his identification with the Party.
73. Schapiro, *Party*, p. 224.
74. Similarly in 1922 he allowed the Deputy Chairman of the Council of People's Commissars to take over the job, if not the title, of head of government. See Tumarkin, *Lenin*, p. 119; Hough and Fainsod, *Soviet Union*, pp. 119–20, and Schapiro, *Party*, pp. 285–6.
75. Tumarkin, *Lenin*, p. 119; Schapiro, *Party*, p. 242. As early as 1922 there was a clear eroding of his ability to have his will respected by the Party and regime. For 'on a number of important issues he was by 1922 in sharp disagreement with his colleagues . . . and his views were circumvented or ignored' (ibid., p. 224).
76. Tumarkin, *Lenin*, pp. 209, 210–11.
77. Fainsod, *Russia*, p. 180.

78. Schapiro, *Party*, pp. 244–5.
79. Hough and Fainsod, *Soviet Union*, p. 131.
80. Fainsod, *Russia*, p. 184; Schapiro, *Party*, p. 322. The stacking of the Central Committee with Stalin's supporters was facilitated by the almost doubling in size of the Central Committee in 1923–5 to a total of 106 full or candidate members (ibid., pp. 278, 288, 299).
81. See Hough and Fainsod, *Soviet Union*, pp. 144–6.
82. Ibid., p. 145.
83. The composition of the Politburo was taking on a more 'Secretarial' hue as some of Stalin's fellow central Secretaries, and even key regional secretaries, were included in an expanded Politburo of nine full members and almost as many candidate members.
84. B. D. Wolfe, *Khrushchev and Stalin's Ghost* (New York, 1957), p. 241; Hough and Fainsod, *Soviet Union*, p. 146; Tucker, *Stalin*, p. 148.
85. Tucker, *Stalin*, p. 262.
86. Fainsod, *Russia*, p. 474.
87. Schapiro, *Party*, pp. 253, 254–5; Fainsod, *Russia*, pp. 181–2. In fact in 1923 this department acquired some new control over appointments within the civil service (Schapiro, *Party*, p. 321).
88. Schapiro, *Party*, p. 320; Fainsod, *Russia*, p. 224.
89. Schapiro, *Party*, p. 320.
90. Tucker, *Stalin*, p. 124. Originally it was the Special Section of the Secretariat's Secret Department but the whole Department was renamed the Special Section in 1934. On the personal secretariat see ibid., pp. 123–5, 272, 458; Schapiro, *Party*, pp. 319, 399.
91. R. C. Tucker, 'The Rise of Stalin's Personality Cult', *The American Historical Review*, 84, 2 (April, 1979), p. 364; Tucker, *Stalin*, p. 160. See also Tumarkin, *Lenin*, pp. 248–51.
92. Louis Fischer in *The Nation* (13 August, 1930), p. 176. Quoted by Tucker, 'The Rise of Stalin's Personality Cult', p. 348.
93. Getty, *Purges*, p. 11.
94. Wolfe, *Khrushchev*, p. 241.
95. Tucker, 'The Rise of Stalin's Personality Cult', p. 348.
96. Ibid.; Hough and Fainsod, *Soviet Union*, p. 152.
97. Tucker, *Stalin*, pp. 328–31.
98. Ibid., p. 332. Volkogonov, too, believes Stalin enjoyed genuine popularity among 'the masses' (D. Volkogonov, *Stalin: Triumph and Tragedy*, tr. H. Shukman (London, 1991), p. 263).
99. Volkogonov, *Stalin*, p. 578; Wolfe, *Khrushchev*, pp. 214, 228, 234, 236.
100. Tucker, *Stalin*, p. 332.
101. Ibid., p. 475.
102. Fainsod, *Russia*, p. 433. In 1934 the State Political Administration (OGPU), which was in charge of the regime's political police, had been merged into the Commissariat of Internal Affairs (ibid., pp. 427, 433; Hough and Fainsod, *Soviet Union*, p. 171).
103. Getty, *Purges*, p. 47 table 2.2.

104. Schapiro, *Party*, pp. 420–1.
105. Volkogonov, *Stalin*, p. 307. Tucker agrees with these figures (*Stalin*, p. 660 n. 132).
106. Tucker, *Stalin*, p. 514. The reasons behind Stalin's purge of the military are still not clear to historians (Getty, *Purges*, p. 168). On the purge of the military see Schapiro, *Party*, p. 421; Tucker, *Stalin*, pp. 345, 349, 514; Fainsod, *Russia*, p. 480.
107. Tucker, *Stalin*, p. 514; Fainsod, *Russia*, p. 480.
108. Fainsod, *Russia*, p. 478; Tucker, *Stalin*, pp. 445, 124.
109. Schapiro, *Party*, p. 511.
110. Ibid., p. 621.
111. Tucker, *Stalin*, p. 477.
112. Wolfe, *Khrushchev*, pp. 120, 240.
113. Schapiro, *Party*, p. 498; Hough and Fainsod, *Soviet Union*, p. 178.
114. Volkogonov, *Stalin*, pp. 415, 451, 525.
115. Wolfe, *Khrushchev*, p. 218; Schapiro, *Party*, p. 510.
116. Getty, *Purges*, p. 21.
117. See ibid.
118. Hough and Fainsod, *Soviet Union*, p. 167; Schapiro, *Party*, p. 452.
119. Getty, *Purges*, p. 21.
120. These regional Party secretaries were the secretaries of the top layers of the Party's territorial subdivisions: not only the territories (*krai*) and regions (*oblast*) within the huge Russian Republic and the larger of the other republics but also the smaller non-Russian republics of this supposedly federal Union of Soviet Socialist Republics. Each of these regional units had four or five Party secretaries, the most senior of whom was the 'first secretary', the Party leader of the region (Schapiro, *Party*, pp. 447–8). In 1939 there was a total of 333 of these regional secretaries but in the mid-1930s there were a lot fewer regional subdivisions and perhaps less than half as many secretaries as at the end of the decade (ibid.; Fainsod, *Russia*, p. 196; Getty, *Purges*, p. 254 n. 69). A large region could have as many as a hundred districts and each district would have three secretaries and be led by a first secretary (Getty, *Purges*, p. 28; Schapiro, *Party*, p. 448). But 'at any level, the first secretary was the effective head of government in that area' (Getty, *Purges*, p. 26).
121. Getty, *Purges*, p. 24.
122. Ibid., pp. 36–7. For this paragraph see also ibid., pp. 24–5.
123. Ibid., p. 145.
124. Ibid., pp. 142–3, 153–4. See also Tucker, *Stalin*, pp. 428–30.
125. See Getty, *Purges*, pp. 154, 162.
126. Ibid., pp. 168, 173, 257 n. 5.
127. Ibid., pp. 194–5.
128. Schapiro, *Party*, p. 455.
129. Ibid., p. 511.
130. On the lack of Party control over the NKVD police see B. Moore, Jr, *Terror and Progress – USSR: Some Sources of Change and Stability in the Soviet Dictatorship* (New York, 1954), p. 29.

131. Hough and Fainsod, *Soviet Union*, p. 167. However, 'this is accurate in a partial sense at best' (ibid.).
132. Schapiro, *Party*, p. 511.
133. Fainsod, *Russia*, p. 390; Hough and Fainsod, *Soviet Union*, pp. 179, 170.
134. Ibid., pp. 178–9.
135. Getty, *Purges*, p. 167; Schapiro, *Party*, p. 423.
136. Fainsod, *Russia*, p. 481.
137. On the military in the 1940s see ibid.
138. Colton, *Commissars*, p. 14.
139. Ibid., pp. 25, 95–109, 70–2, 76, 78–80.
140. Ibid., p. 62.

5 A Survey of the Communist Regimes from the 1940s to 1980s

1. See R. F. Staar, *The Communist Regimes in Eastern Europe* (Stanford, 1971) and G. and N. Swain, *Eastern Europe since 1945* (Basingstoke and London, 1993).
2. Ibid., pp. 149, 152, 160.
3. Ibid., p. 72. See ibid., pp. 72–3 and 138 on the 'self-management' system.
4. Staar, *Communist Regimes*, p. 194.
5. Swain, *Eastern Europe*, pp. 160–1.
6. D. McLellan, *Marxism after Marx: An Introduction* (London, 1980), p. 238.
7. J. D. Spence, *The Search for Modern China* (New York and London, 1990), p. 579. See also J. C. F. Wang, *Contemporary Chinese Politics: An Introduction* (Englewood Cliffs, NJ, 1992), pp. 15–16.
8. Wang, *Politics*, p. 22.
9. However, by the 1990s *chuch'e* was being officially depicted as an entirely new ideology, with no mention made of Marxism–Leninism (R. A. Scalapino, *The Last Leninists: The Uncertain Future of Asia's Communist States* (Washington, DC, 1992), p. 57.

6 Third World Case Studies

1. D. Austin, *Politics in Ghana 1946–1960* (London, New York, Toronto, 1964), p. 12.
2. See ibid., chapter 3 on the 1951 election, chapter 5 on the 1954 election, and chapters 6 and 7 on the opposition CPP and the 1956 election.
3. Ibid., p. 30.
4. Ibid., p. 386.
5. Ibid., pp. 394–5.
6. C. Legum, 'Socialism in Ghana: A Political Interpretation', in W. H. Friedland and C. G. Rosberg, Jr, (eds), *African Socialism* (Stanford and London, 1964), p. 140; M. Owusu, *Uses and Abuses of Political*

Power: A Case Study of Continuity and Change in the Politics of Ghana
(Chicago and London, 1970), p. 262.

7. Kofi Baako in articles in the CPP Journal in April– July 1961 and
   quoted by P. E. Sigmund, Jr, (ed), *The Ideologies of the Developing
   Nations* (New York and London, 1963), p. 188.
8. Quoted by Legum, 'Socialism', p. 141.
9. Ibid., p. 142.
10. Quoted by T. P. Omari, *Kwame Nkrumah: The Anatomy of an Afri-
    can Dictatorship* (London, 1970), p. 121.
11. See Legum, 'Socialism', pp. 155–6, on Consciencism.
12. From articles in the CPP Journal in April–July 1961 and quoted in
    Sigmund, *Ideologies*, p. 194.
13. T. Jones, *Ghana's First Republic 1960–1966: The Pursuit of the Politi-
    cal Kingdom* (London, 1976), pp. 82, 86–8.
14. The use of detention had become so chaotic and capricious that
    'Members of the opposition probably formed a small proportion
    of those detained' as 'the act became a device by which prominent
    party men got rid of small fry who for one reason or another stood
    in their way' (ibid., p. 33). On preventive detention see ibid., pp.
    30–4; Owusu, *Uses and Abuses*, p. 278.
15. Austin, *Politics*, pp. 171, 207, 46.
16. Jones, *Ghana's First Republic*, p. 35.
17. On the Regional Commissioners see ibid., p. 69; B. Amonoo, *Ghana
    1957–1966: The Politics of Institutional Dualism* (London, 1981), pp.
    72–6, 78, 11. On the District Commissioners see ibid., pp. 102,
    103, 106, 111–12; Jones, *Ghana's First Republic*, pp. 69, 71–2; Owusu,
    Uses and Abuses, pp. 288, 309–11.
18. Owusu, *Uses and Abuses*, p. 291.
19. Amonoo, *Ghana*, pp. 18, 85.
20. Owusu, *Uses and Abuses*, p. 289.
21. Ibid., pp. 328–9; Jones, *Ghana's First Republic*, p. 90; Amonoo, *Ghana*,
    p. 167. In fact the CPP became a party motivated by patronage
    rather than ideology. This included such prosaic forms of patronage
    as providing jobs for Party members as junior staff of local (-govern-
    ment) councils.
22. Amonoo, *Ghana*, pp. 13, 14.
23. Ibid.
24. Owusu, *Uses and Abuses*, p. 297.
25. Jones, *Ghana's First Republic*, p. 53.
26. Amonoo, *Ghana*, p. 60.
27. Jones, *Ghana's First Republic*, pp. 53–4. Actually in the last years of
    the regime control over administrative policy making was being
    concentrated in the hands of the small group of senior civil servants
    who worked in the President's official residence, Flagstaff House,
    as officials of the Office of the President and had access to Nkrumah
    on a daily basis (ibid., p. 55).
28. Amonoo, *Ghana*, pp. 75, 73, 74, 164.
29. Though the reputation of the Party as a whole suffered when its
    RC and DC officials' personal rule extended into various forms of

corruption (Jones, *Ghana's First Republic*, pp. 71, 78; Amonoo, *Ghana*, pp. 108–9). For a sympathetic explanation of the instrumental attitude – in terms of patronage and corruption – of the Party's founding or long-standing members towards the CPP in power see Owusu, *Uses and Abuses*, p. 299.

30. S. Baynham, *The Military and Politics in Nkrumah's Ghana* (Boulder and London, 1988), chapter 2 and pp. 47, 94, 79, 140–1; Jones, *Ghana's First Republic*, p. 276.

31. Baynham, *The Military*, pp. 137, 138, 73, 139.

32. The President's Own Guard Regiment originated in 1960 as a largely ceremonial force of elderly soldiers that was known as the Presidential Guard Company. After the August 1962 attempt on his life Nkrumah ordered an expansion of the Guard into a battalion of active-service soldiers and renamed it the President's Own Guard Regiment. At the end of 1963 he ordered the establishment of a second POGR battalion, and in 1965 the POGR was officially detached from the army's chain of command. Moreover, preference was shown to the POGR in the procuring of military equipment, including the purchase of its own, distinctive uniforms. As the POGR's new weaponry and distinctive uniforms were largely of Soviet origin, the difference between the POGR and the largely British-equipped regular army became physically obvious. The training of the POGR officers was also of Soviet origin, for many of the seventy-six officer cadets Nkrumah had had trained in the Soviet Union were posted to the POGR (ibid., pp. 137–9; 132).

33. Ibid., pp. 135–6, 137.

34. Ibid.

35. He also strengthened his position at the head of the Party by acting as supreme arbiter of factional disputes. By allowing factions to express themselves, and balancing one against another, Nkrumah made himself the indispensable arbiter (Jones, *Ghana's First Republic*, p. 60).

36. Omari, *Kwame Nkrumah*, p. 82; Jones, *Ghana's First Republic*, p. 27; Owusu, *Uses and Abuses*, p. 280.

37. Amonoo, *Ghana*, p. 42.

38. Omari, *Kwame Nkrumah*, p. 85; H. L. Bretton, *The Rise and Fall of Kwame Nkrumah: A Study of Personal Rule in Africa* (London, 1966), p. 88; A. R. Zolberg, *Creating Political Order: The Party-States of Africa* (Chicago, 1966), p. 110; Legum, 'Socialism', p. 136.

39. Zolberg, *Creating Political Order*, p. 110. A sacred chiefly stool – the equivalent of a throne – was included among the Presidency's paraphernalia but this seems more a case of adding monarchical prestige to the Presidency than to Nkrumah personally (ibid.).

40. Omari, *Kwame Nkrumah*, p. 2.

41. Jones, *Ghana's First Republic*, pp. 262–8.

42. Baynham, *The Military*, p. 148.

43. Ibid., pp. 187–93, 182, 184–5.

44. Ibid., p. 205.

45. R. W. Johnson, 'Guinea', in J. Dunn (ed.), *West African States: Failure and Promise* (Cambridge, 1978), p. 37.

46. R. S. Morgenthau, *Political Parties in French-Speaking West Africa* (Oxford, 1964), p. 231.
47. R. W. Johnson, 'Sékou Touré and the Guinean Revolution', *African Affairs*, 69, 277 (October, 1970), p. 357; Johnson, 'Guinea', 57.
48. C. Legum (ed.), *Africa Contemporary Record*, xi (New York and London, 1978–9), p. B639.
49. C. F. Andrain, 'Guinea and Senegal: Contrasting Types of African Socialism', in W. H. Friedland and C. G. Rosberg (eds), *African Socialism* (Stanford and London, 1964), p. 160; Johnson, 'Sékou Touré', p. 354.
50. L. Adamolekun, *Sékou Touré's Guinea: An Experiment in Nation Building* (London, 1976), p. 5.
51. L. Kaba, 'Guinean Politics: A Critical Historical Overview', *The Journal of Modern African Studies*, 15, 1 (1977), p. 31.
52. Andrain, 'Guinea', p. 173.
53. Touré's conception of democratic centralism showed a greater concern for fostering mass participation than most other conceptions of this often much distorted principle of Party organization (Kaba, 'Guinean Politics', p. 31).
54. Johnson, 'Sékou Touré', pp. 359–60.
55. C. Rivière, *Guinea: The Mobilization of a People* (Ithaca and London, 1977), pp. 109, 190–8; Adamolekun, *Sékou Touré's Guinea*, p. 64.
56. Johnson, 'Guinea', pp. 63, 55.
57. See also Johnson, 'Sékou Touré', p. 361.
58. Legum, *Africa*, i (1968–9), pp. 504, 505; Johnson, 'Sékou Touré', p. 355.
59. Kaba, 'Guinean Politics', p. 32; Johnson, 'Sékou Touré', p. 361.
60. See Legum, *Africa*, xi (1978–9), p. B640; L. Kaba, 'Guinea: Myth and Reality of Change', *Africa Report*, 26, 3 (May–June, 1981), pp. 55, 56. See Legum, *Africa*, xiii (1980–1), pp. B497, B502; and xv (1982–3), pp. B458, B463, on economic liberalization; and see xii (1979–80), p. B509, xiii (1980–1), p. B497, xiv (1981–2), p. B427, and xv (1982–3), p. B548, on political liberalization. Anti-government rioting broke out in Conakry on 27 August and continued in other parts of the country for several days, with a further and more violent outburst in October in several centres leading to a state of emergency being declared and the army being placed on alert (Legum, *Africa*, x (1977–8), p. B656, B657).
61. Rivière, *Guinea*, pp. 232, 234–5; Adamolekun, *Sékou Touré's Guinea*, p. 133; V. Azarya and N. Chazan, 'Disengagement from the State in Africa: Reflections on the Experience of Ghana and Guinea', *Comparative Studies in Society and History*, 29, 1 (January, 1987), p. 125. See Adamolekun, *Sékou Touré's Guinea*, p. 139, on Party dominance over the Islamic religion in the late 1960s and early 1970s.
62. Quoted by Legum, *Africa*, xiii (1980–1), p. B498, from a December 1980 speech to Conakry University graduates.
63. Kaba, 'Guinean Politics', pp. 29, 32. 'Plot of 1965'.
64. L. Adamolekun, 'Politics and Administration in West Africa: The

Guinean Model', *Journal of Administration Overseas*, 8,4 (October, 1969), p. 8 and see also pp. 24, 25.

65. Adamolekun, *Sékou Touré's Guinea*, Appendix C, p. 224. My emphasis.
66. Johnson, 'Guinea', p. 51.
67. See Adamolekun, *Sékou Touré's Guinea*, pp. 22, 16–17.
68. L. G. Cowan, 'Guinea', in G. M. Carter (ed.), *African One-Party States* (Ithaca, 1962), p. 178.
69. Adamolekun, *Sékou Touré's Guinea*, Appendix C, p. 226.
70. See Johnson, 'Guinea', p. 54, on Touré's frustration.
71. Ibid., p. 55.
72. Ibid., p. 64.
73. Cowan, 'Guinea', p. 207.
74. Adamolekun, *Sékou Touré's Guinea*, p. 134.
75. Ibid., p. 18.
76. Ibid., p. 37.
77. Ibid., pp. 37, 38.
78. Adamolekun, 'Politics and Administration', organizational chart on p. 239. My emphasis. On this relationship at regional and district level see also ibid., pp. 239, 241; Adamolekun, *Sékou Touré's Guinea*, pp. 31–3, 37, 136; Johnson, 'Guinea', p. 54. In later years the balance of power seemed to have moved in favour of the federal secretary but there was no change in the official descriptions of what ought to be the relationship between him and his state equivalent – and there was still constant rivalry between the federal secretaries and the Governors. It has been pointed out, though, that the balanced authority (and mutual supervision) of federal secretary and state Governor helped to guarantee Touré's central control of administration (ibid.).
79. See Adamolekun, *Sékou Touré's Guinea*, pp. 21, 29, 30; Johnson, 'Guinea', p. 55.
80. The PRLs were still subject to some supervision by regional Party and state officials and were still subject to the absolutist authority of the national leader (see Adamolekun, *Sékou Touré's Guinea*, pp. 30–1).
81. See E. F. Pachter, 'Contra-Coup: Civilian Control of the Military in Guinea, Tanzania, and Mozambique', *The Journal of Modern African Studies*, 20, 4 (1982), p. 597; Johnson, 'Guinea', p. 52; Pachter, 'Contra-Coup', p. 600.
82. Johnson, 'Guinea', p. 64.
83. See Adamolekun, *Sékou Touré's Guinea*, pp. 140, 141, 146.
84. Johnson, 'Guinea', p. 64.
85. Ibid., pp. 64, 227–8 n. 51.
86. See ibid., Appendix C, for the Party Statutes and p. 229 for those pertaining to the Secretary General.
87. Rivière, *Guinea*, p. 216.
88. Johnson, 'Guinea', p. 59.
89. Rivière, *Guinea*, p. 95.
90. Johnson, 'Guinea', p. 59.

91. Ibid.
92. Adamolekun, *Sékou Touré's Guinea*, p. 172.
93. Legum, *Africa*, xvi (1983–4), p. B444.
94. The targets were: leading chiefs and trade union opponents (1960), intellectuals and teachers (1961), traders (1965), state employees (May and September 1967), the military and senior civil servants (1969, 1970, 1971), and the Peul (Fulani) tribe (1976) (ibid., p. B443).
95. Johnson, 'Guinea', p. 57; Legum, *Africa*, iv (1971–2), p. B571, and see also ix (1976–7), p. B589; iv (1971–2), pp. B570–1, B573.
96. Even opposition groups in exile claimed no more than 5000 people were arrested, which was a large number in a small country of fewer than 5 million people but was proportionately far fewer than the number arrested in the Soviet Union in 1937–8 (ibid., p. B572).
97. Azarya and Chazan, 'Disengagement', p. 115. Thus by 1976 only six of the seventeen members of the 1958 Political Bureau had survived politically (Legum, *Africa*, ix (1976–7), p. B593; Cowan, 'Guinea', p. 183).
98. Azarya and Chazan, 'Disengagement', p. 115; Johnson, 'Guinea', p. 58; Legum, *Africa*, xv (1982–3), p. B459, and xvi (1983–4), p. B443.
99. Azarya and Chazan, 'Disengagement', p. 115.

7 The Quasi-Fascist Examples

1. The following description of the Spanish political system is derived from J. H. Rial, *Revolution from Above: The Primo de Rivera Dictatorship in Spain, 1923–1930* (London and Toronto, 1986), pp. 17–24.
2. Ibid., pp. 45–46, 49; S. G. Payne, *Politics and the Military in Modern Spain* (Stanford and London, 1967), pp. 193, 204, 224. On the coup and the junta's decrees see S. Ben-Ami, *Fascism from Above: The Dictatorship of Primo de Rivera in Spain, 1923–1930* (Oxford, 1983), pp. 60–5; Rial, *Revolution*, p. 64.
3. Quoted by Payne, *Politics*, p. 202; S. Ben-Ami, 'The Dictatorship of Primo de Rivera: A Political Reassessment', *Journal of Contemporary History*, 12 (1977), p. 65. For this paragraph see also Ben-Ami, *Fascism*, pp. 75, 71.
4. Ben-Ami, *Fascism*, pp. 9–13 (esp. 10). However, a further reason for the support Primo de Rivera received from civilian conservatives, including the King, was that the parliament and the government were becoming more truly representative of popular opinion (ibid., pp. 21–2). Thus the reforming liberal government deposed by the coup had aroused strong antiparliamentary feelings among conservatives and in the mind of the King.
5. Ben Ami, *Fascism*.
6. Ibid., p. 175. See also R. Carr, *Spain, 1808–1975* (Oxford, 1982), p. 566.

7. Quoted by Payne, *Politics*, p. 202. 'Primo believed in the regenerationist myth that Spanish society was held in check by a corrupt system of bossism that extended from Madrid down to the smallest *pueblos*' and 'that *caciquismo* was a conspiracy perpetuated by the few against the many' (Rial, *Revolution*, pp. 126, 81). See Ben-Ami, *Fascism*, pp. 91–5, on the crusade against *caciquismo*.

8. Ben-Ami, *Fascism*, p. 178. To his followers the 'paramount values' of *Primoderriverismo* were (a) this leadership principle of rule by Primo de Rivera the Dictator and (b) 'the principle of "Spain above all"' (ibid.). And the idea of Primo de Rivera's regenerative mission, like his supporters' (positive) references to him as the 'Dictator' and to his regime as the Dictatorship, belonged more to the personality cult than to the ideology.

9. Ibid., pp. 194–5. See ibid., pp. 199–200, 202, on Primo's attack on Catalonian autonomy.

10. Ibid., p. 102.

11. Ibid., p. 202. See also ibid., chapter III, section 2, 'Regeneration Through God – The Genesis of the National-Catholic State', and Rial, *Revolution*, p. 62, on favouritism to Church.

12. Ben-Ami, *Fascism*, p. 282. On Primo's corporative system and policy for winning over the working class see ibid., pp. 283–5, 292–3, 295; Rial, *Revolution*, pp. 68, 206.

13. As well as the Socialists' being allowed to dominate workers' corporativist representation, workers were also given many much publicized indications of the regime's concern for (urban) workers through a series of what were really quite modest measures in the areas of social insurance and labour law (Ben-Ami, *Fascism*, p. 289; Rial, *Revolution*, pp. 200–1).

14. Ben-Ami, *Fascism*, p. 287.

15. Ibid., p. 182. On Primo's and supporters' attitudes towards parliamentary democracy see ibid., pp. 181, 193–4, 367; Rial, *Revolution*, p. 111; Carr, *Spain*, pp. 566, 566 n. 2.

16. Ben–Ami, *Fascism*, p. 136.

17. Ibid., p. 178; S. Ben-Ami, 'The Forerunners of Spanish Fascism: Unión Patriótica and Unión Monárquica', *European Studies Review*, 9 (1979), p. 52.

18. For this paragraph see also Ben-Ami, 'The Dictatorship', p. 81 n. 6; Ben-Ami, *Fascism*, pp. 368–9, 152, 208, 285; Rial, *Revolution*, pp. 60, 105.

19. Ben-Ami, *Fascism*, pp. 152, 148; Ben-Ami, 'The Forerunners', p. 54.

20. Rial, *Revolution*, p. 105. On the state's provincial Governors' influence see Ben-Ami, *Fascism*, pp. 137, 149, 149 n. 107.

21. Ben-Ami, *Fascism*, pp. 90, 95; Rial, *Revolution*, p. 54; Payne, *Politics*, pp. 228, 205–6.

22. Payne, *Politics*, p. 206. On the delegados see also ibid., pp. 228–30, 233; Ben-Ami, *Fascism*, pp. 95–8, 99, 137; Rial, *Revolution*, pp. 80–3, 216.

23. Ben-Ami, *Fascism*, p. 208; Payne, *Politics*, p. 233.

24. On the junta see Rial, *Revolution*, p. 52; Payne, *Politics*, p. 204.

25. Payne, *Politics*, pp. 244, 228. See also ibid., pp. 228, 230; Ben Ami, *Fascism*, p. 357.

26. Payne, *Politics*, pp. 244, 249. See ibid., pp. 244–7, 250–1, on the conspiracies and disillusionment within the military from late 1928 to early 1930.

27. Ibid., pp. 233–4.

28. Ben-Ami, *Fascism*, p. 213.

29. On the personality cult and the referendum see ibid., pp. 166, 157, 162, 164, 214–15; Rial, *Revolution*, pp. 59, 112.

30. Ben-Ami, *Fascism*, p. 167.

31. Ibid., pp. 338–43, 349–54.

32. Ibid., pp. 319–33, 355.

33. See Carr, *Spain*, chapter 15, and M. Blinkhorn, 'Introduction: Problems of Spanish Democracy, 1931–9', in M. Blinkhorn (ed.), *Spain in Conflict 1931–1939: Democracy and its Enemies* (London, 1986).

34. S. M. Ellwood, 'Falange Española: From Fascism to Francoism', in M. Blinkhorn (ed.), *Spain in Conflict 1931–1939: Democracy and Its Enemies* (London, 1986), p. 214.

35. S. G. Payne, *The Franco Regime, 1936–1975* (Madison, 1987), pp. 113–14; P. Preston, *The Politics of Revenge: Fascism and the Military in Twentieth-Century Spain* (London, 1990), pp. 138, 135; Payne, *Politics*, pp. 369–70.

36. Payne, *The Franco Regime*, pp. 115–16; Payne, *Politics*, pp. 371–2.

37. See S. M. Ellwood, *Spanish Fascism in the Franco Era: Falange Española de las Jons, 1936–76* (Basingstoke and London, 1987), pp. 42, 44; Preston, *Revenge*, p. 112.

38. Ellwood, *Spanish Fascism*, p. 44; Payne, *Politics*, p. 377.

39. On Falangist ideology see Ellwood, *Spanish Fascism*, pp. 13–15; S. G. Payne, *Falange: A History of Spanish Fascism* (Stanford and London, 1962), pp. 11–19.

40. For this paragraph see Payne, *The Franco Regime*, pp. 492–3, 514, 393, 395, 395 n. 28, 554.

41. On economic policy see ibid., pp. 464, 470–1, 473, 476.

42. On Traditionalist background and ideology see M. Blinkhorn, 'Right-Wing Utopianism and Harsh Reality: Carlism, the Republic and the "Crusade"', in M. Blinkhorn (ed.), *Spain in Conflict 1931–1939: Democracy and Its Enemies* (London, 1986), pp. 183, 185, 187; Carr, *Spain*, pp. 149–54, 617, 645.

43. Carr, *Spain*, pp. 705, 719; Payne, *The Franco Regime*, pp. 320, 323, 337–8. On these measures, the Cortes, and emphasis on Catholicism see ibid., pp. 323–4, 362–9, 372, 374–5, 420–1; Carr, *Spain*, pp. 707, 721; Payne, *Falange*, p. 246; Ellwood, *Spanish Fascism*, pp. 96–8.

44. Payne, *The Franco Regime*, p. 455.

45. Ellwood, *Spanish Fascism*, pp. 59–60.

46. Payne, *The Franco Regime*, pp. 176, 220. On attached organizations see Payne, *Falange*, pp. 203, 212; Ellwood, *Spanish Fascism*, pp. 90 n. 10, 62–3; Payne, *The Franco Regime*, pp. 187, 181, 262–3.

47. Payne, *Falange*, p. 201.

48. Payne, *The Franco Regime*, p. 324. The Organic Law of 1966 did allow a form of election to almost a fifth of the seats, but these 'family representatives' faced difficult nominating procedures which reduced the need for FET selection or electoral support (ibid., pp. 515, 515 n. 50).

49. Ellwood, *Spanish Fascism*, p. 76; Payne, *The Franco Regime*, p. 181.

50. Payne, *Politics*, p. 378; Payne, *Falange*, pp. 201, 212.

51. Payne, *Falange*, p. 202; Payne, *The Franco Regime*, pp. 290, 522. But by the 1960s most Governor/chiefs were uninterested in the FET's Falangist heritage and a few were openly hostile, refusing to wear the party's blue-shirted uniform on any occasion (ibid.).

52. Payne, *Falange*, p. 202; Preston, *Revenge*, pp. 114, 126.

53. *Encyclopaedia Britannica* (1963 edition), xxi, p. 141; Payne, *The Franco Regime*, pp. 432 table 18.2, 431.

54. Payne, *The Franco Regime*, pp. 327, 528.

55. See M. G. Garcia, 'The Armed Forces: Poor Relation of the Franco Régime', in P. Preston (ed.), *Spain in Crisis: The Evolution and Decline of the Franco Régime* (Hassocks, 1976), pp. 27, 30; Preston, *Revenge*, p. 134; Payne, *The Franco Regime*, p. 236.

56. See Preston, *Revenge*, p. 137.

57. The reduced prominence of the military's contribution to the regime can be seen in the decline in the number of military men who had held ministerial posts by the end of the regime's life in the 1970s – the overall total had fallen to little more than a third (Garcia, 'The Armed Forces', p. 25).

58. Payne, *Politics*, p. 374.

59. Preston, *Revenge*, pp. 138–9. See also Payne, *The Franco Regime*, p. 243.

60. Payne, *The Franco Regime*, p. 567. On military spending see ibid., p. 566 table 21.3; Garcia, 'The Armed Forces', p. 42; Preston, *Revenge*, chapter 6.

61. See Carr, *Spain*, p. 706 n. 1; Payne, *The Franco Regime*, pp. 234, 586.

62. Payne, *Falange*, p. 201.

63. See Ellwood, *Spanish Fascism*, p. 70; Payne, *The Franco Regime*, pp. 118, 193–4, 234, 235 n. 4; Preston, *Revenge*, p. 114.

64. Carr, *Spain*, p. 696.

65. Ibid., p. 704.

8   Third World Socialist Case Studies

1. R. Stephens, *Nasser: A Political Biography* (London, 1971), p. 112.

2. A. Perlmutter, *Egypt the Praetorian State* (New Brunswick, 1974), p. 19; R. W. Baker, *Egypt's Uncertain Revolution under Nasser and Sadat* (Cambridge, Mass., and London, 1978), p. 31.

3. Quoted ibid.

4. R. H. Dekmejian, *Egypt under Nasir: A Study in Political Dynamics* (London and Albany, 1971), pp. 42, 113.

5. Ibid., p. 250; P. J. Vatikiotis, *Nasser and His Generation* (London, 1978), p. 288.

6. Dekmejian, *Egypt*, p. 106.
7. Baker, *Revolution*, pp. 176–7.
8. Ibid., p. 68.
9. Ibid., p. 103.
10. Ibid., p. 176. According to the 1962 Charter, 'the revolutionary solution to the problem of land in Egypt is by increasing the number of landowners' (ibid., p. 199).
11. Dekmejian, *Egypt*, pp. 142, 132.
12. Ibid., p. 134. The Egyptian regime's ideology was not secularist. While it eventually abolished the Islamic law *sharia* courts in 1956 (without any apparent public opposition), it required religious instruction to be given in all schools and maintained several traditional Islamic trappings to its rule (P. J. Vatikiotis, *The Egyptian Army in Politics: Pattern for New Nations?* (Bloomington, 1961), p. 193; J. C. Hurewitz, *Middle East Politics: The Military Dimension* (Boulder, 1982; first published 1969), p. 130).
13. Baker, *Revolution*, p. 190. However, strikes were illegal (Vatikiotis, *Nasser*, p. 219).
14. For this paragraph see Dekmejian, *Egypt*, pp. 138, 140–1.
15. For this paragraph see Vatikiotis, *Egyptian Army*, pp. 103–4, 112, 109–10. Also ibid., p. 108 and I. Harik, *The Political Mobilization of Peasants: A Study of an Egyptian Community* (Bloomington and London, 1974), p. 69, on pyramidal structure of committees, and Vatikiotis, *Egyptian Army*, pp. 111, 113, 139, on functional associations.
16. Vatikiotis, *Egyptian Army*, pp. 108–9, 112; Harik, *Political Mobilization*, p. 69.
17. Baker, *Revolution*, p. 68.
18. Dekmejian, *Egypt*, p. 146. Harik states that the ASU 'comprised all adult citizens' (I. Harik, 'The Single Party as a Subordinate Movement', *World Politics*, 26, 1 (October 1973), p. 87).
19. Dekmejian, *Egypt*, p. 146; Baker, *Revolution*, pp. 100–1.
20. Dekmejian, *Egypt*, pp. 145, 152; Harik, 'Single Party', pp. 90, 92–4, 95 chart 2, 97.
21. Dekmejian, *Egypt*, p. 155.
22. Baker, *Revolution*, p. 114.
23. Harik, 'Single Party', pp. 89, 93–4; Perlmutter, *Praetorian State*, pp. 168–70; Baker, *Revolution*, p. 109.
24. Dekmejian, *Egypt*, p. 254; Baker, *Revolution*, p. 85.
25. Dekmejian, *Egypt*, pp. 149, 152.
26. Ibid., pp. 172–3, 184.
27. Ibid., pp. 221–2, 220 table 21.
28. Baker, *Revolution*, pp. 85, 58. What is more, from the late 1950s onwards a large number of the military men taking posts in the Cabinet or civil service were military technocrats, who had been trained as engineers, lawyers, doctors, and so forth, and therefore presumably were more than usually effective performers of a governing role.
29. Hurewitz, *Middle East Politics*, p. 131.

30. Ibid., p. 143.
31. Ibid; Baker, *Revolution*, p. 55.
32. Baker, *Revolution*, p. 55. This figure applies to the army officer corps after it had been purged of *ancien régime* supporters in the aftermath of the coup (ibid.).
33. See Vatikiotis, *Nasser*, pp. 154, 197–8, 298, on his being a personal ruler.
34. For this paragraph see ibid., p. 160; Dekmejian, *Egypt*, p. 255; Perlmutter, *Praetorian State*, p. 175.
35. See Baker, *Revolution*, pp. 51–7, 59; Vatikiotis, *Egyptian Army*, p. 223; Hurewitz, *Middle East Politics*, p. 133.
36. Baker, *Revolution*, pp. 93, 95; Stephens, *Nasser*, pp. 358–61; Vatikiotis, *Nasser*, pp. 164 n. 177–9.
37. Baker, *Revolution*, p. 95.
38. For this paragraph see ibid., pp. 110, 109.
39. For this paragraph see ibid., pp. 111, 112, 113.
40. Dekmejian, *Egypt*, pp. 155, 154; Hurewitz, *Middle East Politics*, p. 133. See also Vatikiotis, *Nasser*, pp. 198, 293, for Nasser as the source of law.
41. Ibid., pp. 290, 16; Vatikiotis, *Egyptian Army*, p. 236; Vatikiotis, *Nasser*, p. 290.
42. Perlmutter, *Praetorian State*, pp. 77, 111, 143, 176; Dekmejian, *Egypt*, p. 146; Vatikiotis, *Nasser*, pp. 12, 154, 297–8, 293, 295.
43. Baker, *Revolution*, p. 114; Vatikiotis, *Nasser*, p. 296.
44. Baker, *Revolution*, pp. 88, 116.
45. Hurewitz, *Middle East Politics*, p. 142.
46. A. Goldschmidt, Jr, *Modern Egypt: The Formation of a Nation-State* (Boulder, 1988), p. 128. 'Although the ASU seems to have played a guiding role in the demonstrations, the immensity of popular support surpassed that of a staged affair' (Dekmejian, *Egypt*, p. 245).
47. Dekmejian, *Egypt*, p. 252; Perlmutter, *Praetorian State*, p. 183; Stephens, *Nasser*, p. 512; Vatikiotis, *Nasser*, pp. 163–4.
48. Perlmutter, *Praetorian State*, pp. 183–4; Stephens, *Nasser*, pp. 514–15.
49. Dekmejian, *Egypt*, p. 259; Harik, *Political Mobilization*, p. 97.
50. See Stephens, *Nasser*, p. 544, on the ASU in theory now being the source of policy.
51. Ibid., p. 538.
52. Hurewitz, *Middle East Politics*, pp. 142–3; Vatikiotis, *Nasser*, pp. 172, 297.
53. For this paragraph see R. Butwell, 'Ne Win's Burma: At the End of the First Decade', *Asian Survey*, 12, 10 (October 1972), p. 902; J. Silverstein, *Burma: Military Rule and the Politics of Stagnation* (Ithaca and London, 1977), pp. 87–8, 90.
54. Not until 1971 did the government title itself the Government of the Union of Burma and acquire a Prime Minister (Silverstein, *Burma*, pp. 90–2).
55. The description of this tract is taken from the analysis by Silverstein, *Burma*, pp. 81, 84–6.
56. The description of this tract is taken from the analysis by Silverstein,

ibid., pp. 81–4, and by D. I. Steinberg, *Burma's Road toward Development: Growth and Ideology under Military Rule* (Boulder, 1981), pp. 29–31.

57. For this paragraph see Steinberg, *Burma's Road*, p. 35; R. H. Taylor, *The State in Burma* (Honolulu, 1987), pp. 350–2.

58. For this paragraph see Steinberg, *Burma's Road*, pp. 36–7, 58; Butwell, 'Ne Win's Burma', pp. 908–9; J. A. Wiant, 'Burma: Loosening up on the Tiger's Tail', *Asian Survey*, 13,2 (1973), p. 185.

59. For this paragraph see Taylor, *The State*, p. 361; Steinberg, *Burma's Road*, p. 30 and chapter 3; D. I. Steinberg, *The Future of Burma: Crisis and Choice in Myanmar* (Lanham, New York and London, 1990), pp. 21, 28.

60. For this paragraph see Silverstein, *Burma*, pp. 85–6.

61. Taylor, *The State*, p. 363.

62. Wiant, 'Burma', pp. 179–80.

63. Quoted ibid., p. 180.

64. Even earlier than this the new regime had suggested, unsuccessfully, that the existing political parties combine and form a new party which would be led by the Revolutionary Council.

65. Silverstein, *Burma*, pp. 101, 99.

66. Ibid., p. 122.

67. Ibid., p. 101.

68. For membership statistics see ibid., p. 103 table 5; *Keesing's Contemporary Archives*, p. 23959; *Far Eastern Economic Review Asia 1971 Year Book*, p. 107; *FEER Asia 1972 Year Book*, p. 112.

69. Taylor, *The State*, pp. 322–5.

70. Ibid., pp. 321–2.

71. *FEER Asia 1972 Year Book*, p. 112.

72. Although the social role of the Party was not mentioned in the new Constitution, an important and time-consuming duty of the Party and its attached organizations was to educate members and non-members in the regime's socialist programmes and policies (Taylor, *The State*, pp. 325–6); the lack of support for Burmese socialism shown by the people in the late 1980s suggests that this effort at indoctrination was not very effective.

73. Silverstein, *Burma*, p. 122. See also Steinberg, *Burma's Road*, p. 70, on how these candidates were unopposed.

74. Steinberg, *Burma's Road*, p. 67; Silverstein, *Burma*, p. 122.

75. Steinberg, *The Future*, p. 11.

76. Steinberg, *Burma's Road*, p. 165.

77. Steinberg, *The Future*, p. 25.

78. J. F. Guyot, 'Bureaucratic Transformation in Burma', in R. Braibanti (ed.), *Asian Bureaucratic Systems Emergent from the British Imperial Tradition* (Durham, NC, 1966), p. 437. Around 2000 civil servants were retired in the initial purge (Steinberg, *Burma's Road*, p. 164).

79. J. W. Henderson *et al.*, *Area Handbook for Burma* (Washington, DC, 1971), pp. 285, 286.

80. See Silverstein, *Burma*, pp. 92, 137, 138 n. 23; Steinberg, *Burma's Road*, pp. 70, 65, 164.

81. Wiant, 'Burma', p. 180; Silverstein, *Burma*, p. 106. The new General-Secretary, General San Yu, was the army's Chief of Staff and the Minister of Defence (Butwell, 'Ne Win's Burma', p. 904).
82. See Silverstein, *Burma*, p. 93; Taylor, *The State*, p. 314; Butwell, 'Ne Win's Burma', p. 902.
83. At the town and village the non-military representatives would not be civil servants but local leaders who had been selected to hold the post of township officer or village headman (Henderson *et al.*, *Handbook*, p. 154).
84. Taylor, *The State*, p. 314; Silverstein, *Burma*, p. 93.
85. Taylor, *The State*, p. 314; Wiant, 'Burma', p. 182; Butwell, 'Ne Win's Burma', p. 902; Silverstein, *Burma*, p. 94. See also ibid., p. 94 n. 21 for an official description of their wide range of duties.
86. Silverstein, *Burma*, p. 132; Steinberg, *Burma's Road*, p. 69.
87. Although by 1978 nearly 90 per cent of the military, some 143 000 of them, were full or candidate members, they constituted less than 10 per cent of the party's total membership (D. I. Steinberg, *Burma: A Socialist Nation of Southeast Asia* (Boulder, 1982), p. 89).
88. Taylor, *The State*, p. 320 table 50.
89. R. H. Taylor, 'Burma', in Z. H. Ahmad and H. Crouch (eds), *Military–Civilian Relations in South-East Asia* (Singapore, 1985), p. 43.
90. Taylor, *The State*, p. 366; Steinberg, *The Future*, p. 11.
91. Steinberg, *Burma's Road*, p. 190; Taylor, *The State*, p. 366.
92. Steinberg, *The Future*, p. 11. See also Taylor, *The State*, p. 367.
93. Taylor, *The State*, pp. 369–70; Steinberg, *Burma's Road*, pp. 143–4.
94. Ibid., p. 74.
95. Taylor, *The State*, pp. 366–7; J. A. Wiant, 'Tradition in the Service of Revolution: The Political Symbolism of Taw-hlan-ye-khit', in F. K. Lehman (ed.), *Military Rule in Burma since 1962: A Kaleidoscope of Views* (Singapore, 1981), p. 61. For the rest of this paragraph see Steinberg, *Burma's Road*, pp. 184–5; Steinberg, *The Future*, p. 9; Taylor, *The State*, p. 366.
96. Steinberg, *The Future*, p. 31.
97. Ibid., p. 12.

9 Third World 'Multi-Party' Case Studies

1. R. A. Potash, *The Army & Politics in Argentina, 1928–1945: Yrigoyen to Perón* (Stanford, 1969), pp. 240, 249.
2. R. J. Alexander, *Juan Domingo Perón: A History* (Boulder, 1979), p. 37; A. Stepan, *The State and Society: Peru in Comparative Perspective* (Princeton, 1978), p. 94.
3. Alexander, *Perón*, p. 38.
4. On Perón's trade union strategy see ibid., pp. 38–41.
5. R. A. Potash, *The Army and Politics in Argentina, 1945–1962: Perón to Frondizi* (Stanford, 1980), p. 45.
6. Ibid., pp. 47, 48.
7. Ibid., p. 102.

8. Ibid., pp. 58–9, 61.
9. G. I. Blanksten, *Perón's Argentina* (Chicago, 1953), p. 281.
10. Ibid., pp. 281–2, and 283–92 on Justicialismo.
11. Ibid., p. 292, quoting from R. A. Mende, *El Justicialismo* (Buenos Aires, 1950), pp. 94–6. Original emphasis removed.
12. Blanksten, *Perón's Argentina*, p. 297.
13. Ibid., p. 293.
14. Ibid., pp. 317–18. See ibid., on the concept of *descamisados*.
15. See R. D. Crassweller, *Perón and the Enigmas of Argentina* (New York and London, 1987), pp. 229, 252, and Potash, *1945–1962*, p. 106, on this. The concept or ideal of the 'organized community' was in fact the background or foundation concept of the famous April 1949 speech in which he first delineated the doctrine of Justicialismo (Crassweller, *Perón*, p. 229).
16. Potash, *1945–1962*, p. 165. See also Alexander, *Perón*, p. 100.
17. See Potash, *1945–1962*, pp. 164–5, for the extension of the CGE in 1953–4 and founding of the CGP in 1953, and ibid., pp. 171–2, for the founding of the UES in 1954. However, by the fall of the regime the CGE and CGP had yet to incorporate all the business and professional groups, and the UES and CGU had not yet won a grasp on youth (Alexander, *Perón*, pp. 58–9).
18. Crassweller, *Perón*, p. 230.
19. See also ibid., p. 231.
20. Ibid., pp. 252–3.
21. Alexander, *Perón*, p. 97; Potash, *1945–1962*, p. 170; Crassweller, *Perón*, p. 251.
22. Crassweller, *Perón*, p. 251.
23. Blanksten, *Perón's Argentina*, pp. 363–4.
24. On these weapons see ibid., pp. 364–5; Potash, *1945–1962*, pp. 103–4, 103 n. 32, 139 n. 2; Alexander, *Perón*, pp. 55–7.
25. Alexander, *Perón*, p. 56. In October 1949 harsh punishment was prescribed for the offence of offending a public official's dignity, and this *desacato* law was used, for example, in 1950 to imprison the Radical party's parliamentary leader (Potash, *1945–1962*, pp. 103–4, 103 n. 32).
26. Potash, *1945–1962*, p. 133.
27. Alexander, *Perón*, pp. 100, 57.
28. W. Little, 'Party and State in Peronist Argentina, 1945–1955', *Hispanic American Historical Review*, 53, 4 (November 1973), p. 658; Blanksten, *Perón's Argentina*, p. 342.
29. Blanksten, *Perón's Argentina*, pp. 339–40, 336; Little, 'Party and State', pp. 658–9.
30. On this non-democratic centralism and the accompanying disciplinary organs and attitudes see Little, 'Party and State', pp. 653–5, 654 n. 17; Blanksten, *Perón's Argentina*, pp. 336, 338–9.
31. Blanksten, *Perón's Argentina*, p. 341; Crassweller, *Perón*, p. 212.
32. Blanksten, *Perón's Argentina*, p. 340; Alexander, *Perón*, p. 61.
33. Potash, *1945–1962*, p. 146.
34. Little, 'Party and State', p. 658. The female Party's success as a

mobilizer of support for Perón can be seen in the elections of November 1951, the first in which women had the right to vote, where there was a higher turnout among females than males and female voters gave Perón a higher percentage of their vote – about 64 per cent as compared to only about 61 per cent of the male vote (Potash, *1945–1962*, p. 139).

35. On the Peronists' post-1946 election victories see Potash, *1945–1962*, pp. 90, 138, 139, 158, 158 n. 45; Crassweller, *Perón*, p. 242.

36. Little, 'Party and State', p. 657.

37. Blanksten, *Perón's Argentina*, p. 341.

38. Potash, *1945–1962*, p. 121; Crassweller, *Perón*, p. 214.

39. Potash, *1945–1962*, p. 143 n. 11; Crassweller, *Perón*, p. 251.

40. On Perón's strategy of politicization rather than Party-ization of the military see Potash, *1945–1962*, pp. 107, 116, 140, 153 n. 35.

41. Ibid., p. 113.

42. Blanksten, *Perón's Argentina*, p. 310.

43. Potash, *1945–1962*, pp. 48, 54 n. 20, 93, 98–9, 191, 192 n. 48.

44. See ibid., pp. 112, 112 n. 52, 107, 115–16, 149.

45. Ibid., pp. 111–12, 107–8, 76, 81–2, 79, 76, 59, 82.

46. Ibid., p. 107. My emphasis. See also ibid., pp. 113–14.

47. Ibid., p. 166. By then, too, there were indications that promotion to the rank of Brigadier-General would now be denied to any Colonel who was clearly not a supporter of Peronist doctrine (ibid.).

48. Ibid., pp. 181–2, 102, 131–2, 140–1.

49. Little, 'Party and State', p. 653.

50. Blanksten, *Perón's Argentina*, p. 336; Little, 'Party and State', pp. 654–5.

51. See for example Crassweller, *Perón*, p. 216.

52. See ibid., pp. 209–11.

53. Ibid., p. 211.

54. Ibid.

55. Potash, *1945–1962*, p. 146; Crassweller, *Perón*, p. 246.

56. Potash, *1945–1962*, pp. 166–9.

57. Ibid., pp. 200–2. Similarly, the small-scale attempted coup by navy and air force units on 16 June had attracted no army support and been quickly stamped out (ibid., pp. 187–9).

58. Ibid., p. 202.

59. Ibid., pp. 202–8.

60. See Crassweller, *Perón*, pp. 289–90, and Potash, *1945–1962*, p. 205 on the political inaction of the workers.

61. H. Crouch, *The Army and Politics in Indonesia* (Ithaca and London, 1978), chapters 7, 8.

62. See ibid., chapters 9, 10.

63. For this paragraph see ibid., pp. 24–5; M. L. Rogers, 'Depoliticization of Indonesia's Political Parties: Attaining Military Stability', *Armed Forces and Society*, 14, 2 (Winter 1988), p. 254; D. Jenkins, 'The Evolution of Indonesian Army Doctrinal Thinking: The Concept of *Dwifungsi*', *Southeast Asian Journal of Social Science*, 11, 2 (1983), pp. 20, 20 n. 19, 27; M. R. J. Vatikiotis, *Indonesian Poli-*

tics under Suharto: Order, Development and Pressure for Change (London and New York, 1993), p. 71.

64. Jenkins, 'The Evolution', p. 22.
65. Ibid., p. 24.
66. Vatikiotis, *Politics*, p. 33.
67. Ibid., pp. 33, 48, 45, 34.
68. Ibid., p. 53; M. Rudner, 'The Military in Indonesian Development Planning, 1969–1974', in H. Z. Schiffrin (ed.), *Military and State in Modern Asia* (Jerusalem, 1976), pp. 202–3, 205, 209–11.
69. For this paragraph see Vatikiotis, *Politics*, pp. 57, 34, 49, 37–40.
70. R. W. Liddle, 'The Economics of *Ekonomi Pancasila*: Some Reflections on a Recent Debate', *Bulletin of Indonesian Economic Studies* (March 1982), p. 96. Quoted by G. B. Hainsworth, 'The Political Economy of Pancasila in Indonesia', *Current History*, 82, 483 (April 1983), p. 170.
71. Vatikiotis, *Politics*, p. 49.
72. Rogers, 'Depoliticization', p. 262. The following description of the Pancasila is derived from the analysis by D. E. Weatherbee, *Ideology in Indonesia: Sukarno's Indonesian Revolution* (New Haven, 1966), pp. 25–9.
73. L. Suryadinata, *Military Ascendancy and Political Culture: A Study of Indonesia's Golkar* (Athens, Ohio, 1989), pp. 119–23.
74. Vatikiotis, *Politics*, p. 94.
75. For this paragraph see Rogers, 'Depoliticization', pp. 266–7; R. Mortimer, 'Golkar', in H. Fukui (ed.), *Political Parties of Asia and the Pacific* (Singapore, 1985), pp. 393, 395; Suryadinata, *Military*, pp. 125, 127–8, 145.
76. By 1992 membership had apparently reached 35 million, approaching 20 per cent of the population (Suryadinata, *Military*, p. 155).
77. Ibid., p. 57; D. Reeve, *Golkar of Indonesia: An Alternative to the Party System* (Singapore, 1985), pp. 341, 326.
78. Suryadinata, *Military*, pp. 40, 153–7; Vatikiotis, *Politics*, pp. 87, 160.
79. Rogers, 'Depoliticization', p. 259.
80. Reeve, *Golkar*, pp. 333, 338, 339; U. Sundhaussen and B. R. Green, 'Indonesia: Slow March into an Uncertain Future', in C. Clapham and G. Philip (eds), *The Political Dilemmas of Military Regimes* (London and Sydney, 1985), p. 105.
81. Vatikiotis, *Politics*, pp. 94, 103.
82. Hainsworth, 'The Political Economy', p. 169 n. 9. See also Suryadinata, *Military*, p. 131. In the 1980s further restrictions were placed upon the parties' activities, including disallowing the Muslim PPP from appealing to voters on the basis of religion (ibid., pp. 113, 111, 130, and chapter 8, especially pp. 129–30, on the PPP).
83. Reeve, *Golkar*, p. 337.
84. Crouch, *Army*, p. 267. For an example of patronage being used in the lead up to the 1987 elections see Suryadinata, *Military*, p. 131.
85. Rogers, 'Depoliticization', p. 261.

86. Suryadinata, *Military*, pp. 111–12; Reeve, *Golkar*, p. 355. For an example of the village headman's ability to control or secure votes see Vatikiotis, *Politics*, p. 11.
87. Vatikiotis, *Politics*, p. 77; Crouch, *Army*, p. 270.
88. Rogers, 'Depoliticization', pp. 259–60.
89. For examples see Reeve, *Golkar*, pp. 334–5, 340; Suryadinata, *Military*, chapter 5, and pp. 103, 117, 119.
90. Suryadinata, *Military*, pp. 127, 146. However, Golkar's ability to perform this role effectively was limited by the absence of any attached organizations aimed at youth, women, labour, and the like. In the 1970s the regime set up a raft of organizations that were each to be 'single vehicles' for organizing labour, peasants, fishermen, women, and youth/students – supposedly by incorporating and amalgamating existing groups inside and outside Golkar as well as attracting new members (Reeve, *Golkar*, pp. 328–9). However, in theory these new organizations were not attached to Golkar (though run by Golkar loyalists) and they proved to be so ineffective as instruments of control or simply as organizations that they could never have assisted Golkar perform a social role in the 1980s (ibid., pp. 331–2, 346–53).
91. By 1973 the military presence in the Cabinet had been reduced to only four of the twenty-two Ministers – though they still held the two key Ministries of Defence and Security and of Internal (or Home) Affairs (Crouch, *Army*, pp. 241–2). By the late 1970s the military presence had grown to include half of the Cabinet but by 1988 only five of the Cabinet were military men (Vatikiotis, *Politics*, pp. 70, 62).
92. Suryadinata, *Military*, pp. 108, 119; Vatikiotis, *Politics*, p. 62.
93. Reeve, *Golkar*, p. 342.
94. Suryadinata, *Military*, p. 56. The name of the councils differed from level to level and from one English translation to the next, such as 'supervisors' councils' or 'advisory boards' (ibid.; Reeve, *Golkar*, p. 359 n. 7).
95. Reeve, *Golkar*, p. 326.
96. Ibid., p. 342; Suryadinata, *Military*, pp. 100, 145, and 99 on retired Generals.
97. On the *karyawan* system see U. Sundhaussen, 'Decision-making within the Indonesian Military', in H. Z. Schiffrin (ed.), *Military and State in Modern Asia* (Jerusalem, 1976), pp. 190, 192; Jenkins, 'The Evolution', p. 26.
98. Vatikiotis, *Politics*, pp. 179, 71.
99. Crouch, *Army*, p. 242.
100. Vatikiotis, *Politics*, pp. 70–1.
101. For this paragraph see ibid., p. 76; Sundhaussen, 'Decision-making', pp. 185–9, 190, 195.
102. Sundhaussen, 'Decision-Making', p. 192.
103. It has been suggested that 'there is a sense in which the secret of Suharto's grip on power is less the power of the gun and more that of the purse' (Vatikiotis, *Politics*, p. 52). He and his immedi-

ate family have become very wealthy – in the billions of US dollars – and he has used that wealth to bolster his political position. Operating through *yayasans*, 'charitable foundations' that are not subject to any form of public accounting, he has been a major source of funds for Golkar, has paid monthly or annual supplementary allowances to all top-ranking civil servants, provided aid funds to all of the country's districts, and bought off political challengers (ibid., pp. 51, 112, 52, 58).

104. For this paragraph see Reeve, *Golkar*, pp. 326, 342; Suryadinata, *Military*, pp. 100, 125, 146.
105. Suryadinata, *Military*, pp. 146, 151.
106. Vatikiotis, *Politics*, pp. 104, 176, 112, 64.
107. Ibid., pp. 140, 157, 3.
108. Ibid., pp. 31, 152, 29.
109. Ibid., p. 4.
110. Sundhaussen and Green, 'Indonesia', p. 100.
111. Vatikiotis, *Politics*, p. 69.
112. In order to remove Sudharmono from the general chairmanship, the military had a number of officers retire from active service to take Golkar posts in the regions and so ensure the military's control of a large majority of the regional delegates elected to the 1988 Congress, which elected the slate of central officials (Suryadinata, *Military*, pp. 138–9; Vatikiotis, *Politics*, p. 87).

10 From Party-State to Military-Party Regime

1. L. W. Pye, *Warlord Politics: Conflict and Coalition in the Modernization of Republican China* (New York, Washington, and London, 1971), p. 12. Beneath the layer of provincial warlords there were many smaller warlords (some 1300 have been identified) and hordes of ordinary bandits preying on the population (H-M. Tien, *Government and Politics in Kuomintang China 1927–1937* (Stanford, 1972), p. 9).
2. J. E. Sheridan, *China in Disintegration: The Republican Era in Chinese History, 1912–1949* (New York and London, 1975), pp.159–62.
3. T-S. Ch'ien, *The Government and Politics of China, 1912–1949* (Cambridge, Mass., 1961; first published 1950), p. 98; R. E. Bedeski, 'The Tutelary State and National Revolution in Kuomintang Ideology, 1928–31', *The China Quarterly*, 46 (April–June, 1971), p. 316 n. 12.
4. J. K. Fairbank, *The Great Chinese Revolution: 1800–1985* (London, 1988), p. 153.
5. Ch'ien, *The Government*, p. 113.
6. Bedeski, 'The Tutelary State', p. 312.
7. Sheridan, *China*, p. 144.
8. Ch'ien, *The Government*, p. 114; Bedeski, 'The Tutelary State, p. 313. Sun initially argued, even before the First World War, that 'the

twentieth century was the age of democracy, and that China should be up-to-date and part of that age' (Sheridan, *China*, p. 145).

9. Bedeski, 'The Tutelary State', p. 114.
10. L. E. Eastman, *The Abortive Revolution: China under Nationalist Rule, 1927–1937* (Cambridge, Mass., 1974), p. 237; Ch'ien, *The Government*, p. 115.
11. Bedeski, 'The Tutelary State', p. 314. Sun's suggested method of dealing with the problem of land reform was appropriating and using unearned increases in land value to gradually equalize land holdings (Ch'ien, *The Government*, p. 115).
12. Bedeski, 'The Tutelary State', p. 320.
13. Ibid., pp. 334, 320.
14. Ch'ien, *The Government*, p. 297.
15. Ibid., p. 136.
16. Bedeski, 'The Tutelary State', p. 321.
17. Ibid., p. 314; Eastman, *Revolution*, pp. 217, 216.
18. Fairbank, *Revolution*, p. 225.
19. See H-S. Ch'i, *Nationalist China at War: Military Defeats and Political Collapse, 1937–45* (Ann Arbor, 1982), p. 13, on the ambitions to develop a military–industrial base. Military needs were so pressing that throughout the regime's history military expenditure always consumed at least half of the annual budget (Ch'ien, *The Government*, p. 190).
20. Tien, *Government*, pp. 14, 18. On the repression of other parties see Ch'ien, *The Government*, pp. 370, 427 n. 2. See his chapter 3 on the non-Communist parties.
21. Tien, *Government*, p. 28.
22. Ibid. These membership figures include both regular and probationary members; thus in 1935 there were 347 000 regular and 149 000 probationary members.
23. Ibid., p. 29. See also Sheridan, *China*, p. 214.
24. Ch'ien, *The Government*, pp. 124, 123.
25. Tien, *Government*, pp. 31, 32.
26. Eastman, *Revolution*, p. 69. Indeed Chiang actually told the leaders of the New Life Movement that it was because the Party could not function as the 'integrating force' China needed that their Movement had been established (Sheridan, *China*, p. 218).
27. Tien, *Government*, p. 18; Ch'ien, *The Government*, pp. 147–8.
28. On these organs – the Standing Committee and Political Council – see Ch'ien, *The Government*, pp. 120–1, 139, 140, 142–3.
29. Ibid., p. 143.
30. Ibid., pp. 148, 223, 243.
31. Ibid., pp. 147, 125; Tien, *Government*, p. 50; Ch'ien, *The Government*, p. 147. However, if the provincial or county government was under the control of a Kuomintang warlord or a different faction of the Party, such intervention would be resisted and a struggle for power between Party and state officials could develop (Ch'ien, *The Government*, p. 147).
32. On the Kuomintang's Party-ized army see ibid., p. 117; Sheridan, *China*, p. 214; Ch'i, *Nationalist China*, p. 94.

33. Ch'i, *Nationalist China*, p. 94; L. E. Eastman, *Seeds of Destruction: Nationalist China in War and Revolution 1937–1949* (Stanford, 1984), p. 210).
34. Tien, *Government*, p. 28.
35. Ch'ien, *The Government*, p. 96.
36. Ibid., p. 91.
37. P. M. Coble, *Facing Japan: Chinese Politics and Japanese Imperialism, 1931–1937* (Cambridge, Mass., 1991), p. 38.
38. Ch'i, *Nationalist China*, pp. 7–8.
39. Eastman, *Revolution*, p. 272.
40. See Tien, *Government*, pp. 96–8 and chapters 2, 6; Ch'i, *Nationalist China*, p. 20; Ch'ien, *The Government*, p. 184.
41. Ch'ien, *The Government*, p. 98.
42. Ibid., p. 41.
43. Ibid., pp. 42, 108–12.
44. Ibid., p. 96; Ch'i, *Nationalist China*, p. 21; Tien, *Government*, p. 180. See also Tien, *Government*, p. 5.
45. Tien, *Government*, p. 181. 'The civil [state] administrative bureaucracy did a lot of paperwork but had no real chance to implement policy' (ibid., p. 43).
46. Ibid., p. 98.
47. Ibid., p. 43. 'The formal party organs did not make decisions; they merely approved measures already decided on' (ibid.).
48. Ibid., pp. 18, 41.
49. Tien, *Government*, p. 41.
50. See ibid., pp. 50–2; Eastman, *Revolution*, p. 166.
51. Eastman, *Revolution*, p. 61.
52. There was also a separate, élite society comprising the top-ranking leadership, known as the Action, Power or Vigorously Carry-Out Society, and a third, intermediate grouping of either second-ranking leaders and/or élite military officers – known as a Revolutionary Youth (Comrades) Association or as the Green Association. (See Ch'i, *Nationalist China*, pp. 200–1; Tien, *Government*, p. 57; Eastman, *Revolution*, pp. 59–60.)
53. On the Blue Shirts see Eastman, *Revolution*, pp. 36, 55, 57–9, 62; Tien, *Government*, pp. 56, 57, 64; Ch'i, *Nationalist China*, p. 201.
54. Eastman, *Revolution*, p. 64; Tien, *Government*, p. 61.
55. Tien, *Government*, p. 61. In 1938 Chiang officially disbanded them as an organization, though they continued on unofficially as a faction within the regime (Eastman, *Revolution*, p. 79).
56. Coble, *Facing Japan*, p. 277. Chiang was formally only vice-chairman of both bodies but their chairmen, respectively Hu Han-min and Wang Ching-wei, were both overseas (ibid.).
57. Ch'ien, *The Government*, p. 185.
58. Ch'i, *Nationalist China*, p. 229.
59. Ch'ien, *The Government*, p. 186.
60. Ch'i, *Nationalist China*, p. 184.
61. Eastman, *Revolution*, p. 67.
62. Ibid. There was even less philosophical content to the ninety-six

detailed rules of personal behaviour – including several relating to personal hygiene – that were issued to exemplify and supplement *li-i-lieu-ch'ih* (ibid.; Sheridan, *China*, p. 218).

63. Ibid., pp. 218, 216–17.
64. Ibid., p. 219.
65. Ibid.
66. W. G. Hahn, *Democracy in a Communist Country: Poland's Experience since 1980* (New York, 1987), chapter 1; D. S. Mason, 'The Polish Party in Crisis, 1980–1982', *Slavic Review*, 43, 1 (Spring 1984), pp. 30, 33–4, 38.
67. Mason, 'Polish Party', p. 37.
68. Ibid., pp. 44, 38; Hahn, *Democracy*, chapters 2–4; A. A. Michta, *Red Eagle: The Army in Polish Politics, 1944–1988* (Stanford, 1990), pp. 82–3.
69. Michta, *Red Eagle*, pp. 59, 74–9, 72, 97.
70. For the rest of this paragraph see ibid., pp. 85, 92–3, 86, 91, 99, 123–9, 97, 118, 110–11, 131.
71. J. B. de Weydenthal *et al.*, *The Polish Drama: 1980–1982* (Lexington and Toronto, 1983), pp. 237–8; G. Sanford, *Military Rule in Poland: The Rebuilding of Communist Power, 1981–1983* (London and Sydney, 1986), p. 118. See also A. Cook, 'The Absence of Subjective Civilian Control Over the Military in Communist Cuba, China and Poland', MA thesis (Victoria University of Wellington, 1994) on the shift to military rule.
72. De Weydenthal, *Drama*, pp. 243, 237; Hahn, *Democracy*, pp. 226, 228; Sanford, *Military Rule*, p. 209.
73. De Weydenthal, p. 243; Michta, *Red Eagle*, pp. 210, 182, 132; Sanford, *Military Rule*, pp. 198, 201.
74. Sanford, *Military Rule*, pp. 121, 140, 211.
75. Ibid., p. 72; J. Rupnik, 'The Military and "Normalisation" in Poland', in P. G. Lewis (ed.), *Eastern Europe: Political Crisis and Legitimation* (London and Sydney, 1984), p. 155; de Weydenthal, *Drama*, p. 244.
76. Sanford, *Military Rule*, p. 201; Rupnik, 'The Military', p. 155; de Weydenthal, *Drama*, pp. 238, 243–4. See also ibid., p. 239 on the militarization of the factories.
77. Sanford, *Military Rule*, pp. 200, 202; Hahn, *Democracy*, p. 226. See also ibid., p. 229 on the central organs' being largely excluded from decision making.
78. Quoted by Rupnik, 'The Military', p. 155.
79. See Hahn, *Democracy*, p. 233; de Weydenthal, *Drama*, pp. 246–7; Michta, *Red Eagle*, pp. 177, 136, 142.
80. Michta, *Red Eagle*, pp. 182–3. He had also relinquished the post of Minister of Defence to his closest military associate (ibid.).
81. Ibid., p. 143.
82. Sanford, *Military Rule*, pp. 210, and 143, 153, on 1982 additions.
83. Ibid., p. 198; Michta, *Red Eagle*, p. 132.
84. For this paragraph see Hahn, *Democracy*, pp. 228–9; Sanford, *Military Rule*, p. 174; Michta, *Red Eagle*, pp. 178, 183.

85. Michta, *Red Eagle*, p. 172.
86. Ibid., p. 192. For the rest of this paragraph see ibid.; Hahn, *Democracy*, p. 234.
87. Michta, *Red Eagle*, pp. 131, 138–9, 141.
88. Ibid., p. 139.
89. Sanford, *Military Rule*, p. 124.
90. Ibid., p. 125; de Weydenthal, p. 249.
91. Michta, *Red Eagle*, p.146.

11   From Military-Party to Party-State Regime

1. E. Lieuwen, *Mexican Militarism: The Political Rise and Fall of the Revolutionary Army, 1910–1940* (Albuquerque, 1968), pp. 75, 78.
2. Ibid., pp. 85–95.
3. M. C. Needler, 'The Political Development of Mexico', *American Political Science Review*, 55, 2 (June 1961), p. 308.
4. F. Brandenburg, *The Making of Modern Mexico* (Englewood Cliffs, 1964), p. 10.
5. On these provisions see J. Bazant, *A Concise History of Mexico from Hidalgo to Cárdenas, 1805–1940* (Cambridge, 1977), pp. 149–51, 167; E. P. Stevens, 'Mexico's PRI: The Institutionalization of Corporatism?', in J. M. Malloy (ed.), *Authoritarianism and Corporatism in Latin America* (Pittsburgh, 1977), pp. 234, 245; *Encyclopaedia Britannica* (1963 edition), xv, pp. 382–3.
6. *Encyclopaedia Britannica*, p. 382.
7. Bazant, *History*, pp. 178–9. For this paragraph see also ibid., pp. 175–9; Brandenburg, *Mexico*, p. 76.
8. Bazant, *History*, p. 188.
9. R. E. Scott, *Mexican Government in Transition*, revised edition (Urbana, 1964), p. 137.
10. For this paragraph see ibid., p. 122; Lieuwen, *Militarism*, p. 102; J. A. Hellman, *Mexico in Crisis* (New York and London, 1978), pp. 31–2; Brandenburg, *Mexico*, pp. 63–4.
11. For this paragraph see Brandenburg, *Mexico*, p. 65; Scott, *Government*, p. 124.
12. See Scott, *Government*, pp. 132–3; Hellman, *Mexico*, pp. 43–5, 41, 49; Stevens, 'Mexico's PRI', p. 233; Brandenburg, *Mexico*, p. 86; Lieuwen, *Militarism*, p. 125.
13. Lieuwen, *Militarism*, p. 125. Membership in the regime party thus returned to the indirect (and automatic) form of a person's being a member of one of the organizations or associations affiliated to the Party and incorporated into one of its sectors.
14. L. V. Padgett, 'Mexico's One-Party System: A Re-evaluation', *American Political Science Review*, 51, 4 (December 1957), p. 996.
15. Scott, *Government*, p. 135. For this paragraph see also ibid., pp. 132, 134–5; Padgett, 'One-Party System', p. 996; Brandenburg, *Mexico*, p. 91.
16. See Scott, *Government*, p. 136; Padgett, 'One-Party System', p. 997.
17. Lieuwen, *Militarism*, p. 108.

18. An important regional *caudillo*, such as General Cedillo of the state of San Luis Potosí, controlled his state's PNR committee's choice of candidates for the federal Congress as well as for public offices within his state – and the national committee of the PNR automatically ratified these choices (D. Ankerson, *Agrarian Warlord: Saturnino Cedillo and the Mexican Revolution in San Luis Potosí* (DeKalb, 1984), pp. 160–1).
19. See Lieuwen, *Militarism*, p. 107; Brandenburg, *Mexico*, p. 135.
20. Ankerson, *Warlord*, pp. 196, 151.
21. Ibid., p. 196.
22. Lieuwen, *Militarism*, pp. 118–19, 122.
23. Ibid.
24. Scott, *Government*, p. 134.
25. Lieuwen, *Militarism*, pp. 124–5.
26. Ibid. p. 143.
27. Ankerson, *Warlord*, p. 132.
28. Scott, *Government*, p. 123.
29. Lieuwen, *Militarism*, p. 104.
30. Bazant, *History*, p. 187.
31. Lieuwen, *Militarism*, p. 130.
32. Ibid., p. 122.
33. Ibid., pp. 130–1; Brandenburg, *Mexico*, pp. 92–3.
34. Brandenbürg, *Mexico*, p. 93; Lieuwen, *Militarism*, pp. 136–8.
35. Bazant, *History*, p. 188.
36. Brandenburg, *Mexico*, p. 94.
37. Lieuwen, *Militarism*, p. 143.
38. Brandenburg, *Mexico*, pp. 95, 100.
39. Scott, *Government*, p. 140; Brandenburg, *Mexico*, p. 101.
40. Brandenburg, *Mexico*, p. 94.
41. Scott, *Government*, p. 136.
42. Ibid., p. 137.
43. Ibid., pp. 136–7.
44. Ibid., pp. 137–8; Brandenburg, *Mexico*, p. 92.
45. 'Mexicans avoid personal dictatorship by retiring their dictators every six years' (Brandenburg, *Mexico*, p. 141).
46. I. L. Horowitz, 'Military Origins of the Cuban Revolution', *Armed Forces and Society*, 1, 4 (August 1975), p. 407; E. Gonzalez, *Cuba under Castro: The Limits of Charisma* (Boston, 1974), pp. 93, 107, 153, 153 n. 16, 154.
47. Gonzalez, *Cuba*, pp. 133, 133 n. 38; S. Balfour, *Castro* (London and New York, 1990), p. 80.
48. Gonzalez, *Cuba*, pp. 133, 148, 152, 143, 150.
49. Balfour, *Castro*, pp. 146, 151–2.
50. W. M. LeoGrande, 'Party Development in Revolutionary Cuba', *Journal of Inter-American Studies and World Affairs*, 21, 4 (November 1979), pp. 459–63.
51. Ibid., pp. 467, 467 table 1.
52. Ibid., pp. 472, 476.
53. Ibid., p. 476. Not until after 1973 would the Politburo begin meeting even twice a month (J. I. Dominguez, *Cuba: Order and Revolution* (Cambridge, Mass., 1978), p. 332).

54. LeoGrande, 'Party Development', pp. 280–6; Dominguez, *Cuba*, pp. 365–7; L. A. Perez, 'Army Politics in Socialist Cuba', *Journal of Latin American Studies*, 8, 2 (1976), pp. 266–7.
55. Gonzalez, *Cuba*, pp. 96, 98, 102; W. M. LeoGrande, 'Civil–Military Relations in Cuba: Party Control and Political Socialization', *Studies in Comparative Communism*, 11, 3 (Autumn, 1978), pp. 285, 289; Perez, 'Army Politics', p. 266. On party–state relations in Cuba see A. Cook, 'The Absence of Subjective Civilian Control Over the Military in Communist in Cuba, China and Poland', MA thesis (Victoria University of Wellington, 1994).
56. Balfour, *Castro*, pp. 91, 100, 109; Gonzalez, *Cuba*, pp. 179–81, 220, 204.
57. See Gonzalez, *Cuba*, chapter 8; Balfour, *Castro*, pp. 100–1.
58. Gonzalez, *Cuba*, pp. 104, 172–3, 228–9 n. 13 and n. 14; LeoGrande, 'Civil–Military', p. 287; Perez, 'Army Politics', pp. 268–9.
59. Balfour, *Castro*, p. 97; Gonzalez, *Cuba*, pp. 207, 209, 166; Perez, 'Army Politics', p. 270.
60. Balfour, *Castro*, p. 110. See ibid., pp. 98, 100, on the political blow to Castro.
61. Gonzalez, *Cuba*, pp. 212–13, 215–16, 218, 225; Balfour, *Castro*, pp. 104, 108, 116; M. Azicri, *Cuba: Politics, Economics and Society* (London and New York, 1988), pp. 242–3.
62. E. Gonzalez, 'Political Succession in Cuba', *Studies in Comparative Communism*, 9, 1 and 9, 2 (Spring/Summer, 1976), p. 295.
63. Dominguez, *Cuba*, p. 321; Gonzalez, 'Political Succession', p. 89.
64. Dominguez, *Cuba*, pp. 350–3, 359.
65. Ibid., pp. 352, 373.
66. Azicri, *Cuba*, p. 200.
67. LeoGrande, 'Civil–Military', p. 287.
68. J. I. Dominguez, 'Revolutionary Politics: The New Demands for Orderliness', in J. I. Dominguez *et al.* (eds), *Cuba: Internal and International Affairs* (Beverley Hills, 1982), p. 53.
69. Azicri, *Cuba*, p. 96.
70. Ibid., pp. 89, 90 table 4.2, 96.
71. Balfour, *Castro*, p. 167.

12 From Party-State to Military-Party to Democratic Regime: Turkey since 1908

1. B. Lewis, *The Emergence of Modern Turkey* (London, New York, Toronto, 1961), p. 105.
2. *Encyclopaedia Britannica* (1963 edition), iv, p. 653. Article on the Caliphate.
3. For this paragraph see D. Kushner, *The Rise of Turkish Nationalism, 1876–1908* (London, 1977); D. A. Rustow, 'The Military: Turkey', in R. E. Ward and D. A. Rustow (eds), *Political Modernization in Japan and Turkey* (Princeton, 1964), p. 375.
4. Lewis, *The Emergence*, p. 191; F. Ahmad, *The Young Turks: The*

Committee of Union and Progress in Turkish Politics, 1908–1914 (Oxford, 1969), p. 18.

5. Lewis, *The Emergence*, p. 208. On the CUP revolt and its aftermath see Ahmad, *The Young Turks*.
6. Ahmad, *The Young Turks*, p. 144.
7. Ibid., p. 130.
8. For this paragraph see also ibid., pp. 54, 142.
9. Ibid., p. 159.
10. Ibid., pp. 16, 62; Lewis, *The Emergence*, p. 208. 'The Young Turks seem to have been less concerned with political theory than their 19th-century predecessors' and in general 'were little interested in ideologies and social panaceas as such' (Lewis, *The Emergence*, p. 227).
11. Ahmad, *The Young Turks*, pp. 157–8.
12. For this paragraph see ibid., pp. 133, 136, 154; Kushner, *The Rise of Turkish Nationalism*, pp. 47, 98.
13. Ahmad, *The Young Turks*, p. 155.
14. Lewis, *The Emergence*, p. 374.
15. J. P. D. B. Kinross, *Atatürk: The Rebirth of a Nation* (London, 1965), pp. 43, 47; D. A. Rustow, 'The Army and the Founding of the Turkish Republic', *World Politics*, 11, 4 (July 1959), p. 543 n. 74; Kinross, *Atatürk*, pp. 170–1; E. Özbudun, 'The Nature of the Kemalist Political Regime', in A. Kazancigil and E. Özbudun (eds), *Atatürk: Founder of a Modern State* (London, 1981), p. 82. Many members of the nationalist First Grand National Assembly of 1920 were former members of the CUP (ibid., pp. 80–1).
16. P. Dumont, 'The Origins of Kemalist Ideology', in J. M. Landau (ed.), *Atatürk and the Modernization of Turkey* (Boulder and Leiden, 1984), p. 41. Kemalism is also sometimes called Atatürkism (F. Ahmad, *The Making of Modern Turkey* (London and New York, 1993), p. 61).
17. W. F. Weiker, *Political Tutelage and Democracy in Turkey: The Free Party and its Aftermath* (Leiden, 1973), pp. 257, 219–20.
18. Ibid., p. 221.
19. Lewis, *The Emergence*, p. 280; Weiker, *Political Tutelage*, p. 219.
20. D. E. Webster, *The Turkey of Atatürk: Social Process in the Turkish Reformation* (Philadelphia, 1939), p. 297.
21. For this paragraph see S. M. Akural, 'Kemalist Views on Social Change', in J. M. Landau (ed.), *Atatürk and the Modernization of Turkey* (Boulder and Leiden, 1984), pp. 126–7; S. J. and E. K. Shaw (eds), *History of the Ottoman Empire and Modern Turkey, Vol. II: Reform, Revolution, and Republic: The Rise of Modern Turkey, 1808–1975* (Cambridge, 1977), p. 385; F. W. Frey, 'Education: Turkey', in R. E. Ward and D. A. Rustow (eds), *Political Modernization in Japan and Turkey* (Princeton, 1964), p. 217; Özbudun, 'The Nature', p. 96; Dumont, 'The Origins', p. 38.
22. However, the official religious functionaries, the *ülema*, were eventually restored to their former status of members of the state apparatus by being made officials or functionaries of the state's

Directory of Religious Affairs (Özbudun, 'The Nature', p. 96).
23. For this paragraph see Dumont, 'The Origins', p. 28; F. W. Frey, *The Turkish Political Elite* (Cambridge, Mass., 1965), pp. 336 n. 35, 338 n. 38, 337; Lewis, *The Emergence*, p. 285.
24. For this paragraph see Dumont, 'The Origins', pp. 29–31; Akural, 'Kemalist Views', pp.130–2, 134.
25. For this paragraph see Weiker, *Political Tutelage*, pp. 244–5; Dumont, 'The Origins', pp. 31, 33.
26. Dumont, 'The Origins', p. 34.
27. Akural, 'Kemalist Views', p. 141.
28. However, there was no strong consensus in the Party over economic matters and it tolerated discussion and disagreement over economic doctrine. 'In this sense, étatism was not considered nearly as sacred as, for example, republicanism and secularism' (Özbudun, 'The Nature', p. 89). On statism and economic/social policy see Dumont, 'The Origins', p. 39; Shaw and Shaw (eds), *The Rise*, pp. 389, 394; Ahmad, *The Making*, pp. 63–4, 97–100.
29. Weiker, *Political Tutelage*, pp. 188–9; Özbudun, 'The Nature', p. 81.
30. On the first period see Frey, *Political Elite*, pp. 325–7, 330–1, 334–5; Kinross, *Atatürk*, pp. 372, 382, 391–5; Rustow, 'The Army', p. 548; Weiker, *Political Tutelage*, pp. 47–9; G. S. Harris, 'The Role of the Military in Turkish Politics', Part 1, *Middle East Journal*, 19, 1 (Winter 1965), pp. 58–9, 59 n. 12; Lewis, *The Emergence*, p. 261. On the second period see Weiker, *Political Tutelage*.
31. Özbudun, 'The Nature', p. 93; Shaw and Shaw (eds), *The Rise*, p. 383.
32. Weiker, *Political Tutelage*, p. 213; F. Ahmad, *The Turkish Experiment in Democracy, 1950–1975* (Boulder, 1977), p. 1.
33. Webster, *Turkey*, p. 177; *Britannica*, xxii, p. 612 table 2.
34. For this paragraph see also Webster, *Turkey*, pp. 174–6.
35. For this paragraph see ibid., pp. 174, 177, 173; Weiker, *Political Tutelage*, p. 207.
36. Webster, *Turkey*, p. 177, Article 38. My emphasis. See also Articles 138, 139.
37. A. T. Payaslioglu, 'Political Leadership and Political Parties: Turkey', in R. E. Ward and D. A. Rustow (eds), *Political Modernization in Japan and Turkey* (Princeton, 1964), p. 421. See also Özbudun, 'The Nature', p. 93.
38. Ahmad, *The Making*, p. 76.
39. Webster, *Turkey*, p. 173. On the Party's propagating deficiencies see Weiker, *Political Tutelage*, pp. 198, 171, 179, 180 table 1; Webster, *Turkey*, pp. 186–91; Özbudun, 'The Nature', p. 94.
40. I. Turan, 'Continuity and Change in Turkish Bureaucracy: The Kemalist Period and After', in J. M. Landau (ed.), *Atatürk and the Modernization of Turkey* (Boulder and Leiden, 1984), pp. 110–11; Payaslioglu, 'Political Leadership', p. 421; Webster, *Turkey*, p. 178; Shaw and Shaw (eds), *The Rise*, p. 380.
41. Weiker, *Political Tutelage*, pp. 213–14; Webster, *Turkey*, p. 111.
42. Webster, *Turkey*, p. 111; Weiker, *Political Tutelage*, pp. 213–14.

43. Turan, 'Continuity and Change', p. 110.
44. Weiker, *Political Tutelage*, pp. 214, 193. They redivided the two hierarchies into separate and independent structures, with the exception that the Secretary-General of the Party was to be *ex officio* a member of the Cabinet (ibid.).
45. See Harris, 'The Role', pp. 55, 55 n. 3; Rustow, 'The Military', p. 380.
46. Rustow, 'The Army', pp. 545–6. On the rest of this paragraph see Harris, 'The Role', pp. 57–8; Ahmad, *The Making*, p. 9.
47. Rustow, 'The Army', pp. 549, 549–50; Harris, 'The Role', p. 57. It is true that the wider, political and social role assigned publicly to the military shrank during the later 1920s and the 1930s. In February 1924 Kemal declared that 'Our Republic respects only the will of the people *and the guidance of the military*'; by February 1931 he was including in a speech the assertion that the nation 'considers its army *the guardian of its ideals*'; and by 1937 he was proclaiming only that the army was the 'great school of national discipline' and would '*help and assist* especially in our economic, cultural and social struggles' (Harris, 'The Role', p. 56 n. 4). All my emphases.
48. Frey, *Political Elite*, p. 181 table 7.5, 283 table 10.5; Rustow, 'The Military', p. 385. Ex-officers still provided 26 per cent of the Cabinet Ministers in the 1935–9 period.
49. Rustow, 'The Military', p. 366.
50. Harris, 'The Role', p. 56.
51. Rustow, 'The Military', p. 381; Harris, 'The Role', p. 54 n. 2. The only other Turk to hold such a high rank was his close ally, Fevzi Çakmak, who was made a Marshal in 1924 when he became the Turkish Republic's first Chief of the General Staff (*Britannica*, iv, p. 589).
52. Harris, 'The Role', p. 59; Rustow, 'The Military', p. 366.
53. Harris, 'The Role', p. 58.
54. See Webster, *Turkey*, Appendix D, pp. 297–306, on the Turkish Constitution.
55. Ibid., p. 173. He had been given this permanent tenure at the 1931 Congress, having held the post uninterruptedly since 1923 (Weiker, *Political Tutelage*, pp. 201, 199).
56. Webster, *Turkey*, p. 150.
57. Even a foreign observer referred to him occasionally as the Great Chief or Great Leader (ibid., pp. 151, 290, 291, x). However, there was 'almost no effort to build a personality cult around Atatürk himself' in the civics textbooks of the era (Özbudun, 'The Nature', p. 93).
58. Lewis, *The Emergence*, p. 283; Rustow, 'The Army', p. 513 n. 2; Kinross, *Atatürk*, pp. 473–4.
59. Lewis, *The Emergence*, pp. 284, 288; Kinross, *Atatürk*, p. 499.
60. Ahmad, *The Turkish Experiment*, p. 7.
61. Ibid.; Lewis, *The Emergence*, p. 300.
62. Quoted by Ahmad, *The Turkish Experiment*, p. 9.

63. For this paragraph see Ahmad, *The Making*, pp. 103, 105–7, 109–10, 99.
64. See ibid., pp. 111–14, 11, 129, 136–7, 147–8, 152–3, 186–7.
65. For example, socialist but still not yet Communist parties were permitted, the right to strike was acknowledged, and there were guarantees of political and civil liberties (ibid., pp. 11, 129).

Bibliography

Adamolekun, L., 'Politics and Administration in West Africa: The Guinean Model', *Journal of Administration Overseas*, 8, 4 (October 1969).

Adamolekun, L., *Sékou Touré's Guinea: An Experiment in Nation Building* (London, 1976).

Ahmad, F., *The Young Turks: The Committee of Union and Progress in Turkish Politics, 1908–1914* (Oxford, 1969).

Ahmad, F., *The Turkish Experiment in Democracy, 1950–1975* (Boulder, 1977).

Ahmad, F., *The Making of Modern Turkey* (London and New York, 1993).

Akural, S. M., 'Kemalist Views on Social Change', in J. M. Landau (ed.), *Atatürk and the Modernization of Turkey* (Boulder and Leiden, 1984).

Alexander, R. J., *Juan Domingo Perón: A History* (Boulder, 1979).

Amonoo, B., *Ghana, 1957–1966: The Politics of Institutional Dualism* (London, 1981).

Andrain, C. F., 'Guinea and Senegal: Contrasting Types of African Socialism', in W. H. Friedland and C. G. Rosberg (eds), *African Socialism* (Stanford and London, 1964).

Ankerson, D., *Agrarian Warlord: Saturnino Cedillo and the Mexican Revolution in San Luis Potosí* (DeKalb, 1984).

Austin, D., *Politics in Ghana, 1946–1960* (London, New York, Toronto, 1964).

Azarya, V. and Chazan, N., 'Disengagement from the State in Africa: Reflections on the Experience of Ghana and Guinea', *Comparative Studies in Society and History*, 29, 1 (January 1987).

Azicri, M., *Cuba: Politics, Economics and Society* (London and New York, 1988).

Baako, K., articles in the CPP Journal in April–July 1961 and included in P. E. Sigmund, Jr, (ed.), *The Ideologies of the Developing Nations* (New York and London, 1963).

Baker, R. W., *Egypt's Uncertain Revolution under Nasser and Sadat* (Cambridge, Mass., and London, 1978).

Balfour, S., *Castro* (London and New York, 1990).

Baynham, S., *The Military and Politics in Nkrumah's Ghana* (Boulder and London, 1988).

Bazant, J., *A Concise History of Mexico from Hidalgo to Cárdenas, 1805–1940* (Cambridge, 1977).

Bedeski, R. E., 'The Tutelary State and National Revolution in Kuomintang Ideology, 1928–1931', *The China Quarterly*, 46 (April–June 1971).

Ben-Ami, S., 'The Dictatorship of Primo de Rivera: A Political Reassessment', *Journal of Contemporary History*, 12 (1977).

Ben-Ami, S., 'The Forerunners of Spanish Fascism: Unión Patriótica and Unión Monárquica', *European Studies Review*, 9 (1979).

Ben-Ami, S., *Fascism from Above: The Dictatorship of Primo de Rivera in Spain, 1923–1930* (Oxford, 1983).

Blanksten, G. I., *Perón's Argentina* (Chicago, 1953).

Blinkhorn, M., 'Introduction: Problems of Spanish Democracy, 1931–9', in M. Blinkhorn (ed.), *Spain in Conflict 1931–1939: Democracy and Its Enemies* (London, 1986).

Blinkhorn, M., 'Right-Wing Utopianism and Harsh Reality: Carlism, the Republic and the "Crusade"', in M. Blinkhorn (ed.), *Spain in Conflict 1931–1939: Democracy and Its Enemies* (London, 1986).

Bracher, K. D., *The German Dictatorship: The Origins, Structure and Consequences of National Socialism* (Harmondsworth, 1973).

Brandenburg, F., *The Making of Modern Mexico* (Englewood Cliffs, 1964).

Bretton, H. L., *The Rise and Fall of Kwame Nkrumah: A Study of Personal Rule in Africa* (London, 1966).

Brooker, P., *The Faces of Fraternalism: Nazi Germany, Fascist Italy, and Imperial Japan* (Oxford, 1991).

Broszat, M., *The Hitler State* (London, 1981).

Buchheim, H., 'The SS – Instrument of Domination', in H. Krausnick, H. Buchheim *et al.*, *Anatomy of the SS State* (London, 1968).

Butwell, R., 'Ne Win's Burma: At the End of the First Decade', *Asian Survey*, 12, 10 (October 1972).

Carr, R., *Spain, 1808–1975* (Oxford, 1982).

Chamberlin, W. H., *The Russian Revolution, 1917–1921, ii* (New York, 1954).

Ch'i, H-S., *Nationalist China at War: Military Defeats and Political Collapse, 1937–1945* (Ann Arbor, 1982).

Ch'ien, T-S., *The Government and Politics of China, 1912–1949* (Cambridge, Mass., 1961; first published 1950).

Coble, P. M., *Facing Japan: Chinese Politics and Japanese Imperialism, 1931–1937* (Cambridge, Mass., 1991).

Colton, T. J., *Commissars, Commanders, and Civilian Authority: The Structure of Soviet Military Politics* (Cambridge, Mass., 1979).

Cook, A., 'The Absence of Subjective Civilian Control Over the Military in Communist Cuba, China and Poland', MA thesis (Victoria University of Wellington, 1994).

Cowan, L. G., 'Guinea', in G. M. Carter (ed.), *African One-Party States* (Ithaca, 1962).

Crassweller, R. D., *Perón and the Enigmas of Argentina* (New York and London, 1987).

Crouch, H., *The Army and Politics in Indonesia* (Ithaca and London, 1978).

De Grand, A. J., *The Italian Nationalist Association and the Rise of Fascism* (Lincoln and London, 1978).

Dekmejian, R. H., *Egypt under Nasir: A Study in Political Dynamics* (London and Albany, 1971).

Demeter, K., *The German Officer-Corps in Society and State, 1650–1945*, tr. A. Malcolm (London, 1965).

De Weydenthal, J. B., *et al.*, *The Polish Drama: 1980–1982* (Lexington and Toronto, 1983).

Dominguez, J. I., *Cuba: Order and Revolution* (Cambridge, Mass., 1978).

Dominguez, J. I., 'Revolutionary Politics: The New Demands for Orderliness', in J. I. Dominguez *et al.* (eds) *Cuba: Internal and International Affairs* (Beverley Hills, 1982).

Dumont, P., 'The Origins of Kemalist Ideology', in J. M. Landau (ed.), *Atatürk and the Modernization of Turkey* (Boulder and Leiden, 1984).

Eastman, L. E., *The Abortive Revolution: China under Nationalist Rule, 1927–1937* (Cambridge, Mass., 1974).

Eastman, L. E., *Seeds of Destruction: Nationalist China in War and Revolution 1937–1949* (Stanford, 1984).

Ellwood, S. M., 'Falange Española: From Fascism to Francoism', in M. Blinkhorn (ed.), *Spain in Conflict 1931–1939: Democracy and Its Enemies* (London, 1986).

Ellwood, S. M., *Spanish Fascism in the Franco Era: Falange Española de las Jons, 1936–76* (Basingstoke and London, 1987).

Fainsod, M., *How Russia Is Ruled* (Cambridge, Mass., 1967).

Fairbank, J. K., *The Great Chinese Revolution: 1800–1985* (London, 1988).

Far Eastern Economic Review Asia Year Book (1971, 1972, 1990).

Finer, H., *Mussolini's Italy* (London, 1935).

Finer, S. E. (ed.), *Five Constitutions: Contrasts and Comparisons* (Harmondsworth, 1979).

Frey, F. W., 'Education: Turkey', in R. E. Ward and D. A. Rustow (eds), *Political Modernization in Japan and Turkey* (Princeton, 1964).

Frey, F. W., *The Turkish Political Elite* (Cambridge, Mass., 1965).

Fried, R. C., *The Italian Prefect* (New Haven, 1963).

Garcia, M. G., 'The Armed Forces: Poor Relation of the Franco Régime', in P. Preston (ed.), *Spain in Crisis: The Evolution and Decline of the Franco Régime* (Hassocks, 1976).

Gentile, G., 'The Problem of the Party in Italian Fascism', *Journal of Contemporary History*, 19 (1984).

Germino, D., *The Italian Fascist Party in Power: A Study in Totalitarian Rule* (Minneapolis, 1959).

Getty, J. A., *Origins of the Great Purges: The Soviet Communist Party Reconsidered, 1933–1938* (Cambridge, 1985).

Goldschmidt, A., Jr, *Modern Egypt: The Formation of a Nation-State* (Boulder, 1988).

Gonzalez, E., *Cuba under Castro: The Limits of Charisma* (Boston, 1974).

Gonzalez, E., 'Political Succession in Cuba', *Studies in Comparative Communism*, 9, 1 and 9, 2 (Spring – Summer, 1976).

Gregor, A. J., *The Ideology of Fascism* (New York, 1969).

Grill, J. H., *The Nazi Movement in Baden, 1920–1945* (Chapel Hill, 1983).

Guyot, J. F., 'Bureaucratic Transformation in Burma', in R. H. Braibanti (ed.), *Asian Bureaucratic Systems Emergent from the British Imperial Tradition* (Durham, NC, 1986).

Hahn, W. G., *Democracy in a Communist Country: Poland's Experience Since 1980* (New York, 1987).

Hainsworth, G. B., 'The Political Economy of Pancasila in Indonesia', *Current History*, 82, 483 (April 1983).

Harik, I. F., *The Political Mobilization of Peasants: A Study of an Egyptian Community* (Bloomington and London, 1974).

Harik, I. F., 'The Single Party as a Subordinate Movement: The Case of Egypt', *World Politics*, 26, 1 (October 1977).

Harris, G. S., 'The Role of the Military in Turkish Politics', Part 1, *Middle East Journal*, 19, 1 (Winter, 1965).

Hellman, J. A., *Mexico in Crisis* (New York and London, 1978).

Henderson, J. W., *et al.*, *Area Handbook for Burma* (Washington, DC, 1971).

Hiden, J. and Farquharson, J., *Explaining Hitler's Germany: Historians and the Third Reich* (London, 1989).

Hitler, A., *Mein Kampf*, tr. D. C. Watt (London, 1974).

Horowitz, I. L., 'Military Origins of the Cuban Revolution', *Armed Forces and Society*, 1, 4 (August 1975).

Hough, J. F. and Fainsod, M., *How the Soviet Union Is Governed* (Cambridge, Mass., and London, 1979).

Hurewitz, J. C., *Middle East Politics: The Military Dimension* (Boulder, 1982; first published 1969).

Jenkins, D., 'The Evolution of Indonesian Army Doctrinal Thinking: The Concept of *Dwifungsi*', *Southeast Asian Journal of Social Science*, 11, 2 (1983).

Johnson, R. W., 'Sékou Touré and the Guinean Revolution', *African Affairs*, 69, 227 (October 1970).

Johnson, R. W., 'Guinea', in J. Dunn (ed.), *West African States: Failure and Promise* (Cambridge, 1978).

Jones, T., *Ghana's First Republic 1960–1966: The Pursuit of the Political Kingdom* (London, 1976).

Kaba, L., 'Guinean Politics: A Critical Historical Overview', *The Journal of Modern African Studies*, 15, 1 (1977).

Kaba, L., 'Guinea: Myth and Reality of Change', *Africa Report*, 26, 3 (May–June 1981).

Kater, M., *The Nazi Party: A Social Profile of Members and Leaders, 1919–1945* (Oxford, 1983).

Keesing's Contemporary Archives.

Kershaw, I., *The 'Hitler Myth': Image and Reality in the Third Reich* (Oxford, 1987).

Kinross, J. P. D. B., *Atatürk: The Rebirth of a Nation* (London, 1965).

Knox, M., *Mussolini Unleashed, 1939–1941* (Cambridge, 1982).

Koehl, R., 'Feudal Aspects of National Socialism', *American Political Science Review*, 54, 4 (December 1960).

Kushner, D., *The Rise of Turkish Nationalism, 1876–1908* (London, 1977).

Legum, C., 'Socialism in Ghana: A Political Interpretation', in W. H. Friedland and C. G. Rosberg, Jr, (eds), *African Socialism* (Stanford and London, 1964).

Legum, C. (ed.), *Africa Contemporary Record* (New York and London), i (1968–9), iv (1971–2), ix (1976–7), x (1977–8), xi (1978–9), xii (1979–80), xiii (1980–1), xiv (1981–2), xv (1982–3), xvi (1983–4).

Leogrande, W. M., 'Civil-Military Relations in Cuba: Party Control and Political Socialization', *Studies in Comparative Communism*, 11, 3 (Autumn, 1978).

Leogrande, W. M., 'Party Development in Revolutionary Cuba', *Journal of Inter-American Studies and World Affairs*, 21, 4 (November 1979).

Lewis, B., *The Emergence of Modern Turkey* (London, New York, and Toronto, 1961).

Liddle, R. W., 'The Economics of *Ekonomi Pancasila*', *Bulletin of Indonesian Economic Studies* (March 1982).

Lieuwen, E., *Mexican Militarism: The Political Rise and Fall of the Revolutionary Army, 1910–1940* (Albuquerque, 1968).

Little, W., 'Party and State in Peronist Argentina, 1945–1955', *Hispanic American Historical Review*, 53, 4 (November 1973).

Lyttelton, A. (ed.), *Italian Fascisms from Pareto to Gentile* (London, 1973).

Lyttelton, A., *The Seizure of Power: Fascism in Italy, 1919–1929* (London, 1973).

Mason, D. S., 'The Polish Party in Crisis, 1980–1982', *Slavic Review*, 43, 1 (Spring, 1984).

McLellan, D., *Marxism after Marx: An Introduction* (London, 1980).

Melograni, P., 'The Cult of the Duce in Mussolini's Italy', in G. L. Mosse (ed.), *International Fascism* (London, 1979).

Michta, A. A., *Red Eagle: The Army in Polish Politics, 1944–1988* (Stanford, 1990).

Moore, B., Jr, *Terror and Progress – USSR: Some Sources of Change and Stability in the Soviet Dictatorship* (New York, 1954).

Morgenthau, R. S., *Political Parties in French-Speaking West Africa* (Oxford, 1964).

Mortimer, R., 'Golkar', in H. Fukui (ed.), *Political Parties of Asia and the Pacific* (Singapore, 1985).

Mussolini, B., 'The Doctrine of Fascism' (first published 1932), in A. Lyttelton (ed.), *Italian Fascisms from Pareto to Gentile* (London, 1973).

Needler, M. C., 'The Political Development of Mexico', *American Political Science Review*, 55, 2 (June 1961).

Noakes, J., 'The Nazi Party and the Third Reich: The Myth and Reality of the One-Party State', in J. Noakes (ed.), *Government, Party and People in Nazi Germany* (Exeter, 1980).

Omari, T. P., *Kwame Nkrumah: The Anatomy of an African Dictatorship* (London, 1970).

O'Neill, R. J., *The German Army and the Nazi Party, 1933–1939* (London, 1966).

Orlow, D., *The History of the Nazi Party, 1933–1945* (Pittsburgh, 1973).

Owusu, M., *Uses and Abuses of Political Power: A Case Study of Continuity and Change in the Politics of Ghana* (Chicago and London, 1970).

Özbudun, E., 'The Nature of the Kemalist Political Regime', in A. Kazancigil and E. Özbudun (eds), *Atatürk: Founder of a Modern State* (London, 1981).

Pachter, E. F., 'Contra-Coup: Civilian Control of the Military in Guinea, Tanzania, and Mozambique', *The Journal of Modern African Studies*, 20, 4 (1982).

Padgett, L. V., 'Mexico's One-Party System: A Re-evaluation', *American Political Science Review*, 51, 4 (December 1957).

Payaslioglu, A. T., 'Political Leadership and Political Parties: Turkey', in R. E. Ward and D. A. Rustow (eds), *Political Modernization in Japan and Turkey* (Princeton, 1964).

Payne, S. G., *Falange: A History of Spanish Fascism* (Stanford and London, 1962).

Payne, S. G., *Politics and the Military in Modern Spain* (Stanford and London, 1967).

Payne, S. G., *The Franco Regime, 1936–1975* (Madison, 1987).

Perez, L. A., 'Army Politics in Socialist Cuba', *Journal of Latin American Studies*, 8, 2 (1976).

Perlmutter, A., *Egypt the Praetorian State* (New Brunswick, 1974).

Peterson, E. N., *The Limits of Hitler's Power* (Princeton, 1969).

Pipes, R., *The Russian Revolution* (New York, 1990).

Plamenatz, J., *German Marxism and Russian Communism* (London, 1954).

Potash, R. A., *The Army and Politics in Argentina, 1928–1945: Yrigoyen to Perón* (Stanford, 1969).

Potash, R. A., *The Army and Politics in Argentina, 1945–1962: Perón to Frondizi* (Stanford, 1980).

Preston, P., *The Politics of Revenge: Fascism and the Military in Twentieth-Century Spain* (London, 1990).

Pye, L. W., *Warlord Politics: Conflict and Coalition in the Modernization of Republican China* (New York, Washington, and London, 1971).

Reeve, D., *Golkar of Indonesia: An Alternative to the Party System* (Singapore, 1985).

Rial, J. H., *Revolution from Above: The Primo de Rivera Dictatorship in Spain, 1923–1930* (Fairfax, London, and Toronto, 1986).

Rivière, C., *Guinea: The Mobilization of a People* (Ithaca and London, 1977).

Rogers, M. L., 'Depoliticization of Indonesia's Political Parties: Attaining Military Stability', *Armed Forces and Society*, 14, 2 (Winter, 1988).

Rudner, M., 'The Military in Indonesian Development Planning, 1969–1974', in H. Z. Schiffrin (ed.), *Military and State in Modern Asia* (Jerusalem, 1976).

Rupnik, J., 'The Military and "Normalisation" in Poland', in P. G. Lewis (ed.), *Eastern Europe: Political Crisis and Legitimation* (London and Sydney, 1984).

Rustow, D. A., 'The Army and the Founding of the Turkish Republic', *World Politics*, 11, 4 (July 1959).

Rustow, D. A., 'The Military: Turkey', in R. E. Ward and D. A. Rustow (eds), *Political Modernization in Japan and Turkey* (Princeton, 1964).

Sanford, G., *Military Rule in Poland: The Rebuilding of Communist Power, 1981–1983* (London and Sydney, 1986).

Sarti, R. (ed.), *The Ax Within: Italian Fascism in Action* (New York, 1974).

Scalapino, R. A., *The Last Leninists: The Uncertain Future of Asia's Communist States* (Washington, DC, 1992).

Schapiro, L., *The Origin of the Communist Autocracy* (London, 1955).

Schapiro, L., *The Communist Party of the Soviet Union* (London, 1970).

Schapiro, L., *Totalitarianism* (London, 1972).

Schönbaum, D., *Hitler's Social Revolution: Class and Status in Nazi Germany, 1933–1939* (New York, 1967).

Scott, R. E., *Mexican Government in Transition*, revised edition (Urbana, 1964).

Service, R., *The Bolshevik Party in Revolution* (London, 1979).

Shaw, S. J., and Shaw, E. K., *History of the Ottoman Empire and Modern Turkey, Vol. II: Reform, Revolution, and Republic: The Rise of Modern Turkey, 1808–1975* (Cambridge, 1977).

Sheridan, J. E., *China in Disintegration: The Republican Era in Chinese History, 1912–1949* (New York and London, 1975).

Sigmund, P. E., (ed.), *The Ideologies of the Developing Nations* (New York and London, 1963).

Silverstein, J., *Burma: Military Rule and the Politics of Stagnation* (Ithaca and London, 1977).

Smith, D. M., *Mussolini* (London, 1981).

Spence, J. D., *The Search for Modern China* (New York and London, 1990).

Staar, R. F., *The Communist Regimes in Eastern Europe* (Stanford, 1971).

Steinberg, D. I., *Burma's Road toward Development: Growth and Ideology under Military Rule* (Boulder, 1981).

Steinberg, D. I., *Burma: A Socialist Nation of Southeast Asia* (Boulder, 1982).

Steinberg, D. I., *The Future of Burma: Crisis and Choice in Myanmar* (Lanham, New York and London, 1990).

Steiner, H. A., *Government in Fascist Italy* (New York and London, 1938).

Stepan, A., *The State and Society: Peru in Comparative Perspective* (Princeton, 1978).

Stephens, R., *Nasser: A Political Biography* (London, 1971).

Stevens, E. P., 'Mexico's PRI: The Institutionalization of Corporatism?', in J. M. Malloy (ed.), *Authoritarianism and Corporatism in Latin America* (Pittsburgh, 1977).

Sundhaussen, U., 'Decision-making within the Indonesian Military', in H. Z. Schiffrin (ed.), *Military and State in Modern Asia* (Jerusalem, 1976).

Sundhaussen, U. and Green, B. R., 'Indonesia: Slow March into an Uncertain Future', in C. Clapham and G. Philip (eds), *The Political Dilemmas of Military Regimes* (London, 1985).

Suryadinata, L., *Military Ascendancy and Political Culture: A Study of Indonesia's Golkar* (Athens, Ohio, 1989).

Swain, G. and Swain, N., *Eastern Europe since 1945* (Basingstoke and London, 1993).

Tannenbaum, E. R., *Fascism in Italy: Society and Culture, 1922–1945* (London, 1973).

Taylor, R. H., 'Burma', in Z. H. Ahmad and H. Crouch (eds), *Military-Civilian Relations in South-East Asia* (Singapore, 1985).

Taylor, R. H., *The State in Burma* (Honolulu, 1987).

Tien, H-M, *Government and Politics in Kuomintang China 1927–1937* (Stanford, 1972).

Tucker, R. C., 'The Rise of Stalin's Personality Cult', *The American Historical Review*, 84, 2 (April 1979).

Tucker, R. C., *Stalin in Power: The Revolution from Above 1928–1941* (New York and London, 1990).

Tumarkin, N., *Lenin Lives!: The Lenin Cult in Soviet Russia* (Cambridge, Mass., and London, 1983).

Turan, I., 'Continuity and Change in Turkish Bureaucracy: The Kemalist Period and After', in J. M. Landau (ed.), *Atatürk and the Modernization of Turkey* (Boulder and Leiden, 1984).

Unger, A. L., *The Totalitarian Party: Party and People in Nazi Germany and Soviet Russia* (London, 1974).

Vatikiotis, M. R. J., *Indonesian Politics under Suharto: Order, Development and Pressure for Change* (London and New York, 1993).

Vatikiotis, P. J., *The Egyptian Army in Politics: Pattern for New Nations?* (Bloomington, 1961).

Vatikiotis, P. J., *Nasser and His Generation* (London, 1978).

Volkogonov, D., *Stalin: Triumph and Tragedy*, tr. H. Shukman (London, 1991).

Wang, J. C. F., *Contemporary Chinese Politics: An Introduction* (Englewood Cliffs, NJ, 1992).

Weatherbee, D. E., *Ideology in Indonesia: Sukarno's Indonesian Revolution* (New Haven, 1966).

Webster, D. E., *The Turkey of Atatürk: Social Process in the Turkish Reformation* (Philadelphia, 1939).

Webster, R. A., *The Cross and the Fasces* (Stanford, 1960).

Wegner, B., 'The "Aristocracy of National Socialism": The Role of the SS in National Socialist Germany', in H. W. Koch (ed.), *Aspects of the Third Reich* (Basingstoke, 1985).

Weiker, W. F., *Political Tutelage and Democracy in Turkey: The Free Party and Its Aftermath* (Leiden, 1973).

White, S., *After Gorbachev* (Cambridge, 1993).

Wiant, J. A., 'Burma: Loosening up the Tiger's Tail', *Asian Survey*, 13, 2 (1973).

Wiant, J. A., 'Tradition in the Service of Revolution: The Political Symbolism of Taw-hlan-ye-khit', in F. K. Lehman (ed.), *Military Rule in Burma since 1962: A Kaleidoscope of Views* (Singapore, 1981).

Wolfe, B. D., *Khrushchev and Stalin's Ghost* (New York, 1957).

Zolberg, A. R., *Creating Political Order: The Party-States of Africa* (Chicago, 1966).

Index